The Architects of London
and their buildings from 1066 to the present day

Frontispiece. The Horse Guards, Whitehall (c.1748–59) designed by William Kent

The Architects of
LONDON

and their buildings from 1066 to the present day

ALASTAIR SERVICE

WITH PHOTOGRAPHS BY W. J. TOOMEY
AND OTHERS

THE ARCHITECTURAL PRESS : LONDON

Notes on the Indication of Existing Buildings and on Dating

The numbers on the maps indicate the position of buildings illustrated in the book by their Plate numbers. The names of buildings given in **bold type** in individual chapters are for the use of those who want to go and see them—bold type indicates that a building exists at the time of writing.

The dates given for buildings have been made as accurate as possible, bearing in mind that historical research is constantly yielding new information for precise dating. In general, I have tried to give the year of design as the first date and the year of completion as the second. Where only one year is given, either the building was designed and completed in that year, or only one date is known.

A.S.

First published in 1979 by The Architectural Press Ltd: London

British Library Cataloguing in Publication Data

Service, Alastair, b.1933
  The architects of London and their buildings from 1066 to the present day.
  1. Architects—Great Britain   2. Historic buildings—England—London   3. London—Buildings
  I. Title
  720'.92'2   NA996

  ISBN 0-85139 044 7

Filmset and printed in Great Britain by BAS Printers Limited, Over Wallop, Hampshire

Contents

Author's Preface and Acknowledgements

This book tells the story of the major buildings and architectural styles of modern London through the careers and designs of some of its most important architects from the early 1600s until the 1970s. Their significant buildings known to survive in London are briefly described in the relevant chapters and their location is given clearly wherever possible. Among architectural historians, the current fashion is for history by building-types. All the same, historians will find this a useful book of reference and it is to be hoped that the wider public interested in architecture will find my approach in this book a great deal more interesting.

Architects do not make cities. They do not decide on building sites nor on what sort or height of buildings are to be erected there. Nor do they (usually) pay for the buildings. But architects and current architectural ideas do decide on the appearance of the building, the visual contribution it makes to the city around it, the design of the spaces within and often the materials and structure. People who were not formally trained architects have designed and built many of the world's greatest buildings and most of its houses and work-places. But the centres of most modern cities have had their character built up by the designs of a few generations of architects, each reacting to the ideas of their time about what is fine and beautiful, and about what type of buildings express the fashionable tastes of the public, or at least of the clients, in that period. London is no exception. The way it looks today is the choice of clients and developers as regards the size of the buildings and their overall shape; but it is the choice of three hundred and fifty years of architects' designs as regards the quality, texture and detail of the buildings and of the streets.

The character of the architect can be important, too. It is likely that Classicism would have arrived in England much later had it not been for the courtly ambitions and aesthetic arrogance of Inigo Jones. The Regent's Park terraces would not have been built without the *entrepreneurial* side of John Nash's personality, nor the Albert Memorial without Gilbert Scott's self-righteous determination. Most of all, whatever the stylistic or structural ideas of his age which a designer may adopt, his own individuality will decide the way he interprets and realizes them. Thus the Neo-Classical buildings of Soane and of Smirke are entirely different from each other, as are the Victorian Gothic works of Butterfield and of Scott.

Apart from Henry Yevele, master mason during the building of the nave of Westminster Abbey from 1375 to 1400, the first significant individual London designer was Inigo Jones, architect of the 1619 Banqueting House in Whitehall. From Jones, the book moves on through the work of Sir Christopher Wren and the English Baroque architects to William Kent and the Palladian Classicism of the seventeenth century. After Robert Adam's decorative revolution came the period of Greek-influenced Neo-Classicism, with buildings such as the British Museum, and the great originality of Sir John Soane's work around the year 1800. The picturesque romantic Classicism of John Nash and his Regent's Park terraces was followed by the Victorian age, with Barry and Pugin's Houses of Parliament and the High Victorian Gothic of Gilbert Scott, Butterfield and Street. At the end of the nineteenth century, Norman Shaw became the dominant architect and a mixing of styles was followed by an attempt to find a new style free of all historical copyism. In the full imperial pride of Edwardian England, a revival of freely adapted English Baroque flourished in the capital of the Empire and developed into a late splendour in the 1920s work of Sir Edwin Lutyens and the Neo-Georgian architects. Finally, Charles Holden's London University Senate House of 1931 signalled the end of the attempt to develop a specifically English new style, and International Modernism was introduced from abroad, finding success in various Anglicised forms after the Second World War.

Many fine architects have necessarily been omitted from the chapters on individual designers, in order to keep the book to a useful size. But the thirty-eight included the major stylistic and other developments in the architecture of the capital during the period.

The studies of individuals' lives and works incorporate some of the research of countless architectural historians, to whom I pay tribute and give my thanks. They are named in the references and bibliography at the end of the book, but I must acknowledge here that without the scholarship of H. M. Colvin and of Sir Nikolaus Pevsner it would have been impossible to write the book. As it was, when I started my research in 1967 for this work (which I set out to do because it was a book I wanted to own and use myself) I found that too little was known of the buildings and architects of the end of the nineteenth century and the Edwardian period. The work in which this involved me led to the publication of articles and two books on that period before I could complete this one.

I also want to name and thank some of the many people who have given me help, especially Robert Thorne, who read the whole manuscript and suggested many improvements; Marcus Binney, who made suggestions about the chapter on Sir Robert Taylor; Gavin Stamp, who read and made amendments to the chapters on Sir Gilbert Scott, William Butterfield and G. E. Street; Andrew Saint, for the correct dates of Norman Shaw's buildings; Maxwell Fry and Sir Denys Lasdun, for providing the hard facts about their buildings and dates; David Walker, for his information about the life of Sir John Burnet; Margaret Crowther, for her careful editing of the book; Bill Toomey, for many fine photographs; Venetia Maas, for her scrupulous typing of the manuscript; the staff of the library of the RIBA for their endless patience and helpfulness, and Louisa, Nicholas and Sophie for putting up with the subject for many years, as well as much help.

For ease of reading, I have not included footnotes in the text giving the sources of each quotation, date and reference, but the chief sources are listed under each chapter and architect's name at the end of the book. The book is intended to encourage and enable people to visit the buildings of architects who interest them and so the address of each is given in the text. I have stated which buildings I know to have been demolished, but my visits to the hundreds of works mentioned have been spread over a decade of much redevelopment. If a reader finds that a building, described in this book as surviving, has disappeared when he or she visits it, please let me know and then become an active member of one of the preservation groups such as the Victorian Society, the Georgian Group, the Society for the Protection of Ancient Buildings, the Ancient Monuments Society, or "Save".

Alastair Service

Photographic Credits

The photographs in this book were taken by W. J. Toomey, with the following exceptions: *The Architects' Journal* 202 (photo by Jo Reid), 203 (photo by Sam Lambert); *The Architectural Review* 111 (photo by de Burgh Galwey), 157 (photo by Peter Baistow), Berthold Lubetkin portrait, 160, 185; Brecht-Einzig 199; Camera Press Maxwell Fry portrait (photo by Tom Blau); M. Carpentian 198; Christopher Dalton 42, 43, 45; Department of the Environment 112; John Donat 193; Greater London Council 10, 13, 197, 201; Sir Denys Lasdun 46 (photo by BEHR Photography), portrait (photo by Anthony Crickmay), 194, 195, 196 (photos by Donald Mill); Mewès and Davis 162; National Monuments Record 1, 2, 5, 6, 7, 9, 19, 20, 22, 34, 38, 48, 64, 73, 74 (© Bank of England), 77, 105, 118, 119, 122, 127, 141, 172; National Portrait Gallery, Wren, Hawksmoor, Archer, Gibbs, Kent, Dance, Soane, Smirke, Wyatt, Burton, Bentley, Lutyens, Holden; RIBA, Jones, Vanbrugh, Burlington, Taylor, Chambers, Adam, Nash, Barry, Scott, Butterfield, Street, Shaw, Waterhouse, Webb; John Rose and John Dyble 21; Alastair Service 3, 54, 71, 75, 80, 84, 86, 101, 104, 126, 128, 129, 138, 142, 145, 147, 148, 150, 154, 155, 173, 174, 175, 180, 186, 187, 189, 190, 192, 200.

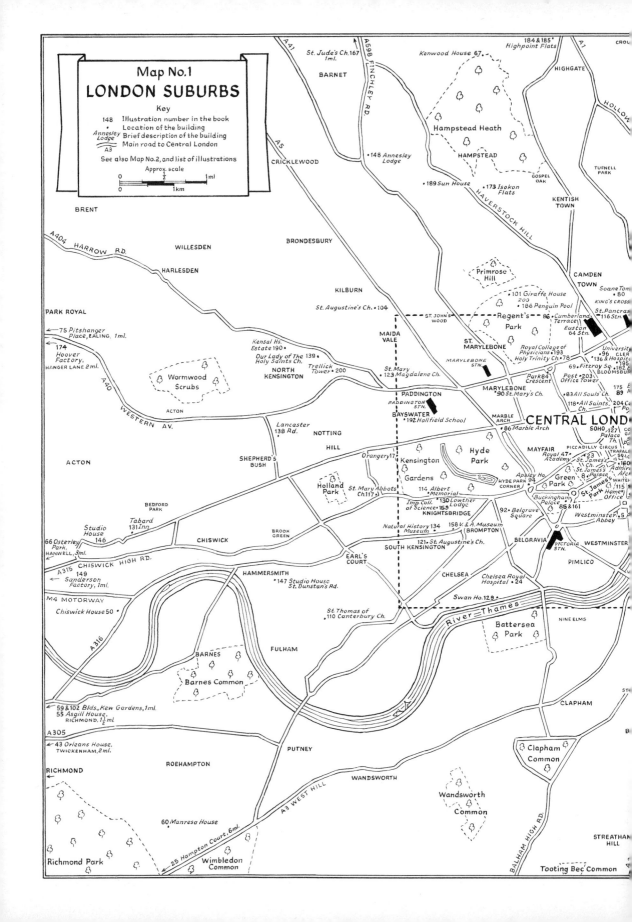

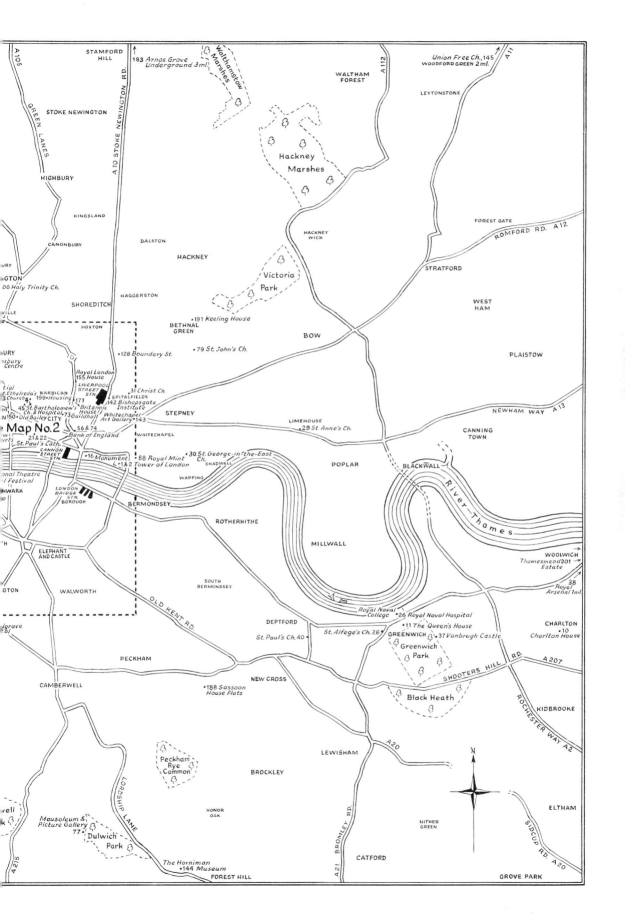

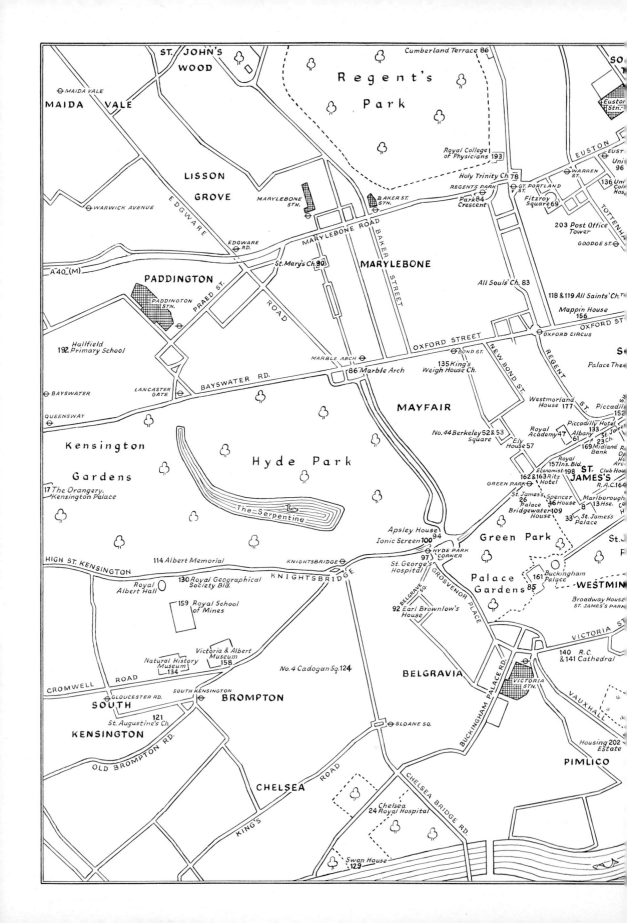

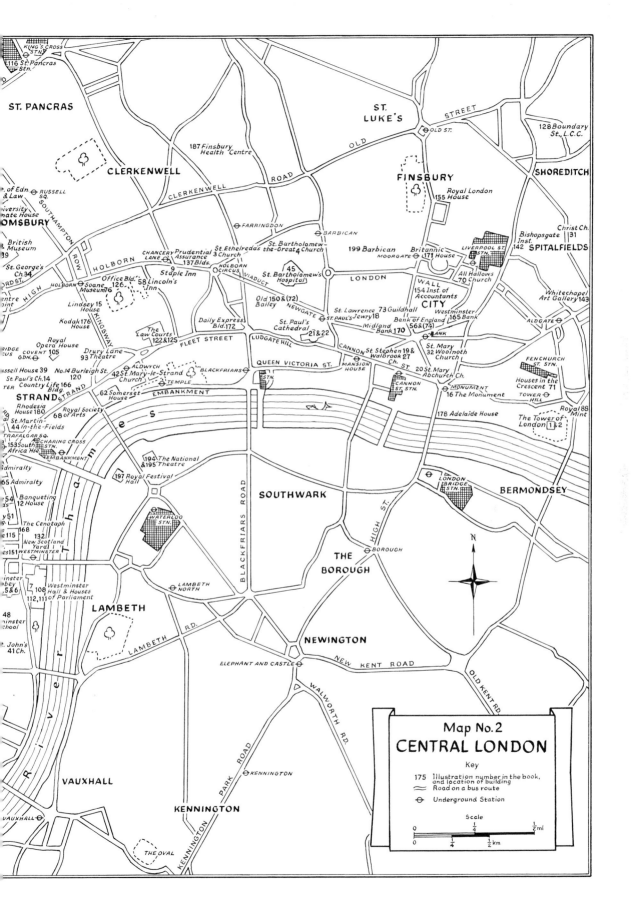

1
Early London and the Gothic Masons

Architects, as such, begin in London with Inigo Jones. The city's surviving architecture, however, goes back far further than that. Roman London was one of the great cities of the Western Empire. The remains of its Forum and Basilica, a huge apsed and aisled hall of *c.* A.D. 100 with a length of 500 feet, lie far beneath the modern buildings running east–west under Leadenhall Market and Cornhill in the City. The ruins of two Imperial Roman structures can be seen above ground level. The lower walls of a basilica-plan temple of the Mithraic religion, dating perhaps from the third century A.D., have been excavated and reassembled outside Bucklersbury House, Queen Victoria Street in the City. Fragments of the Roman Wall of London, probably dating from about A.D. 200, can be seen at several points, one of the best just north of the highway called London Wall extension, near an office block named Roman House in the Barbican area.

Hardly any traces remain of Saxon buildings in London, but some Norman work can be seen. The original massive keep of the Tower of London, beside Tower Bridge in the City, is called the White Tower. Except for the four high corner turrets, the basic structure is much as it was finished in 1097, thirty years after William the Conqueror had ordered its construction. Apart from the military rooms inside, its St. John's Chapel is the high point of architecture within the White Tower. With its two-level arcade, powerful round piers below and dramatic arches punched straight through above, it is as moving a space as can be found anywhere in London.

The other most notable Norman work to be seen is also religious. There are pieces of original work in the north and south doorways of old St. Pancras Parish Church in Pancras Road (running north between King's Cross and St. Pancras Railway Stations), apart from the Victorian Norman-style work of 1848 by the architects Roumieu and Gough. Much of the Chapel of the Pyx and other fragments of Westminster Abbey probably date from before 1100. The crypt of St. Mary-le-Bow in Cheapside is Norman. And, best of all apart from the chapel in the White Tower, the chancel (started 1123) of St. Bartholomew-the-Great, behind a gatehouse in Smithfield Market, was cleverly restored and roofed by Sir Aston Webb between 1880 and 1900 and the round-arched Norman arcades provide a church of great beauty today.

St. Bartholomew's great crossing arches, of about 1150, are the first pointed arches to survive in London, marking the transition towards the Gothic style. The circular Temple Church, completed in 1185 and now restored after bombing in World War Two, is definitely Gothic in feeling as well as in the shape of the arches—the church was built by the Knights Templar, who doubtless brought the style from abroad.

There are few other early medieval Gothic churches left in central London. St. Ethelreda, Ely Place, off Holborn (*c.* 1300) is a small Roman Catholic church, built as the chapel of the Bishop of Ely's palace and surviving with only restrained restoration. Further out, St. Mary, Stratford-le-Bow, in the East End, is a village parish church of the fourteenth century, but had to be much restored after 1941 bombing. There are medieval fragments among the largely later buildings of Lambeth Palace and Fulham Palace.

The small St. Ethelburga, Bishopsgate, in the City and parts of St. Helen, Bishopsgate, date from about

1 *The White Tower, Tower of London, Tower Hill, City* (*1077–97*). *The tops of the corner turrets were added c. 1400*

1

1400. The Gothic St. Paul's Cathedral was destroyed by the Great Fire in 1666, while the early Gothic Southwark Cathedral (c. 1230–80) has had most of its original character obliterated by the restoration and rebuilding of the 1890s. This leaves Westminster Abbey, where the Gothic replacement of the Norman building started in 1245. The chancel, crossing and transepts were finished by 1258 and the rebuilding of the nave was begun. The names of the successive master masons are in the records. They were Henry of Reyns, John of Gloucester and Robert of Beverley. In 1269 work stopped for a century and the nave was only continued in 1375 under the supervision of the master mason Henry Yevele, who is the earliest London building designer to emerge as an individual personality.

2 *Interior, St. John's Chapel in the White Tower, Tower of London, City (1077–97)*

3

3 *St. Ethelreda, Ely Place, Holborn (c. 1300). The glass was replaced when the building was renovated in the 19th century*

4 *Chancel interior, St. Bartholomew-the-Great, Smithfield Market, City (1123 onwards)*

4

Henry Yevele (c.1320-1400) and the Gothic Masons

Sculptured boss of c. 1400 in the cloisters of Canterbury Cathedral, possibly a portrait of Henry Yevele

The amount of actual designing that was done by Henry Yevele and his fellow master masons will probably never be precisely established, for many of their employers—especially the clerical ones—may have influenced them considerably. But there is enough cohesion in the style of the works carried out by Yevele—such as the great Westminster and Canterbury naves, the royal tombs and Westminster Hall—for us to conclude that the head mason was largely responsible for the designs. The mason's social and professional status was certainly lower than that of the modern architect, but the most successful practitioners rose to positions of some importance and wealth.

Hardly anything is known of Yevele's early years and no accredited portrait of him exists. He was probably born about 1320, possibly in Yeovil or in Derbyshire at Yeaveley (which is how his name is pronounced). His parents' names were Roger and Marion and his father may also have been a mason, since both his sons took up that trade.

During Yevele's youth and apprenticeship, the Early Perpendicular style was being developed, and much ecclesiastical work was in progress. We do not know where this apprenticeship was served, for doubtless he moved around and it was the beginning of a confused period. When he was about seventeen, war broke out with France. In 1346 there was the great success of the Battle of Crécy, but this was followed two years later by the Black Death which reduced the population of England from some four millions to little over two and a half millions by the end of 1349.

At the latest, Yevele presumably came to London soon after the Black Death, for by February 1356 he was sufficiently well known to be one of six masons representing his faction in a demarcation dispute settled in the Guildhall. He must have been a strong character to have been selected for this at the age of about 36.

In 1358 he executed some works for the Black Prince at Kennington Palace (now demolished) and was appointed the Prince's mason the following year. In 1360, after the Peace of Bretigny, he became "Disposer of the King's Works" at Westminster and the Tower of London. This was certainly a meteoric rise and, perhaps to celebrate it, he married his first wife Margaret.

In 1365 he built the Westminster Palace clock tower (demolished) and about this time he seems to have established links with Westminster Abbey, where Abbot Litlyngton had started the new building programme. There seems no reason to connect Yevele with the west and south walks of the cloister (*c.* 1350–66), but it is quite possible that he had a hand in the design of the **Abbot's Residence and Hall** (1360s and 70s) which run from the corner of Dean's Yard almost to the side of the Abbey's west front. Today this range consists of College Hall (now used as a dining room by Westminster School), the Jerusalem Chamber and a number of smaller rooms. All have been altered, but as one approaches through the little courtyard off Dean's Yard, one senses immediately a medieval atmosphere. A covered wooden stairway leads up to College Hall, and inside, in spite of the decorations, gallery and other work added later, the Hall is a wonderfully preserved example of the work of the 1360s and typical of Yevele's time, whether or not he was responsible for

5 *Yevele. Nave interior of 1375–c. 1410, Westminster Abbey*

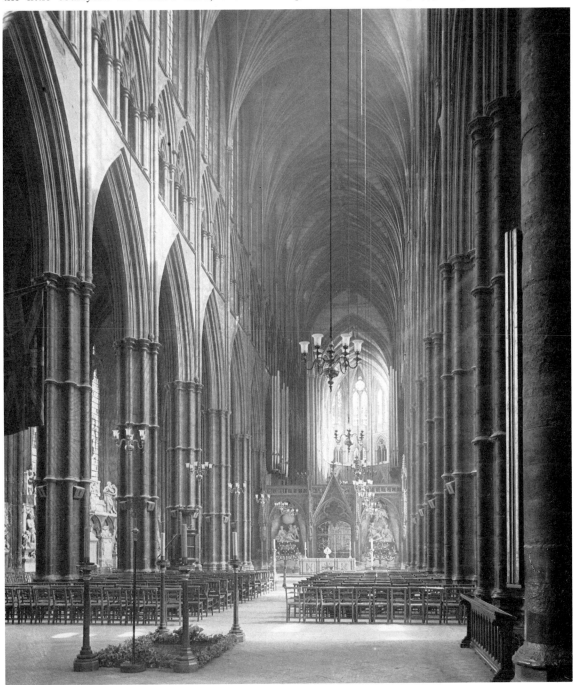

6 Yevele. Tomb-chests of King Richard II (died 1400) and King Edward III (died 1377), Westminster Abbey

it. It has massive walls, each with four windows with contemporary tracery, and a fine span of timbered roof with central lantern and beams on angel corbels. Beyond the far end of the Hall, is the splendid Jerusalem Chamber, but most of what we see there was added later.

The 1370s were the start of the busiest period of Yevele's life. In 1371 he obtained a £600 contract for completing the first part of the **London Charterhouse priory** in Charterhouse Square, Finsbury, though it is now hard to tell what of the surviving fourteenth-century work (chiefly the cloister) was his. He also obtained the first of many commissions for impressing masons for various building works and he may have done other private work as well as official projects. One gets the impression of a man of great ability, pugnacious and with a keen eye for any sort of profitable venture.

In the early 1370s he seems to have received some sort of appointment to Westminster Abbey. The exact nature of this is not clear, for there was another resident mason, and Yevele was King Edward III's employee. But there is no doubt that Yevele was in charge of the rebuilding of **Westminster Abbey nave** which started in 1375 and continued the rest of his life. The work involved the demolition of the Norman nave and its replacement by the high vaulted one seen today. As you approach the main

entrance of the Abbey, the exterior, though altered, is basically Yevele's design up to the level of the top of the great west window. This exterior, with its powerful masses, was completed after Yevele's death but only the design of the tracery of the main window seems to have been altered (for the worse). The towers above were nothing to do with Yevele, being designed by Hawksmoor in the 1730s. From the doorway, the long space of the nave is taken rhythmically and loftily all the way to the crossing, interrupted only by the organ pipes and the polychrome nineteenth-century choir-screen. This great nave cannot be taken as typical of Yevele's design work at the time, but it is a remarkable tribute to his (or Abbot Litlyngton's) good taste. More than a century earlier, the first five bays from the crossing had been rebuilt by the master mason, Robert of Beverley, in the up-to-date style of that time, and Yevele must have decided that to change the style for the westward extension would be a visual disaster. The full length of the nave was therefore completed in the early style, though Yevele was as aware as anyone of the latest developments of his own day. Yevele's work can easily be detected by the absence of the diapered pattern on the walls above the arches. Apart from this, the continuity is unbroken and there are only the smallest changes in detailing.

Two years after this work began, Yevele started work on his other great nave, at Canterbury (the city walls and west gate there are also his work). In the same year the old king died and Yevele's office was confirmed by Richard II in 1378. **Edward III's tomb-chest** at the side of the chancel of Westminster Abbey has been fairly certainly attributed to Yevele on stylistic grounds. It is a masterpiece of its kind, with a finely carved marble chest and an elegantly complicated wooden tester over the serene figure of the King.

Yevele was to prosper more than ever under Richard II, though there were troubled periods before the King came of age, particularly the Peasants' Revolt of 1381. Apart from his major works in hand, at this time Yevele designed the south aisle and porch of St. Dunstan-in-the-East, which was burnt in 1666. We get other glimpses of his increasing importance: later in the decade, there is reference to two shops he owned in the City and he was elected a Common Councillor. His first wife had died and he married his second, Katharine (a widow), with whom he bought some properties in Southwark.

Under the Lords Appellant, many of the royal household salaries were not paid. But in 1389 Richard reached majority and established his rule. Geoffrey Chaucer, the poet, was appointed Clerk of

7 *Yevele with Hugh Herland. Westminster Hall, Houses of Parliament, Westminster (1395–1402)*

Works and in September he was ordered to pay Yevele and others their arrears.

During the 1390s Yevele became steadily richer, obtaining two manors in Kent as well as an estate near Purfleet. Perhaps he was becoming rather a crotchety old man, for he had a bitter quarrel with his step-daughter over her estate, which ended in the Law Courts. He was now in his seventies and still extremely busy. With Hugh Herland and William Wynford, he had been appointed to refurbish the royal castles, as well as having works in hand at Canterbury, Winchester and Westminster.

The greater part of the nave at Canterbury was built in this decade and, in about 1394, the King added yet another major job. This was the almost complete reconstruction of **Westminster Hall**, beside the Houses of Parliament, with the royal carpenter Hugh Herland. It was to be Yevele's last large-scale work.

If possible, the Hall should be entered by the north door from Parliament Square through New Palace Yard. The outside of the entrance from here is again massively impressive and reminds one that Yevele was also a fortifications expert. Much of the detail was altered and restored during the nineteenth century, but the imposing doorway and the powerful towers guarding the gable and vast window between them, are essentially as Yevele designed them.

Entering the door, there is an impression of endlessness, a feeling emphasised by the great flight of steps and wide passageway which Sir Charles Barry added at the far end in the nineteenth century. The old Hall had had three aisles, separated by rows of piers (probably wooden) down its length, and the problem which Yevele and Herland had to solve was how to roof this width in one great span. Together they devised the powerful walls around the older stone-work and the flying buttresses which support the great masterpiece of the hammer-beam roof, the earliest surviving example on this scale. The work was started in 1395 and finished in 1402. The chief source of light is Yevele's splendid windows at either end (Barry moved back and presumably altered the southern one). As a result, there is an austerity about the sheer expanse of masonry on the lower part of the side walls, though the visual richness of the roof overhead avoids any possibility of the huge space feeling dead. Three law courts used to sit simultaneously in various parts of this great hall, and it is unfortunate that it is not used more often for state occasions now.

Yevele gave up his other posts during his last years while the Hall was approaching completion and Canterbury nave was being vaulted. He designed his own tomb in St. Magnus Church, which was also destroyed by the Fire, and spent most of his time at his house in Southwark. He seems to have been rather infirm during his last year or two and was doubtless much upset by the murder of Richard II in February 1400, for Richard had been a great benefactor to him. **Richard II's tomb chest** in which the King and his Queen Anne (who died earlier) were buried, beside that of Edward III on the edge of the chancel in Westminster Abbey, was designed by Yevele, a slightly simpler version of the old King's. Nearby is **Cardinal Langham's tomb**, which is also attributed to Yevele, probably about 1389.

Yevele died on 21st August 1400. Geoffrey Chaucer, his colleague and perhaps his friend, died very shortly afterwards. Yevele left his very extensive properties to his wife Katharine and his Early Perpendicular style to be carried on and developed by his many successors. An example of the late Perpendicular Gothic lies between Yevele's Westminster nave and palace hall, where Robert and William Vertue added a chapel to the east end of the Abbey. In Henry VII's Chapel (1503–c. 1512) there seem to be no solid wall masses; all is light below and heavy whirling complexity in the pendant bosses of the ceiling above. Yevele would indeed have been astounded to see how the Perpendicular style was to be transformed.

2
The Renaissance
and Inigo Jones

During the whole of the sixteenth century, and especially during the reign of Queen Elizabeth, the indigenous styles of English architecture which had developed from late Perpendicular Gothic gradually began to feel the influence of architectural developments abroad, especially those in Holland and France resulting from the Italian Renaissance. The growth of published books made foreign examples easily available to English designers. Moreover, with increasing political stability, more English people travelled abroad than before and saw new types of continental buildings.

Robert Smythson, the great architect-mason of such palatial country houses as Longleat, Wollaton and Hardwick between 1568 and 1597, was only one of many designers whose work made brilliant—if provincial—use of this Renaissance architecture, grafting it onto traditional English building. But if Smythson did work in London, it does not survive.

Among other remnants of Tudor London which do survive, however, some impressive buildings illustrate well the changes in domestic architecture between the fifteenth and the end of the sixteenth centuries. The frontage of Sir Paul Pindar's house, formerly in Bishopsgate, can now be seen in the Victoria and Albert Museum, where it was re-erected when the building was demolished in 1892. Crosby Hall was the Gothic main hall, long and high with a richly timbered roof, of a City of London merchant's house. It was built between 1466 and 1475 and, when the house was to be demolished in 1908, the hall was dismantled and re-erected. It now serves as the main space of the women's hostel named after it on the corner of Danvers Street and Cheyne Walk, Chelsea Embankment. Parts of King Henry VIII's St. James's Palace still remain.

Most poorer London houses of Tudor times were probably timber or half-timbered, and many of them were ramshackle hovels. But the notable houses called Staple Inn in Holborn (dating from 1586) are an extraordinary survival of the half-timbered black and white housing, with overhanging upper levels, oriels and high gables; the frontages were sensibly restored when the interiors were rebuilt in 1937. Inner Temple Gateway, Fleet Street (1610, restored 1906) shows a richer half-timbered style.

Charlton House contains interiors typical of those built more than a century after Crosby Hall. It stands on the top of the hill almost in the centre of Charlton Village, near Greenwich in south-east London. The design has been attributed (without proof) to John Thorpe. Its plan is in the form of two short-armed Es, back to back, with twin ogee-roofed towers at the ends. The brick and stone-dressed walls are a rather austere example of the architecture of Elizabethan and Jacobean mansions, with large areas of mullioned windows. The main doorway, richly sculpted in a florid Renaissance manner, gives entry to a large ground-floor hall running right through the building. The other great space, as expressed in the great high windows on the exterior, is the saloon running from front to back of the top storey. In the saloon, and elsewhere, original ceilings and fireplaces survive as well as Victorian work in the same manner, all submerged beneath the municipal paintwork to be expected from its current use as a Council community centre. The house dates from 1607–12; with Holland House largely destroyed, it is London's only surviving Jacobean Renaissance mansion. It should be better known and better treated.

Ham House, beside the Thames near Richmond, is another of the glories of the outskirts of London, but dates from three different stages with varying

8 The Gatehouse, St. James's Palace (1532)

styles. The basic H-plan belongs to a house of 1610, probably by John Smythson (the son of Robert). Most of the house was rebuilt in 1637–38 and the south range and other works were done in 1673–75; the interiors include some of the finest existing examples of middle seventeenth-century work.

The architectural detail of the main entrance of Charlton House shows how wildly northern Europe used the Classicism of Renaissance Italy. The contrast is emphasised by the chaste purity of a building started only four years after Charlton was completed and not far away. This was The Queen's House at Greenwich, and its architect was the first to introduce the theories and principles of Italian Renaissance Classicism to England direct from the land of their origin.

9 *Elizabethan houses of 1586 at Staple Inn, Holborn*

10 *Charlton House, Charlton Village, near Greenwich (1607–12). An ambitious Jacobean country mansion, now within the outskirts of London*

9

10

Inigo Jones
(1573-1652)

Inigo Jones, portrait

The introduction of Italian Renaissance ideas and their establishment in England as the only civilised form of architecture was the completely personal achievement of Inigo Jones. This arrogant and brilliant man first established the style generally called Palladian in this country, a style which has survived many periods of partial eclipse and lasted well into the present century. His existing buildings are few, but most of them are in London.

Jones's life was an extraordinary one. He was born in 1573—the year after Ben Jonson, with whom his early career was to be so closely involved. He was baptised in Smithfield, London and may have lived nearby, though his family origins were probably Welsh; his father, a comparatively poor cloth-worker, was also called Inigo and the name seems to have Welsh connections rather than Italian.

The early part of his career remains something of a mystery. About 1588 he was apprenticed to a joiner in St. Paul's Churchyard and we know that he was in England in 1597, for he witnessed the will when his father died that year. Shortly afterwards he left for Italy, where he probably spent much time in and around Venice and must have seen the great Masques which the Medici family staged in Florence, for his knowledge of these was to be the foundation of his success in England. His own annotated copy of Palladio's book *Quattro Libri dell' Architettura* is dated 1601, but it appears that for the next year or two he was employed by King Christian IV of Denmark in Copenhagen. In January 1605 he appears abruptly as the producer and designer of the royal Masque called *Masque of Blackness* written by Ben Jonson. He seems to have been primarily the favourite of the Queen, who had a passion for these Masques developed from the Florentine model, with brief plots of highly dramatized allegorical themes, sumptuously staged.

Some of Jones's costume drawings for that first Masque survive, but his first known architectural drawings are dated 1608 and are very crude. One of these was for Lord Salisbury's New Exchange in the Strand. The building was demolished long ago and it is not known whether Jones had a hand in the design eventually built. Meanwhile his Masques were increasing his fame at the Court of the new King James I, and it is possible that he designed the Banqueting House of timber and brick (1609, burnt 1619) which the King added to Whitehall Palace especially for the performance of Masques. Even at this time, when his own knowledge of Italian architecture was negligible, Jones had a reputation of arrogance and for despising what he considered to be the crudity of English ways.

In 1613, after the death of Henry, the Prince of

Wales, whose Surveyor he had been for nearly three years, Jones was granted the reversion of the post of Surveyor of the King's Works. The post was occupied by old Simon Basil, and Inigo must have had every hope that it would be his before long. At about this time he had a stroke of luck. He was invited to act as guide to the young Earl of Arundel on a long tour of Italy. The party spent the autumn in the Palladio country around Venice and Vicenza, then moved south through Florence and several central Italian cities to winter in Rome. They visited Naples and Genoa in the spring of 1614, then travelled slowly home *via* Turin and Paris, arriving back in November.

Only one of his many sketch books of Italian buildings survives from this journey, but the sheer application of the man and his will to learn is obvious. Sir John Summerson has pointed out that it was antique Roman architecture in general and its modern re-creation through the work of Alberti (1404–72) that interested Jones, rather than the designs of Palladio (1508–80) alone. This re-creation was founded theoretically on *The Ten Books of Architecture* (*De Re Architectura*) by Vitruvius, a Roman architect who wrote during the reign of the Emperor Augustus (27 B.C.–A.D. 14). Vitruvius's work is the only ancient Roman treatise on the subject to survive, and its discovery in the Monastery of St. Gall in 1414 gave the Renaissance architects just the sort of venerable authority they needed. Long before the first printed edition of *c.* 1486, copies were circulating. It may be that this interest would have amazed Vitruvius himself and his contemporaries, for he does not seem to have been an especially important architect in his own time. But Alberti and the Italian architects studied his sometimes ambiguous words avidly and interpreted them to suit Renaissance Italy.

Alberti's own *Ten Books of Architecture* (*De Re Aedificatoria*) was written in 1452 and is the earliest surviving major Renaissance treatise on the theory of architecture. It was followed by many others, as well as editions and translations of Vitruvius, leading up to Palladio's *Four Books of Architecture* (1570) and his illustrations for his patron Barbaro's 1556 edition, with commentary, of Vitruvius. Jones certainly visited a great many of Palladio's buildings in 1613, for the latter had died only 33 years before and was the latest in the line of great Italian masters. But the term "Palladian" came into use much later. Jones certainly thought of himself as a modern interpreter of ancient Roman architecture as revealed by Vitruvius. It is worth noting that he rejected both the extremes of later Mannerist work and the interest in powerful Baroque possibilities

opened up by Michelangelo, which pre-occupied contemporary Roman architects such as Maderna, whose nave and frontage of St. Peter's were being built at the Vatican when Jones visited Rome.

Inigo got back to England at the end of 1614 and in September of the following year became the King's Surveyor when Simon Basil died. The Surveyor's duties were largely administrative, and rather strangely, hardly anything had been built since the reign of Queen Elizabeth. All the same, James I liked building, and Sir John Summerson lists twenty-one royal buildings designed by Jones before the King died in 1625, of which four survive. With these works this extraordinary man established beyond doubt in the Court circles that a sophisticated Classical style was the only one fit for a civilized country.

The earliest of the surviving buildings is **The Queen's House**, Greenwich Palace, Greenwich, which was built between 1616 and 1635 (there was an eleven year gap in construction after Queen Anne died in 1619 before it was completed for Henrietta Maria). This was intended as a country villa for Queen Anne. Very oddly, she chose to build it astride the main Dover road, with a block on each side of a bridge across the middle to join the upper floors, thus forming the shape of an H. The open ends of the H were later bridged by Jones's disciple, John Webb, to provide extra rooms, thereby making the building appear to be a simple four sided block. Today, the house presents a serene and even rather dull appearance from outside, but one must remember that the calm elevations at front and back were originally set off by the drama of the deep gap in the middle. The Dover road was moved a long time ago and in the nineteenth century open colonnades were built along the old line of the road to link it with the buildings on either side that make up the Maritime Museum, of which it is now part.

The main entrance to The Queen's House is now from this central passage and the visitor arrives directly in the great cube room. This, the principal room of the house, is galleried all round half way up. It has a handsome beamed ceiling, but otherwise is very plain. To the right, the main spiral staircase leads up to the gallery of the cube room, which acts as the only passage-way to the other parts of the house. The original bridge room in the centre leads over to the other half of the house. Most of the rooms are small, and it is interesting to try and work out how far Inigo went in applying Vitruvius's rules about proportion. For instance, Vitruvius states forthrightly that dining-rooms ought to be twice as long as they are wide and that the height of oblong rooms should generally be half the length and width of the room added together. He gives a great many other instructions as to what proportions are harmonious for various types of rooms.

The next building which Jones designed was the **Banqueting House** of Whitehall Palace, in Whitehall, Westminster (1619–22). When the earlier Banqueting House, in the same position, was burnt down in 1619, the King immediately set about replacing it with a more magnificent building and this, now the only surviving part of the palace, remains Jones's most celebrated building. Within its

basically Italian tradition, it displays much originality.

Approaching the Banqueting House from White-

11 *Inigo Jones. The Queen's House, Greenwich (1616–35). The colonnade marks the route of the old Dover Road, which ran through the middle of the building. Now part of the Royal Maritime Museum*

12 *Inigo Jones. The Banqueting House, Whitehall, Westminster (1619–22), the only surviving part of the Palace of Whitehall*

11

12

hall, the main façade is in fact the side of the hall within, for the entrance at the north end was never properly finished as James I intended to extend the range with further replacements of the old Whitehall Palace. The Whitehall frontage and the one on the other side are of great richness and elegance, with the huge hall itself rising above a low ground floor. Both inside and outside, the main hall is expressed in two levels, to allow for the balcony which runs around the interior. Jones used the Ionic order for the lower columns and pilasters, and the Corinthian for those above. The rather inadequate entrance and staircase were added by James Wyatt, and all the external stonework was conscientiously restored by Soane in 1829.

Inside, the ground floor was originally a sort of grotto in which the King held parties—it has now been remodelled as a simple vaulted area for occasional exhibitions. The great room above was for banquets and masques. The cool splendour of this hall is a reminder that the aim of Renaissance architecture was harmony, not excitement of any strong emotion. The hall is a double cube and originally had the plan of a Basilica without aisles, with a great apse at the far end—now most unfortunately removed. The vast blank floor cries out for the tables which are for some reason kept elsewhere when the room is not in use, but the lofty space above is brought to life by the jutting balcony and the rich ceiling. Rubens' joyous paintings were an after-thought, for which one is grateful. From the far end of the room there is a moment of real excitement, for, looking back, the full majesty of the Ionic portico over the entrance door is apparent. This is the only work which can give an idea of the splendour of the famous Corinthian portico which Jones built for St. Paul's Cathedral.

During the next few years Inigo designed various buildings of which the only survivor is a fine **gateway** originally at Beaufort House, Chelsea (1621) which Lord Burlington bought and re-erected in the grounds of Chiswick House.

The next important survivor is **The Queen's Chapel** at St. James's Palace (1623–27) which now stands within the grounds of Marlborough House, though its entrance faces the old Palace across the road. The Chapel is again a double cube, though this time it is topped with a coffered barrel-vault ceiling. The entrance is deceptively simple, with a frontage which might be that of a private house, though there is a fine pediment above. The entry is under a deep gallery and, emerging into the main body of the

Chapel, the first impression is the blaze of light from the huge Venetian window above the altar—the first of its kind in England. The space is of extreme simplicity, suitable to a chapel, in spite of much gold sculpted ornament. Spatially, the Chapel is enriched by the three comparatively small openings from the deep royal balcony which forms a gallery at the back, whose dim light contrasts with that from the big triple window. The Chapel is only open to the public during services.

Before James I died in 1625 Inigo did other minor work which has been demolished, but Charles I had only been on the throne three years before he and Henrietta Maria started a major building programme. This brought Jones into constant close contact with the King and Queen. He re-built the interior of the Cock Pit at Whitehall Palace as a theatre for the King, while for the Queen he did a great deal of work re-building Somerset House, including the addition of a Chapel, and completing the house at Greenwich. Except for the latter all this is now demolished, and of his work in the late 1620s only two very doubtful attributions remain—some **gate piers** in the grounds of Holland House, Kensington and a **summer house** at Charlton House, Charlton.

There are witnesses of Jones's closeness to the royal couple at about this time. For example, the Papal agent wrote a description of the scene when some Italian paintings arrived to be inspected by the King. The agent tells of Jones putting on his glasses and holding forth at great length about the pictures and their painters—"a very vain man" he comments. All we know about Jones indicates that he was completely self-confident and that his manner was overbearing—even to those who were his social superiors. Ben Jonson refused to work with Jones after 1631 and in *Tale of a Tub* he gives a caricature of him in the character of Medlay. He gives his victim an apparently country accent, which may be irrelevant, but there is a glimpse of a true picture in the way that Medlay insists on managing everything and always talks in confusing and confused mathematical terms. But his protégé, John Webb, tells us emphatically that Jones was not arrogant or ambitious, and this may be accepted as evidence of his behaviour in private life, for which Webb is the only source, and of which even Webb gives us little information. We know that Inigo never married and he seems to have had little to distract him from his work.

Jones became involved with private enterprise in 1631–37, when the Earl of Bedford was granted permission to carry out the development of the first London square at **Covent Garden**, perhaps on the

13 *Inigo Jones. Interior, The Queen's Chapel, Marlborough House, Pall Mall, St. James's (1623–27)*

condition that the Royal Surveyor looked after the design. Jones supplied the designs for houses and Church (though he did not superintend the works).

The general plan was based on recent developments at Livorno (1587) and the Place des Vosges in Paris (1605). The Church is in the centre of one side of the square, originally flanked by two independent houses, while the houses over the great covered arcades which became known as the Piazza ran along two other sides. The south side of the square was occupied by the plain wall of Bedford House.

The design of the houses was largely derived from an illustration in Serlio's book, *L'Architettura*, which showed some French influence, but Jones altered the detail to fit in with the Tuscan style of the whole development. The Tuscan order is an obscure one and Summerson has argued convincingly that it probably seemed to Jones the nearest Classical style to a natural domestic one best suited to civilised town houses. It is in this deliberate use of a primitive order to express a particular intimate type of building that Jones's sophistication is demonstrated.

The houses and arcade were gradually destroyed, the last range as late as 1930. But one part was replaced in 1880 by Bedford Chambers which was based loosely on Jones's original and gives an approximate idea of the appearance.

The Church of St. Paul, Covent Garden was built at the same time (1631–33) and this climax of the Tuscan ensemble around the square still survives. Its famous and lovable portico with the Tuscan columns seven and a half diameters high and the simple beams jutting out to support the pediment, is in fact at the east end of the Church. The entrance is at the other end where there is a rather charming garden.

Inside the Church all is changed and one cannot help thinking that the famous story of Jones saying "you shall have the handsomest barn in England" has come to be more true than he meant. The Church was burnt out in 1795, and although Thomas Hardwick restored the exterior fairly faithfully, the inside was severely simplified. As usual with Jones, the interior space is calm and light, but the original side galleries, which must have made it more spatially interesting, were not re-built.

In the Church of St. Giles-in-the-Fields, St. Giles High Street, off Charing Cross Road, there is a weather-worn **monument** which Jones designed and erected in memory of the poet George Chapman in 1634. It is a simple upright chest with a sculpted scroll across the top—apparently this scroll had a verse of the poet's translation of Homer, but the rain washed this away before the memorial was moved inside.

From this year until the outbreak of Civil War in 1642, Jones was largely occupied with the modernisation of St. Paul's Cathedral, which he gave much Classical detail over the Gothic fabric. The result was odd, but it included the great glory of the Corinthian portico which Wren so admired but was forced to dismantle when re-building after the fire.

Inigo's schemes for a new Whitehall Palace were never executed and his latest surviving building in London is one of the row of speculative houses which were built to his designs in Lincoln's Inn Fields. The survivor is now called **Lindsey House**, numbers 59 and 60 and was built in about 1638. The façade is an immensely distinguished one, using giant Ionic pilasters, which was to supply a model for future English architects. The interiors have been altered. The attribution to Jones is probable, though without documentary evidence.

This brings us to the end of Jones's work in London. In 1642 the Civil Wars started, and even in December 1641 Jones was in trouble with the Puritans because his work at St. Paul's damaged another church, and it seems that he had behaved with an all too typical arrogance in the matter. In 1642 he went north with the King as his Surveyor (he had done some study of fortifications) and was probably with Charles at the outbreak of real war in Nottingham. Presumably he stayed with the King, for Parliament replaced him with another Surveyor in London after taking over the Office of Works, and Jones was captured by Parliamentary forces in 1645. His name was sufficiently well known for this capture to cause some glee, according to John Aubrey. He was roughly treated, stripped and carried away in a blanket—an alarming experience, particularly for a man in his seventies.

His estate was confiscated, but the House of Lords pardoned him the next year and restored his property. This was the end of his career, except for a few last designs for Wilton in 1649. In that same year, Charles I was executed, and one can imagine that Webb is correct in saying that Inigo was heartbroken about this, for Charles had provided rare opportunities for the architect. Jones continued to live quietly until his death in 1652. He was not poor and left a fair fortune to John Webb (at the time of Inigo's capture in 1645, the terms of his fine indicated that his property was worth over £12,000).

The Commonwealth and Protectorate was not a time to encourage the development of architecture in England, and after the Restoration a different Classical style from Inigo's became established for half a century. Later, of course, he would be saluted as the founding father of what came to be called "Palladianism".

14 *Inigo Jones. St. Paul's Church, Covent Garden (1631–33). The interior was somewhat altered in 1871. The arcaded terrace houses designed by Jones around three sides of the square, called The Piazza (of which the church was the dominant feature), have been demolished*

15 *Lindsey House, Nos. 59–60 Lincoln's Inn Fields (1638), attributed to Inigo Jones*

3
Wren and the English Baroque

The successful restoration in 1660 of the Monarchy, in the glamorous person of King Charles II, was followed only a few years later by the Plague of 1665 and the Great Fire of London in 1666. The fire destroyed most of the old City and the re-building presented an extraordinary opportunity for town planning and for architecture. The King appointed a Royal Commission to supervise the re-building of the City. However, none of the ambitious plans for the re-built street pattern of London came to anything much, largely due to the citizens' insistence that they should build their new dwellings on their old individual sites, and most of the houses were re-built without attention to the new Classical architecture. But a clever young scientist with an interest in architecture, Christopher Wren—who had submitted the most far-sighted of these proposals—was entrusted with the re-building of the burned City churches, the Cathedral and later with other important buildings. The story of their building will be told in the chapter on Wren.

In the intellectual atmosphere of the time it was inconceivable that the style of these buildings should be anything but the Classical of the Italian Renaissance, for any mathematician now knew of the Renaissance and Pythagorean theories of the connection between the harmonious proportions of the universe, the earth, the musical scales and the dimensions of architecture. Despite this knowledge, the Classical buildings of London for the next fifty years often ignored the strict rules of Classical proportions, preferring an inventively free Classicism which moved steadily towards the Baroque.

16 *The Monument (to the Great Fire), Fish Street Hill, by London Bridge, City (1671–76). Design attributed to Sir Christopher Wren and to Robert Hooke*

Wren was the dominant figure among quite a number of Classical architects during the last forty years of the seventeenth century. To begin with, there was a small group of survivors from the days of Inigo Jones. These included Jones's own protégé and relative, John Webb (1611–72), who built the original King Charles II Block of the Royal Hospital (now the Royal Naval College) at Greenwich in 1665–68. Then there was Sir Roger Pratt (1620–84), a gentleman architect who was one of the Royal Commissioners specially appointed by the King to supervise the re-building of the City—his large Clarendon House of 1664 in Piccadilly was demolished as early as 1683. History has been kinder to Hugh May (1622–84), for although his Berkeley House of 1664 in Piccadilly has gone, his splendid Eltham Lodge of 1663, off Court Road, at Eltham in south-east London survives in good order as a golf club.

Robert Hooke (1635–1703) was from a background closer to that of Wren himself. He was an eminent scientist and a member of the Royal Society. He shares with Wren the attributions for the design of The Monument (1671–76) to the Great Fire in Fish Street Hill, where it is said to have started, but most of his other buildings have disappeared. William Winde (c. 1645–1722) left the army to become an architect and built Newcastle House at No. 66 Lincoln's Inn Fields (1685–89, much re-built by Lutyens in 1930) and Buckingham House (1703–05, later replaced by Nash's Buckingham Palace).

None of these men could rival Wren's success, and other major figures only started to emerge in the great man's old age—first his own brilliant disciple Nicholas Hawksmoor, then Sir John Vanbrugh, Thomas Archer and James Gibbs. These were the men who created the splendours of English Baroque architecture between 1700 and 1720, in the age of Queen Anne and the Duke of Marlborough's victories, before the return of Palladianism. Of their contemporaries active in London, mention must be made of John James (*c.* 1672–1746), the sound if usually pedestrian architect of St. George's Church, Hanover Square, Mayfair (1712–25), St. Lawrence Whitchurch at Stanmore in the northern suburbs (1714–16), the steeple (1730) of Hawksmoor's St. Alphege at Greenwich, and probably of St. Luke, Old Street, Finbury (1727–33, but now a burnt-out shell). Thomas Ripley (*c.* 1683–1758) was another lesser architect of this period whose chief existing work is the main entrance building of The Admiralty (1723–26), in the courtyard behind Robert Adam's later screen wall in Whitehall.

17 *The Orangery, Kensington Palace, Kensington Gardens, Kensington (1704–5). Probably by Hawksmoor, but also attributed to Vanbrugh and to Wren*

Sir Christopher Wren
1632-1723

Sir Christopher Wren, portrait

While it may be said that Inigo Jones established Classical architecture and Renaissance ideas among court circles in England before the Civil Wars, it was the works and influence of Christopher Wren that spread Classicism and gave it firm roots in a very English form. Wren's London buildings made a mark on the city and its surroundings which has not been exceeded by any architect until modern times and has been approached by only one or two. The list of his works in and around London amounts to seventy buildings designed by him, while about another ten have been attributed to him without documentary proof. Nearly fifty of these buildings still exist—including a cathedral, palatial works for the King, houses, an observatory, monuments and numerous churches—so in Wren's case I shall be selective in those I describe, only listing the other buildings in an appendix at the end of the book.

Quite apart from his architectural work, Wren's contribution to science was tremendous, and his intellect was one of the most intriguing ever produced by this country. He was born on the 20th October 1632 at East Knoyle in Wiltshire, where his father was rector at the time. His father was a high churchman and had been a Fellow of St. John's College, Oxford, so the family had many friends in the academic world. In 1634 the family moved to Windsor, where the father became Dean.

Wren was a delicate boy and had a tutor in his early years. At the age of nine he went to Westminster School under the famous Dr. Busby and studied there for five years during the troubled period of the Civil Wars. He went up to Wadham College, Oxford in 1649 to study astronomy, mathematics and anatomy. Wadham became the centre of a group ranging over every field of scientific experiment, and Wren's strong intellect contributed much, despite his shy personality.

After obtaining his B.A. in 1651 and his M.A. two years later, Wren was elected a Fellow of All Souls College, Oxford at the age of 21. He was short in height and the many portraits of him show a sensitive, clever face. Apart from his theoretical studies, Wren was continuously inventing such ingenious machines as a writing duplicator, a transparent bee-hive and a multiple stocking-weaving loom. In 1657 he was appointed Professor of Astronomy at Gresham College in the City of London; but Cromwell died in the following year and Wren returned to All Souls during the resulting period of unrest. He stayed there until the Restoration of the Monarchy in 1660.

After the Restoration Wren returned to Gresham College and so was able to move in London circles on the verges of the Court and political power. He was one of the most active of the dozen or so Gresham men who organised the Royal Society and obtained a royal charter for it in the year that King Charles II returned to the throne. When the King asked for a model of the moon, Wren made it, and this confirmed him as a favourite in intellectual matters. He refused the King's invitation at that time to survey the defences of Tangier, but this is the first indication that his talents might be employed in practical affairs.

Only two years later Wren (now Professor of Astronomy at Oxford) designed his first building, the Sheldonian Theatre in Oxford, which already shows a typical blend of classical theory with his own practical ingenuity. His understandable naivety in architecture can be seen in the dome and spire he proposed about the same time, when he was asked to survey the old St. Paul's Cathedral, which was again in a decayed state despite the work Inigo Jones had done on it in the 1630s. But in 1665 Wren was able to increase his architectural knowledge by studying works of foreign masters at first hand.

The journey he made to Paris that year at the age of 33 was for the special purpose of studying French architecture, and it seems to have been the only time that Wren went abroad. The timing was fortunate because it meant that Wren was out of England during the year of the Great Plague and also because architecture in France was at a peak with the great works built by Louis XIV and Colbert to celebrate the glory of France. Of the great architects, François Mansart was in the last year of his life, but Louis le Vau was in his prime. Wren also met the great Italian, Bernini, who gave him a few minutes to study his Louvre designs—which were never executed.

Perhaps because of the plague, Wren did not return to England until March 1666, and he immediately produced another design for restoring St. Paul's, including a dome. But in September of that year the whole outlook changed when the Fire of London burned for days, leaving a huge area of the City in ruins and the Cathedral a burnt-out shell of walls.

There was no shyness in Wren's behaviour now. The fire had started on 1st September and ten days later he submitted his plan for re-building central London to the King. This plan was never carried out, or London would now be a city of wide boulevards linking important points such as the Royal Exchange and St. Paul's with a number of large new piazzas. But it was too sweeping for its time—Londoners wanted to re-build their houses where they had previously stood.

All the same, Wren was one of the King's three representatives on the committee of six appointed to supervise the re-building, and three years later he was appointed the King's Surveyor at the age of 37.

The appointment put him in a fairly prosperous financial position for the first time in his life, for it was salaried and with it went a good house beside Whitehall Palace. He immediately took the opportunity to get married in December to Faith Coghill, whom he had probably known for many years. They had two sons and seem to have been quite happy until Faith died of smallpox two years after Wren was knighted in 1673.

Wren had no appointment in the City of London, but as the Royal Surveyor he was entrusted with the designing of the new churches which had to be built for the City and the re-building of St. Paul's Cathedral. In 1670 Parliament passed an Act to raise funds for these buildings by a Coal Tax. Money came in only gradually, but work on the churches started that year. **St. Paul's Deanery** (1670), tucked away in Dean's Court nearly opposite the entrance to the Cathedral, dates from this early period and has been attributed to Wren, but without evidence.

THE CITY OF LONDON CHURCHES

The Great Fire had burned eighty-seven old City churches, and these were replaced by fifty-one new or re-built ones. Wren supplied plans and designs for every one of these fifty-one churches, though his involvement in each varied greatly after the first design stage, and the amount of the detailed execution that can be attributed to him is not always clear.

The sites available were of all sorts of shapes and sizes, so Wren decided to experiment with a wide range of plans. As was typical of his age, Wren's scientific interests did not conflict with the fact that he remained a sincerely religious man all his life, and he shared the contemporary interest in the possibility of involving the congregation more closely in church services. One way of achieving this was to use a centralised plan, rather than putting the altar at one end of a long narrow quadrangular space. He had certainly seen such centralised churches in Paris, Guarini's Sainte Anne among them. And of course he was familiar with the plans of recent centralised Dutch churches (such as the Nieuwe Kerk in Haarlem of 1649) from the many Dutch architectural books available in England. The other important source of architectural books was naturally Italy, and Wren presumably read of the possibilities for centralized planning in the Italian architectural

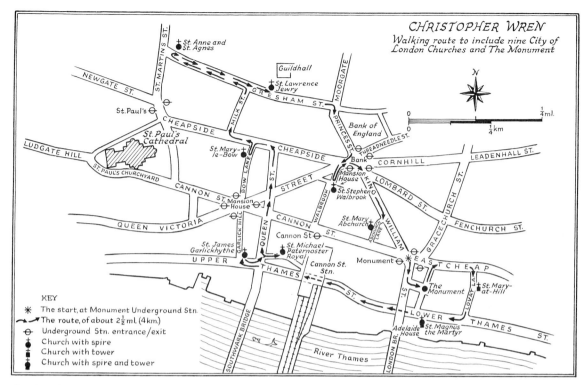

CHRISTOPHER WREN
Walking route to include nine City of
London Churches and The Monument

KEY
* The start, at Monument Underground Stn.
↝ The route, of about 2½ ml. (4 km.)
⊖ Underground Stn. entrance/exit
♦ Church with spire
♦ Church with tower
♦ Church with spire and tower

classics from Alberti onwards. French influence seems to have been rejected and, apart from his Great Model scheme for St. Paul's Cathedral, his work can only be called Baroque after 1695.

The Restoration of the Monarchy and the new Parliament had brought back the Anglican Church as supreme, and the opportunity provided by the Fire to re-build the churches as an expression of the restored faith was timely. But oddly enough, Wren had no recent English prototype churches to look at, for Inigo Jones's two chapels were small affairs for Roman Catholic worship, while St. Paul, Covent Garden was designed more on the lines of an antique temple, without centralisation. Wren was therefore breaking entirely new ground for England.

Of his fifty-one City churches, twenty-four survive in various states of preservation, apart from two others in the West End of London. The variety of their plans is immense, and there are several books which analyse them all. But the best idea of the churches will probably be obtained by examining eight particularly interesting ones which can be taken in during a day's stroll through the City. A map of the suggested route for walking is shown above—it is advisable to visit them on a weekday, since most of the churches are closed during the weekend.

This route starts in Eastcheap near the Monument underground station. The **Monument** itself is just down the hill and may have been designed by Wren

or jointly with that other clever scientist-turned-architect, Robert Hooke. It was built in 1671–76 and is a single huge fluted column, perhaps rather fat, with sculpted flames above the viewing platform on its top.

St. Mary-at-Hill (1670–76) is in Lovat Lane, a small turning a little way along Eastcheap. It is one of the earliest of the churches and though it has been burned it is well restored. Typically of many City churches, it is hidden away, a simple brick building with a small stone-trimmed tower. Beyond a rather cluttered lobby, the central door opens into a subtly lit space of light blue, white and gold. In this church we see at once the Dutch influence on some of Wren's plans—what is in fact a large, roughly rectangular room has been divided up into most delicate and subtle spaces by the four free-standing columns of the central square and the vaults springing from them. A shallow dome in the middle emphasises the centralised plan, while the short arms of an almost Greek (equal-sided) cross, with rounded vaults, radiate from the dome. The daylighting is from a variety of windows, high and low, large and small, giving a subtle glow to the serene open spaces.

At the bottom of Lovat Lane, Lower Thames Street runs to the right, and a short way along stands **St. Magnus the Martyr** (1671–76). Unfortunately, this is now tucked away behind the mass of Adelaide House on the London Bridge approach, and the office block dwarfs even the tall tower and steeple which Wren added in 1705 (this was the last steeple before the series of Italianate Baroque ones, and is based on the 1621 steeple of the Jesuit church in Antwerp).

The imposing doorway is under the tower and the narrow lobby now has a glass screen. This church has quite a different type of plan from St. Mary-at-Hill, more like that of an ancient basilica—there is a high nave with clerestorey, and lower aisles separated from the nave by two rows of Ionic columns, without arches.

Everything emphasises the lines running the length of the church. There are transepts, but these are barely noticed. The windows are again a subtle arrangement, though the light has been dimmed by stained glass windows which should not be there.

Lower Thames Street continues under London Bridge and becomes Upper Thames Street. Near the approach to Southwark Bridge, you can see two of the magnificent Baroque steeples which Wren built in the last twenty years of his life (see the separate section on these steeples, later in this chapter). The first is that of **St. Michael Paternoster Royal**, whose interior was bombed but has been restored. The interior is typical of the simpler calm spaces, with a floating panel ceiling, that Wren turned to in the 1680s, but it is ruined by the jangly coloured windows which were unwisely inserted during its restoration.

Still further on, in Garlick Hill, off Upper Thames Street, is **St. James Garlickhythe** (1676–83), with its fine Baroque steeple added in 1713. The entrance is under the tower. The small domed lobby leads into another darker one. The central door opens into the body of the church, which was dubbed "Wren's Lantern"—all clear glass windows, white columns, walls and ceiling with just a few touches of gold. It originally had another huge clear window at the east end, increasing the "lantern" effect of shining daylight. This interior well demonstrates the benefits to Classical churches of clear glass, rather than the coloured windows suitable for Gothic buildings.

Again, the form is almost a simple quadrangle, transformed into an open-work cross by the free-standing columns and the vaulting—but here the cross is a long one with larger arms. There is little effective centralisation, for the altar is in a small recessed chancel. At the other end, the gallery is piled up impressively to the rear wall. But it is the white luminosity of this church that stays in the mind.

From the approach to Southwark Bridge, Queen Street runs up the hill and goes across Cheapside. A little way to the left in Cheapside is **St. Mary-le-Bow** (1670–73), a church for once in a prominent position whose street façade is treated with the attention it deserves. The famous steeple containing Bow bells was built in 1680 and is the most grandiose of Wren's early steeples, still influenced more by Flemish sources than Italian. The main entrance is through the open loggia under the tower, and a big lobby leads to the rear of the interior at one side, though there is a central entrance around the corner. The interior (restored after bombing) is a disappointment. We do not know how closely Wren's design was followed, but the plan (based on that of Constantine's Basilica in Rome) is interesting and odd, rather than satisfying—a wide nave with very narrow aisles. Again, the coloured windows are unfortunate.

On the other side of Cheapside, Milk Street leads through to Gresham Street. To the left lies the charming, very Dutch-looking church of **St. Anne and St. Agnes** (1676–80) at the end of Gresham Street. The exterior is of rose-red brick and grey tiles, with an odd stumpy steeple added in 1714, though probably designed much earlier.

The interior is one of the most delightful of all Wren's Dutch influenced plans, almost square but divided up into a Greek cross by high vaults which swoop down to low domed corners. It is very intimate and softly lit. The church should be much better known, but its present Lutheran occupants keep it locked up most of the time.

Along Gresham Street in the other direction, you soon come to **St. Lawrence Jewry** (1670–77). This is close to the Guildhall and has a correspondingly imposing exterior. The steeple is early Wren, with obelisks reflecting the spire. There is a tall lobby under the gallery, with doors opening into the cream and gold spaciousness of the church itself. Again, this was restored after bombing, but it has been well done and has already started to mature.

For the first time among Wren churches, this one gives an immediate impression of civic splendour and pomp. Wren left the main part of the church as an uninterrupted open space with a flat ceiling.

The grandeur of this space, with its Corinthian pilastered walls and richly coffered ceiling, has an extra dimension added by the screen of stone columns and carved woodwork which delicately divides off the large chapel on the left. The two spaces seem to play against each other through this screen as the visitor moves about the church.

Gresham Street continues to the corner of the Bank of England, where Princes Street turns to the right and brings you out opposite the Mansion House. Tucked away on the far side of the Mansion House is the architectural *pièce de résistance* of these churches of the 1670s. This is the church of

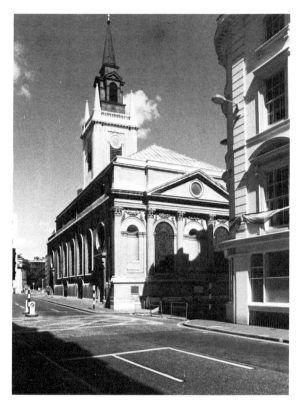

18 *Wren. St. Lawrence Jewry, Gresham Street, City (1670–77)*

19 *Wren. Interior, St. Stephen Walbrook, Walbrook, behind the Mansion House, City (1672–79)*

St. Stephen Walbrook (1672–79) in the small street also called Walbrook. It has a curiously rough and irregular exterior, with a green dome, and on the tower is another of Wren's late Baroque steeples. This one was built in 1717 and the way the stages succeed each other is playful and brilliant.

Some steep stairs from Walbrook lead through a curving lobby, and upon entering the church itself the dome is partly in sight at once—drawing the visitor forward from curiosity. This is another of Wren's open plans within a quadrangular room, though here the high bases of the Corinthian columns emphasise the internal cross strongly at floor-level (in the other centralised churches, the cross-plan only becomes evident when looking upwards).

The creamy dome, splendidly coffered and moulded, opens overhead further into the wide space under it—a space with tremendous life and elegance rising to a bright lantern at the top. Lighting and colouring are very restrained and subtle, with daylight filtering on to the stonework, cream plaster and dark wood. The purely sensual enjoyment of this space is intensified by the gradual understanding of the complex design. Within the open room, Wren

built up a fascinating composition of concentric crosses, squares and an octagon of arches before the circles of the vaulting and the dome are reached.

The brilliance of this church has never been denied. Even when Wren's reputation was at its lowest in the 1720s, there is a nice story of Lord Burlington—the leader of the then new Palladian movement—being astonished by a picture of the interior he saw in Rome and hastening to see it as soon as he got home to London.

The last of these City churches described here takes us to a design of the 1680s. This is **St. Mary Abchurch** (1681–86) hidden away in Abchurch Lane, which runs between King William Street and Canon Street, not far from St. Stephen Walbrook.

This church was a new type of design for Wren. The outside is of brick with stone trimming, restrained but impressive. There is a fine, comparatively early, Wren spire.

The doorway opens immediately into the white walled body of the church, left as a completely uninterrupted square (though slightly irregular through the error of the builders), but it seems to be a circle because of the dark painted dome filling almost the entire area overhead. There are comparatively

20

few windows, but there is one huge one on the most open side of the church which bathes the whole space with daylight.

The treatment is of great simplicity, without even pilasters around the white walls, for the dome is supported by eight arched vaults springing from Corinthian capitals which act like corbels. It is a deeply impressive space, with altar and pulpit embraced within the circle of the dark dome and a fine altar reredos by Grinling Gibbons.

So, after a decade of experiments with complicated plans, Wren returned here to a form of striking simplicity but great richness. He went on to give up centralisation altogether and to develop a type of plan that was to be widely copied in England and abroad. But the chief examples of this are in the West End of London and will be dealt with later.

ST. PAUL'S CATHEDRAL

Wren started work on designs for the Cathedral to replace the burned ruin even before his appointment as the King's Surveyor. The designs went through a number of stages before reaching the final form, and these must be described briefly. In 1668 the Dean asked him to design a completely new Cathedral, though no funds were available yet. He produced the "First Model" the following year. This was criticized for being either too modest or too odd.

So in 1673, Wren produced the "Great Model", which can still be seen in the Cathedral Library. This

20 *Wren. Interior, St. Mary Abchurch, Abchurch Lane, off Cannon Street, City (1681–86)*

21 *Wren. St. Paul's Cathedral, Ludgate Hill, City (1675–1711)*

22 *Interior of St. Paul's Cathedral. The space under the dome, and the subtle effects of its natural lighting, can just be seen in this photograph*

was a tremendously ambitious design, consisting of a vast Greek cross with curving sides and a dome, with a short nave to the west of it. Its curving walls and visual drama link the plan with the Baroque, yet the symmetry (and the criterion that no part could be removed without spoiling the whole) roots it firmly in the Italian Renaissance.

If it had been built, it would have been one of the greatest of all Baroque masterpieces, but "the Chapter and some of the Clergy thought the model not enough of a Cathedral fashion". What the Clergy meant was that they wanted a traditional Gothic form, exactly what Wren wanted to avoid. There is an unconfirmed story that he wept when he heard this decision, which would be a rare show of emotion for Wren but understandable enough. All the same, he set about producing a compromise and in 1674 produced the "Warrant Design", which received the Royal Warrant in 1675.

This long thin design, with a spire on top of its dome, seemed to meet the criticisms—though one

21

22

doubts whether Wren had any intention of completing it like that. He probably did intend to preserve the Inigo Jones Corinthian portico, but he soon set about changing the rest, and in the end the old portico was found to be too damaged for preservation. By the end of 1675, Wren had completed the design he intended to build, though he did not publish it. It had much broader proportions and there was no question of a spire on the dome. Work started in December and it was structurally completed in 1711. By this time he had completely changed the design of the west towers in accordance with his turn to a Baroque style during those late years.

Visiting the Cathedral today, the most impressive approach is from the east, passing along the side of the whole great structure before arriving at the west main entrance. The first impression is that this appears to be a building of two storeys, for which there are good reasons. For one thing the most notable example of a grand street façade in London was that of Inigo Jones's Banqueting House in Whitehall, where again an apparently two-storey exterior contained a high single space. The upper level of Wren's two-storey treatment of the Cathedral also provided a screen for the buttresses supporting the nave roof, and gives the illusion that St. Paul's is a truly classical building of one height throughout—in fact, the hidden buttresses and aisles of a lower height than the nave link the form of the Cathedral firmly with its Gothic predecessor.

The splendour of the exterior walls is crowned by the Dome, which Wren spent many years designing. He had no English model to study, and of course the drawings of Michelangelo's dome of St. Peter's in Rome influenced him. But the solution he finally produced was very much his own, and the tremendous success of the dome from the outside as well as inside is largely due to his technical ingenuity. From the exterior, much of the triumphant feeling of the dome is given by the soaring stone lantern which Wren put on top of it. His problem was how to support the weight of this masonry, and his answer was to build an internal dome and then to erect a great cone of brickwork around and above it, supporting the stone lantern on this cone and supporting the external dome on a timber frame around the sides of the cone. The result is quite different from Michelangelo's design, for the columns and ribs of the St. Peter's Dome and lantern take the eye always upwards. Wren's lantern rides triumphantly on the serene hemisphere of the outer dome itself.

For the main entrance at the west end, Wren never found a really satisfying substitute for the old portico

he had hoped to preserve. The present portico is again of two storeys and is recessed into the mass of the building. This has an oddity to it which is not quite convincing, but it does give the entrance front some drama by contrasting the dark spaces of the portico with the surfaces of the tower walls—and the upper parts of the two western bell towers, which he re-designed thirty years after the Warrant Design, show astonishing spatial inventiveness for a man aged seventy.

Entering the Cathedral at the west end, the proportions of the nave make it slightly disappointing, for instead of each bay being a serene cube crowned by a semi-circular arch, the wall side continues higher than the 42 feet square in plan of each bay. This removes any feeling of calmness from the spaces, without giving enough height to provide any real vertical excitement. But there is an immediate glimpse of the huge space in the dome, a magnet for the eye.

Advancing down the nave, the drum and then the dome itself start to appear. Between the final massive couple of piers, the space flows out on every side and the eyes are drawn into the great expanse in the dome before penetrating into the daylit recesses of the lantern high above. The vividness of this experience does not lessen with repeated visits.

The choir stalls carved by Grinling Gibbons are of great beauty, and there is a formidable array of statues and monuments in the transepts. There are many more of these in the crypt of the Cathedral, where there are simple white vaults and arches, with the fine tomb of Nelson and the ponderous sarcophagus of Wellington. The crypt has an informal splendour of its own, with unexpected fragments as well as the famous tombs. Wren himself is buried here on the right-hand side at the extreme east end. Two simple tablets mark the spot, one of them with the famous epitaph *Lector, si monumentum requiris, circumspice*, which one might translate as "Reader, if you want his monument, look around you".

THE WEST END CHURCHES

Most of the City churches were designed in the 1670s, though the last one was started as late as 1686. But by this time Wren had also developed another type of church plan which was to become a pattern for English and Colonial churches. Two examples of this plan are given in his only surviving West End churches. Both were gutted by bombs during the Second World War, but have been restored.

St. Clement Danes (1680–82) has a prominent

23 Wren. St. James's, Piccadilly (1682–84)

The windows are large, and the amount of clear daylight ensures a joyful atmosphere in the church.

This was the type of plan which Wren described as his conclusion for the most convenient arrangement in an Anglican church. Gibbs later took up the type and through his influence it was copied in many British colonies of the time.

ROYAL AND PUBLIC BUILDINGS

Wren's working life must have been crowded, for he was doing other designs at the same time as the churches, such as **The Royal Observatory**, Blackheath Avenue, Greenwich Park (1675–76) an individualistic octagonal building high in the park above Greenwich Royal Hospital, which combines great charm with its purely functional purpose. The attractive range of brick houses for lawyers at **Nos. 2–7 King's Bench Walk**, Temple was started in 1678, and the designs have sometimes been attributed to Wren. More certainly, he built Pump Court Cloisters in the Temple two years later; these were destroyed by bombs in 1941 and have been re-built.

His wife, Faith, died in the year that St. Paul's Cathedral was started, but two years later in 1677 he was married again to Jane Fitzwilliam. By her he had two more children though sadly he was widowed again in 1679. From then on he remained single, though his household seems to have been comfortably run. Robert Hooke's diary tells of frequent dinners and visits to the theatre with Wren.

Wren's work was still basically that of the King's Surveyor, and with most of his churches designed by the end of 1681, Charles II found a new type of problem for him. In that year he decided to set up a suitable establishment for retired soldiers, and Wren designed the first part of the **Chelsea Royal Hospital** (1681–91) in Royal Hospital Road, Chelsea. This main range, with the wings Wren added in 1686 to enclose three sides of the courtyard, is in a suitably domestic style with just a touch of austerity. Again the style has Dutch origins but it was by this time well established in England as the vernacular Classical style.

All the ranges are in brick with stone trimming and porticoes, the first porticoes where Wren uses a giant order of columns. The main range contains a simple and airy Great Hall and a chapel which was decorated much later. The courtyard now ends in a rather severe terrace, but originally the park ran straight on down to the riverside. Wren added various outbuildings in 1691, and others were built later by Soane. The Chelsea Royal Hospital was

position in the middle of the Strand, near the Law Courts, but even here Wren rejected the opportunity for a really ambitious façade. The doorway is under the tower which James Gibbs added later, and Wren's handsome lobby opens directly into the church.

The plan emphasizes the length of the church, and all the idealistic centralised planning of Wren's earlier designs has gone. But in spite of this impression of a long shape leading up to the altar, the breadth of the church compared to the length and the shortness of the sanctuary allow all the congregation to feel reasonably involved, even those in the gallery which runs round three sides.

The next church using the same type of plan is one of Wren's best-known works. This is **St. James's, Piccadilly** (1682–84). It has an attractive churchyard on Piccadilly and a steeple which is a modern structure based on Wren's own drawings. The rows of five windows on the flanks of the church again indicate a longitudinal plan, which is borne out in the interior. The colouring here is light grey and gold, contrasting with the brown woodwork. Again there is a broad barrel vault over the nave and springy vaulting in a pattern similar to St. Clement Dane's.

24

Wren's first large-scale work in brick and became a prototype for educational and institutional buildings on both sides of the Atlantic.

Wren's position as Royal Surveyor was secure enough to remain unaffected by the political troubles of the 1680s. After James II came to the throne in 1685, Wren built various additions to Whitehall Palace, all of which were later demolished. In the same year, Wren became Member of Parliament for Plympton St. Maurice in Devon for two years, the start of a peculiarly ineffective political career of Tory affiliation. He later became M.P. for another constituency, but both occasions were short-lived and he seems to have taken no active part in Parliamentary affairs.

In 1688 James was deposed and William and Mary were crowned. William disliked the dampness of Whitehall and instructed Wren to transform Nottingham House, Kensington, into a Palace.

This became **Kensington Palace**, Kensington Gardens (1689–95, expanded 1702), and the tastes of the Dutch King of England are clearly reflected in it.

The scale was intimate and the material used was chiefly brick. The main entrance is under the clock-tower (an individualistic design) into Clock Court, and the King's Staircase on the far side of the Court took the visitor up to the Royal Suite. Today, this Court is still a residence of the royal family, and the visitor must enter from the back of the Palace, facing the Round Pond of Kensington Gardens. The Wren range on this side is even more informal than Clock Court—it might be a terrace of private houses. Going directly through the Queen's apartments to the King's Staircase, it is possible to obtain some impression of how domestically Wren designed the Royal Suite for William III, though the surviving decoration of the King's apartment was done after Wren's time (see William Kent and Nicholas Hawksmoor).

The other Palace which Wren worked on for William and Mary was intended to be on a far grander scale. This was **Hampton Court Palace**, near the Thames at East Molesey, and most of the executed work was carried out between 1689 and

1694 when Queen Mary died. The East and South Wings, together with the Fountain Court, were the only parts that were built, so the remainder of Cardinal Wolsey's Tudor palace was fortunately preserved. Wren's work here has a certain magnificence of scale on the garden frontage, but also a curious domestic quietness. The original designs were much more eventful, with façades that advanced and retreated and a central dome as the climax on each side.

24 *Wren. Chelsea Royal Hospital, Royal Hospital Road, Chelsea (1682–91)*

25 *Hampton Court Palace, in the western outskirts of London. The East Wing, built by Wren in 1689–94*

26 *Wren. Royal Naval Hospital, Greenwich. Wren's designs were built in 1696–1702*

25

26

But if his imagination was not given full scope at Hampton Court, he had no such restrictions on his next work for the King, and it is only in this design that we can say Wren became a truly Baroque architect. This was the transformation of the uncompleted Greenwich Palace into a large-scale naval counterpart of the Chelsea Hospital. The **Royal Naval Hospital**, Greenwich, was decided upon in 1694, and Wren designed the whole general lay-out in the following year. It seems possible that it was John Webb's one existing block, powerful and dramatic, that made Wren at last cross the border into undeniably Baroque design. The central parts were built between 1696 and 1702, departing only in detail from Wren's original plans. The long coupled colonnades, twin domes and central ranges on either side of the open vista from the river up to Inigo Jones's The Queen's House, are Wren's great masterpiece of palace architecture and remain the finest group of their sort in Britain. Various parts were built under the direction of Hawksmoor, Vanbrugh, Campbell and others, but the design is essentially one of Wren's greatest achievements. At the age of 63, perhaps encouraged by the youthful enthusiasm of Hawksmoor, he suddenly arrived at a mature English version of the Baroque style—urbane as yet, but Baroque in the way the masses play with each other, in the successive views unfolded dramatically and in the visual tension of the design.

Seen from the river today (or best of all from the Isle of Dogs on the other side of the Thames), the first block on the right is John Webb's original part of King Charles II's palace, which Wren incorporated. The similar block on the left was planned by Wren, but carried out by Colen Campbell. Behind and between these two blocks, the ground rises with a great flight of steps to the William and Mary blocks with their high domes and the great colonnades running along the sides of the narrower space between, until the vista ends with a distant view of Inigo Jones's chaste Queen's House. The contrast between Renaissance and Baroque was never more vividly demonstrated—the calm harmonious proportions of the one with the splendid drama of the other.

Walking away from the river into the centre of the great group, the left-hand dome is over the chapel (interior 1779 by James "Athenian" Stuart), while the King William block under the dome on the right contains the most important interior of the whole complex. This is the famous Painted Hall, and in it Wren used the available space brilliantly. The entrance is to a sunken lobby, from which the vast ceiling of the Hall is glimpsed above through a screen of giant columns and pillars. Going up the fairly steep steps from this lobby, the expanse and length of the Hall grows visibly through this screen, until the painted richness of the main space itself is reached. The surprises have not finished yet. Thornhill's huge painted ceiling runs on up the Hall, and, at the far end, up more steps and lurking behind another screen of columns, is another great space. This is where the High Table is placed during functions—the space is almost a cube, playing against the long shape of the main Hall.

Not far away from the Royal Naval Hospital on the other side of the open space of Blackheath, is another delightful institutional building which has been attributed to Wren. This is **Morden College**, Blackheath (1695–1700), whose driveway runs from one end of the Paragon on the corner of Morden Road. The two-storied buildings are of brick trimmed with stone and stand in extensive grounds. The main façade and inner courtyard are typical of Wren's domestic manner and have great charm.

After 1690, it becomes more difficult to be sure of the amount of detailed design which Wren did for buildings planned in his office. He trusted and was fond of Nicholas Hawksmoor, who had joined the office in 1679 at the age of eighteen. At this time Wren was anxious about his own health, and in 1698 he wrote urging his son to return from abroad "before it pleases God to take me from you". In fact he had another quarter of a century to live and was to become a Member of Parliament for a third short period, in 1701, for Weymouth on this occasion. The Baroque 1698 plans for Whitehall Palace are certainly Wren's. About this time he was supervising repairs on Westminster Abbey and in 1706 enlarged the House of Commons to provide places for the Scottish members on the disbanding of the separate Scottish Parliament.

King William had died in 1702 and Anne became Queen. Wren's school was still dominant architecturally, and although the much younger Vanbrugh had been appointed Comptroller of Works he adored Wren.

These were the years of the Duke of Marlborough's glory and while Vanbrugh and Hawksmoor designed his monumental Palace at Blenheim, it was Wren who designed his London house. The basic reason for this was that the Duchess could not stand the rumbustious Vanbrugh and she went to the grand old man instead. Wren treated her tantrums with avuncular patience, and **Marlborough House** (1709–11) was built in The Mall (it is entered from Pall Mall today). Wren's building still exists, though it is scarcely recognisable. Third and then fourth storeys were piled on top of it later, and the interior has been entirely re-decorated. The outbuildings are also later additions.

THE BAROQUE STEEPLES

These last years of Wren's architectural career saw him withdrawing gradually into old age, but they also saw one of the most extraordinary Indian summers in any architect's work. This last development was brought about by Wren's increasing interest in the Roman Baroque work of Borromini and Bernini and was expressed in the West towers of St. Paul's Cathedral and in his last spires for the City churches.

Some of Wren's earlier spires were quite grandiose, but were still modelled on Dutch and Flemish examples. **St. Mary-le-Bow** (*c.* 1680) and **St. Magnus** (built 1705, but probably designed earlier) are good examples. **St. Augustine**, Watling Street (1695) shows an increasing use of Baroque motifs in the lead spire, but it is only after 1700 that the Roman Baroque influence starts to show itself in the steeples' stonework. At first, he was cautious—the tower of **St. Andrew**, Holborn (1703) has extraordinary bell-stage windows in a fairly straightforward framework. **St. Bride** (1701–03) has four almost identical stages, diminishing in size towards the obelisk on top.

27 *Wren. Steeple, St. Stephen Walbrook, City (1717)*

Christ Church, Newgate Street (1704) shows a new Baroque confidence, though it is still basically rectangular.

After that, Wren designed the West towers of **St. Paul's** in about 1705 (built 1706–08) with the use of many curves and diagonal pairs of columns. It is clear that the ideas behind this design are those of Borromini and Bernini, and it seems likely that Hawksmoor had at least a hand in pushing the old master's interest in that direction. It should be mentioned that we cannot be sure of the order in which the City spires were designed, though we know when they were built.

The last four steeples are the most extraordinary and brilliant of all. The dates of building spread over eight years, but it seems likely that they were designed over a short period. **St. Vedast** (1709–12) has sides which are all curves, some concave, others convex, and great contrasts between solids and voids. This is a fascinating development from Borromini's towers.

St. James, Garlickhythe (1713–17), **St. Michael, Paternoster Royal** (1713) and **St. Stephen Walbrook** (1717) are highly original variations on another theme. The first has coupled columns which make a diagonal cross through the square plan of the steeple, the second is basically round in pattern, and the last has deep voids and corner columns and pillars which seem to dance around the core of the steeple.

The last decade of Wren's life had its troubles, but his writings show that he felt reasonably content. His financial position was comfortable, and he was able to spend nearly £20,000 on a Warwickshire estate for his son. He continued to see his old friends, though most of them died before him, and liked to go for short walks while discussing the latest ideas—a typically English pastime for intellectuals. According to his first biographer Elmes, he worked on a new method of calculating longitude during his very last years.

But after the accession of George I in 1714, architectural fashions changed. Lord Burlington and Colen Campbell spread the neo-Palladian gospel. Wren gradually lost control of the Office of Works and finally lost the Royal Surveyorship in 1719. He lived quietly in his house at Hampton Court after that, making occasional visits to London where he had chambers in St. James's Street. He liked to visit St. Paul's Cathedral and he was still Surveyor of Westminster Abbey.

It was on one of his visits to London in 1723 that Wren caught a bad cold and after he had retired for a nap in his St. James's Street rooms, his servant found that he had died peacefully at the age of 91.

Nicholas Hawksmoor (1661-1736)

Nicholas Hawksmoor, portrait bust

The work and the personal character of Nicholas Hawksmoor make him the most fascinating of all English architects for many lovers of architecture today. His apparent obsession with the expression of strong—even violent—emotion in his buildings, his obvious love of stone and of the stern grandeur of ancient Roman architecture, his integration of the old Gothic tradition with Classicism, his eccentricity and the intensity which enabled his genius to emerge from his working class background and from the shadow of Wren and Vanbrugh: all these aspects of Hawksmoor give him particular appeal.

Hawksmoor was born in East Drayton, Nottinghamshire, in 1661. His family were yeoman farmers who spelt the name "Hawksmore"—Nicholas himself preferred the spelling we usually see. His only obituary says "he was bred a Scholar" but judging by the earliest known example of his handwriting, from about 1680, the scholarship was rough. However, he did learn mathematics, for as a boy he was taken on as a clerk by Samuel Mellish J.P., of Doncaster. There he got to know a plasterer who had some acquaintanceship with Wren. So Hawksmoor came to London at the age of eighteen, and Wren engaged him as his personal clerk in 1679.

At first he was not directly involved with building, but he was soon doing crude architectural sketches. At this time Wren was still designing some City churches, while others were being built, and the walls of St. Paul's Cathedral were rising. We can presume that he took a personal liking to the young man for they worked closely together from the start, and in 1683 Hawksmoor was appointed Deputy Surveyor for the building of Wren's Chelsea Hospital—quite a responsibility at the age of twenty-two.

After this he became increasingly involved in building and design, though he continued to do accounting work for Wren's Office of Works at least until the early 1700s. Wren encouraged him to travel and read widely, though he never left England. In the architectural discussions they had, the older man doubtless passed on a huge amount of knowledge as well as his own fascination with Vitruvius's verbal descriptions of Roman buildings. By 1690 Hawksmoor's drawing and handwriting were excellent.

It was a long apprenticeship, and, though Hawksmoor was Clerk of Works at Kensington Palace from 1689 and in charge of the St. Paul's drawing office from 1691, it is doubtful whether he had the freedom to design more than minor details. But the next year, Wren seems to have given him a free hand in the design of a new building for Christ's Hospital School (now demolished) in the City, though it was officially the work of Wren's office. It was a distinctly sub-Wren design—two brick storeys above a stone arcade—but there were recognizable differences. In 1695 Hawksmoor took on the design of Easton Neston House in Northamptonshire and references to him now changed from "clerk" to Wren's "gentleman" or "draughtsman". It is impossible to get an impression of his personality at this time and one feels that he must have been extraordinarily self-effacing until someone, probably Vanbrugh in the next decade, gave him a modicum of assurance.

It is probable that Hawksmoor also designed the **King's Gallery** (1695–96), the range on the south side of Kensington Palace, and **The Orangery** (1704–05) in the garden there, though there is no documentary proof. He was still Clerk of Works there and although the interior of the King's Gallery is too simple to give a clue, the proportions and severe uprights of the outside, together with the already typically Hawksmoor central feature on the roof, have caused this to be generally accepted as his design. The Orangery is less surely attributed— Wren and Vanbrugh might both have had a hand in the design. It is a delightful building of brown brick trimmed with stone and red brick, in an expansive Baroque style. Dr. Kerry Downes has pointed out that the evidence of the detailing points to Hawksmoor's involvement, and the unexpected contrast of the long interior, cool subtle white spaces, makes it hard to think of any other designer.

Meanwhile, in 1696, Hawksmoor was appointed Clerk of Works for the building of Wren's Greenwich Royal Hospital, and with this new security he married. Little is known of his wife Hester or of his home life, except that they had one daughter, Elizabeth. His obituary says "he was a tender Husband, a loving Father and a most agreeable companion". Many other writers, as well as his own long friendships, confirm that he had a likeable personality and manner. Only in his old age, when he was often ill and was angry at the success of Lord Burlington's reactionary Palladianism, did he become occasionally bitter in his letters. Otherwise, his own intense emotions found their outlet in his architecture.

Dr. Downes, who has done more than anyone else to unravel what is Hawksmoor's work, is inclined to attribute the west side of the **King William Block** at Greenwich Royal Hospital (1699–1707) to Hawksmoor, rather than to Wren or to Vanbrugh. Once again there is no proof and, even though the style is wild for Wren, we know that the old man was experimenting with High Baroque at this time.

On the other hand, the outside range of the **Queen Anne Block** at Greenwich, started in 1700

and finished in 1703, was certainly designed by Hawksmoor. Here he is in his most severely Classical mood, with firm round-topped windows in massive masonry. His inexperience perhaps shows in the way the overall proportions do not quite succeed. The part of the Queen Anne Block on the central vista of the Royal Hospital was built to match the design of John Webb's King Charles Block opposite, while Hawksmoor designed and built the fine loggias at each end of the courtyard inside the Queen Anne Block in 1716. His ambitious plans for the hospital later included a Baroque chapel on the central vista between the Queen's House and Wren's colonnades to close the view dramatically—but the plan came to nothing.

About 1698 he had met John Vanbrugh, the turbulent playwright-soldier, who turned architect the next year and for at least a decade drew heavily on Hawksmoor's expertise. But between 1700 and 1711, Hawksmoor's posts at Greenwich, Kensington and St. Paul's, together with his work with Vanbrugh at Castle Howard and Blenheim, gave him no time to take on many individual commissions himself.

Then in 1711 everything changed. He built a Charity School (now demolished) in Kensington, but much more important was the establishment by a new Tory parliament of the "Commission for Building Fifty New Churches in London". It was Hawksmoor's great chance and he grasped it tenaciously, starting his own individual career at the age of fifty.

It began at Greenwich, when the roof of the old parish church collapsed. Hawksmoor, still Clerk of Works of the Royal Hospital, may have helped to instigate the petition which the parish sent to Parliament. It suggested that the old coal tax for building the City churches had fulfilled that purpose and the funds might now be used for other churches, notably Greenwich. The idea was taken up and developed by the High Churchmen of the Tory Party. Not only was Greenwich to benefit, but fifty new churches were to be built in the spreading suburbs of London, west as well as east. Two surveyors were appointed in 1711 and Hawksmoor retained one of these posts to the end. The other surveyorship changed frequently—first it was William Dickinson (another man from Wren's office), then Gibbs, then John James. Only twelve churches were actually built, though the funds were used to help with three others. Hawksmoor built six of them to his own designs and collaborated on others. They were very different churches from Wren's—much larger on average, and much more ambitious outside.

Hawksmoor's survival as surveyor through the

political upsets in the next few years of government changes, the accession of George I and the 1715 Scottish rebellion, can only be explained by his sheer competence and lack of interest in anything except architecture and building. He was too guarded in manner to make influential enemies and his only portrait, a bust in All Souls College at Oxford made in his old age, shows sensitivity and closeness in the faintly rustic features, as well as determination in the jaw. His mouth was unusually wide, but the deep downward lines from its corners are more likely to express his constant pain from the "stomach gout" rather than the frustration of his last years.

Understandably, **St. Alfege** (1712–18) in Church Street, Greenwich was the first church to be built under the commission. The main road frontage is in fact at the back of the altar end, and the congregation was originally allowed to enter by the extra doors tucked into the tremendous recessed portico here. The plan is that of a Roman cross, with more doors in the transepts. All these churches are notable for the

28 *Hawksmoor. Interior, St. Alfege, Church Street, Greenwich (1712–18)*

number of entrances originally provided. Each of the plans has a main axis along the central line from altar to main door, with cross-axes at right angles— complex patterns around the square or rectangle which is at the heart of each design. They are strikingly different from Wren's church plans, for the High Church had its own ideas about the lay-out for liturgical purposes and Hawksmoor interpreted their ideas in his own original way.

The side walls are severely Roman in feeling, with the great triple keystones Hawksmoor loved— though these do not yet flare as dominatingly as in the slightly later churches. The tower is Hawksmoor's up to church roof level, but the top is an anticlimax designed by John James (Hawksmoor used his own basic design for this tower at St. George in the East).

Entering the church under the west tower is in

itself a succession of spatial experiences. A long low lobby leads under the gallery, and the view of the church starts gradually to unfold. Emerging into the main space itself, the size is unexpectedly large and its height is accentuated by the vast oval panel floating overhead. The galleries run round three sides of the church, and Hawksmoor used no columns to support the roof. As a result, in spite of the emphasis on the length of the church, there is very little obstruction to the view of the altar and the great ceiling embraces the whole rectangular space. The transepts, so noticeable outside, almost disappear behind the side galleries—there can be no question that Hawksmoor liked his interiors to astonish and they are rarely what would be expected from the outside.

This applies particularly to the next churches, the three in the East End which were all started in 1714 and finished at the very end of the 1720s.

St. Anne, Limehouse (1714–30) rears up in the middle of a green churchyard beside an otherwise depressing section of the Commercial Road, Limehouse (on the corner of Three Colt Street). At the west end there is a semicircular porch and above it the broad face of the tower surges up in craggy stages to a complex top which has echoes of Gothic lantern towers. In contrast, the main side windows are extraordinary, punched forcefully into the flat mass of the disciplined walls.

The entrance today is not through the front porch, but to one side. As in Greenwich, there is a feeling of being trapped inside the stonework of the lobbies followed by a release into the serene space of the church itself. The plan is again based on a central rectangle, pointing towards the large calm east window over the altar. The tension expressed by the low arch high above this only sets off the utter peacefulness of the circular ceiling panel.

At **St. George in the East** (1714–29), Cannon Street Road, Stepney the contrast between interior and exterior was reversed. The outside is the most Roman Baroque of Hawksmoor's churches in feeling, like a great galleon floating at anchor among its low surroundings. There is tension between the strong horizontals of the church itself and the vertical lift of the five towers. The main tower's lantern is topped with a circle of Roman (i.e. round) altars on its pinnacles, while the flanking towers are capped with domes. The detailing is done with tremendous *bravura* and the overall impression is of buoyancy and exultation.

The inside of the church was very different, expressive of tension, unrest and even doubt. There was no serene floating ceiling here, but low barrel vaults crossing each other with the same unrestful

29 Hawksmoor. St. Anne, Commercial Road, Limehouse (1714–30)

curve as the main arches.

A visit to the inside today is a depressing experience. It was gutted by bombs in 1941, and after the war an unworthy church structure was fitted inside part of the bare walls.

The other great church started the same year is **Christ Church, Spitalfields** (1714–29) on Commercial Street at the corner of Fournier Street, Stepney—just outside the City. By far the best approach is by foot along Brushfield Street, a side street off Bishopsgate (quite near Liverpool Street Station). From there the church tower looks like a piece of architectural fantasy piling up towards the sky at the end of the street. This broad tower again shows Hawksmoor's powerful, almost grim, vision of ancient Rome—at least up to the clock stage. Above that the soaring broach spire gives another echo of the Gothic which was exaggerated when its Baroque decorations were stripped off by the

30

31

Victorians when the stonework became unsafe.

From either flank of the church, with its monumental walls and windows tautly composed, it can be seen how Hawksmoor built out the sides of the tower with buttresses to give the front view the impressive breadth he wanted.

Within the tall arched portico the war-damaged interior is structurally complete, except for the galleries removed in the nineteenth century. Again there is a contrast with the exterior. The austere masses outside give way to an atmosphere of triumph and light. This church too is planned around a central square and it has a central cross-axis to side doors (now closed). But the high arcades of slender columns and round arches (which become the tunnel vaults of the aisles) lead rhythmically down the centre of the nave, under an isolated entablature suspended across the nave on twin columns, and on to the Venetian window over the altar. This window is the same form as the entrance porch, but now transformed from an almost threatening power into a

30 *Hawksmoor. St. George-in-the-East, Cannon Street Road, Stepney (1714–29)*

31 *Hawksmoor. Christ Church, Spitalfields, Commercial Street, Stepney (1714–29)*

32 *Hawksmoor. St. Mary Woolnoth, King William Street, opposite the Bank of England, City (1716–24)*

33 *Hawksmoor. Arcade building, Stable Yard, St. James's Palace (1716–17)*

32

triumphant harmony. Christ Church is arguably the finest of all London's churches, and it is to be hoped that its long-delayed restoration will be completed soon.

There can be little doubt that in these three 1714 churches Hawksmoor was striving to express a variety of deep emotions, whether religious or humanitarian, which can only be described by stone and space.

The year 1716 brought Hawksmoor the job of building the **Arcade Building** (1716–17) on the north side of the Stable Yard of St. James's Palace, opposite Stafford House—a charming two-storey range of brown brick trimmed with stone and red brick. In the same year he also built the timber Court of Judicature in the Palace of Westminster, which only stood for twenty-two years. However, the **Jewel Tower**, nearly opposite the entrance to the House of Lords, survives in the form in which Hawksmoor restored it, with his bold window surrounds. This work was done in 1718–19.

This year saw the start of his last two London churches. **St. Mary Woolnoth** (1716–24) replaced an old church. It occupies a prominent site on the corner of King William Street and Lombard Street in the City, near the Bank of England, and dominates its surroundings in spite of its small size. If the exteriors of Christ Church and other Hawksmoor churches have a thunderous extrovert quality, St. Mary is introverted but no less powerful. It is like a piece of compressed matter vibrating on its foundations, likely to explode at any moment. The effect is achieved by the heavy rustication of the massive

33

bottom storey, topped by twin towers that seem to have been crushed together. The rustication is carried on in the splendid Lombard Street façade, but the other side was originally hard against another building and is much simpler.

The area is small, and the door leads almost immediately into the body of the church, revealing Hawksmoor's only truly centralised plan. It is a cube topped by a clerestorey whose big semicircular windows provide most of the daylight. There are

typical Hawksmoor low arches and a square panel ceiling, but in this small space he was satisfied with a calm, almost Renaissance, harmony of expression. The original galleries have been removed and their

34 *Hawksmoor. Interior, St. George's Church, Bloomsbury Way, Bloomsbury (1716–31)*

35 *Hawksmoor. West towers, Westminster Abbey (1734–40)*

34

55

front panels have been suspended on the side walls.

The other church of the same year has the most complicated of all his plans. This is **St. George's Church** (1716–31), Bloomsbury Way, Bloomsbury, near the British Museum.

St. George, both inside and out, shows the architect in grand ancient Roman mood—there may be some Vanbrugh influence here. Only at the top of the tower did Hawksmoor let his imagination go free with a Baroque re-creation of the Mausoleum of Halicarnassus—this originally had lions and unicorns fighting on the step-pyramid, below the surviving statue of George I. The lamps on the main entry steps were copied from the tower and show the original state.

The reason for the complicated plan of the church was that the length of the site ran north and south, and Hawksmoor eventually provided a design that could be used with the altar in the true east apse or at the north end. The main entrance today is under the great six-column portico, but the door under the tower is sometimes left unlocked—that entrance faces the original altar apse inside.

The portico doorway enters into the back of the church as the seating is now usually arranged, facing north towards a fine wooden aedicule altar-piece of a later date. The plan is based on a square, with large depressed arches bearing the clerestorey and the floating rectangular ceiling panel high above. When the church was used with the altar in the apse, there was another gallery facing the surviving one.

Whichever way round it is used, the effect of the interior is absorbing and subtle. Receding ranges of columns and arches towards the altar add mysterious spaces, heightened by the light from the slanted windows, while the wall on the tower side plays strange tricks with levels, solids and voids.

From 1718 onwards Hawksmoor started to lose official posts as the Palladian revival, with its love of calm good taste, put his emotional Baroque out of fashion. But he had work up to the end of his life and he left several designs still to be built—including major works in London and Oxford and at Castle Howard. He seems to have lived quite comfortably in his family home on Millbank and he also owned several other houses. All that really plagued him was his acute gout and his fury at the incompetence of the man who followed him in major positions. When Benson succeeded in ousting Wren as the King's Surveyor in 1718, Hawksmoor's acid account of it read "William B——n Esqr in extream Need of an employment, could find nothing at that time but ye Office of Workes to fall upon, soe disguising himself under the pretence of an Architect, got himself made Surveyor Generall".

The churches kept him busy throughout the 1720s and he built the semi-Gothic tower of **St. Michael**, Cornhill in 1718. It is likely that he designed the obelisk tower of **St. Luke**, Old Street in Finsbury (1727–33), though its church was probably by John James. Dr. Downes suggests he may have done the even more eccentric tapering column steeple of St. John, Horsleydown, Bermondsey too, but this has vanished.

Hawksmoor was Surveyor of Westminster Abbey from Wren's death until his own. The year before he died in 1736, he built a house in New Burlington Street, which has been demolished. In the same year he started to build his last major design. This was the **west towers and gable of Westminster Abbey** (designed 1734, built 1735–45), paid for by the Fifty Churches Commission. The towers are an odd but typical blend of Gothic and Classical detail. Ironically, they have become the most widely known of all his works—though few people could tell you the name of their designer.

The mysterious stomach gout finally killed him in March 1736, though his letters show that only a week earlier his obsessive mind was working on a scheme for a stone Westminster Bridge. That was as it should be for a man who cared about little except building. His simple tomb still exists in Shenley churchyard, Hertfordshire, where he asked to be buried.

Sir John Vanbrugh
(1664-1726)

Sir John Vanbrugh, portrait

Vanbrugh could more accurately be described as one of the important architects of Greenwich, rather than of London, for almost all his surviving London buildings are in that area. But his work is of such importance in the history of British architecture that he must have at least a small section to himself. He and Hawksmoor are the two great originals of the English Baroque period and their work is like that of no other country.

Vanbrugh was born in 1664 in London, the fourth of the nineteen children of Giles Vanbrugh (originally the Flemish merchant family of Van Brugg) and Elizabeth Carleton. In 1666 the family moved to Chester, and nothing is known of Vanbrugh's education. In 1686 he was commissioned as an officer in the Earl of Huntingdon's foot regiment at the age of twenty-two. He was posted to the garrison of Guernsey, but the life was too boring for his wild character and he soon resigned. He went to Paris and seems to have become some sort of spy, for in 1690 he was arrested in Calais and imprisoned. Early in 1692 he was released from the Bastille and returned to England, where he was commissioned in the Marines until 1698. During this time, he took up play-writing and his first effort, *The Relapse*, was a tremendous if scandalous success in 1696. It was followed by seven other plays, of which *The Provok'd Wife* of 1697 is the most brilliant. The plays are quick, witty and bawdy, and Vanbrugh began a public controversy with Jeremy Collier to defend them against the attacks of the Puritans.

During this time he got to know many of the writers and politicians of his time, living a rowdy private life in aristocratic London Whig society. Then in about 1698, he seems to have decided that the prevailing puritanism was too depressing for his future as a writer and, perhaps after meeting and talking to Hawksmoor (who was three years older), he suddenly turned his vast energies to architecture with no training at all.

The very next year, with Hawksmoor's help, he started to design Castle Howard in Yorkshire for Lord Carlisle. Carlisle was First Lord of the Treasury and became a powerful lifelong friend for both men. In 1702, he got Vanbrugh the job of Comptroller of the King's Works, making him second only to Wren in the field of official architecture. Curiously enough, Hawksmoor, usually the first to resent the appointment of architectural amateurs, seems not to have minded Vanbrugh's position above him, and indeed, to judge from the surviving letters, the two had affectionate respect for each other's abilities.

Captain Vanbrugh (he still had an army commission) was a fount of strikingly original architectural

36 *Vanbrugh. Goose-Pie House, Whitehall (c. 1700). Demolished. The wing pavilions were added by another architect*

37 *Vanbrugh. Vanbrugh Castle, Maze Hill and Westcombe Park Road, Greenwich (1717–26)*

ideas. His own writings give a good feeling of what he was trying to express—he wanted buildings to have "something of the Castle Air", and he thought that churches should have a "Solemn and Awfull Appearance". He succeeded in putting over these ideas to his powerful political friends of the Whig party and he continued to get official posts, some of them most unexpected. In 1703 he was made one of the directors of Greenwich Hospital, where he became increasingly important. The next year he became Clarenceux King of Arms, to the fury of other heralds whose occupation he had publicly mocked. About Christmas that year, he was commissioned to design Blenheim Palace, the national gift of thanks to the Duke of Marlborough, and while he was working on the plans (again with Hawksmoor) he was also writing his last three plays. With all this work, he still found time to be a leading member of the Whig Kit-Cat Club and a great lover of women.

About 1700 he had built a house for himself in Whitehall (now vanished) which was eccentric enough to be dubbed Goose-Pie House, but after that he specialised in large country houses all over England. In London, he was involved to some extent with the plans for Greenwich and possibly with the Orangery, Kensington Palace (1704, see the chapter on Hawksmoor). His next London work was His

37

Majesty's Opera House, Haymarket (1704–05) which was burned down eighty years later.

His proposals of 1711 to the Commission for Fifty New Churches had some effect on what was built, though the Tory government which controlled the Commission did not like him and grabbed a flimsy excuse for dismissing him as Comptroller in 1713. But Vanbrugh had the last laugh, for when George I succeeded Queen Anne in the next year, the returning Whigs gave him back the post and a knighthood as well.

At this time Vanbrugh built himself a country house called Claremont, south-west of Esher in Surrey, where only some of his outbuildings survive. The **Old Kitchen** in St. James's Palace (1716–18) has been attributed to him, but in the same year that work started there, Vanbrugh also began yet another house for himself, this time at Greenwich. He had been appointed Surveyor of Greenwich Hospital in succession to Wren in 1716. Vanbrugh said later that he could also have had the Royal Surveyorship, but he refused it from affection for the old man.

The house he built himself at Greenwich is still called **Vanbrugh Castle** (1717–26), in Westcombe Park Road. When Vanbrugh wrote of buildings having "something of the Castle Air" he was thinking in terms of massiveness and monumentality, rather than turrets and machicolation. But at Vanbrugh Castle he treated the building as a full medieval fantasy. It stands on the slope overlooking the Royal Hospital, as romantic as a work of the nineteenth century. Inside, the tall doorways and one taut depressed arch are typical of their designer. The exterior is still well preserved, although the interior has been converted.

Three smaller houses were built in Vanbrugh Fields nearby, all of which may have been designed by Vanbrugh himself; none of these survives.

During these same years, he and Hawksmoor were also working on the outer part of the **King William Block** (1703–28) of Greenwich Hospital. It is impossible to sort out who was basically responsible for those massive ranges of brick and stone, with their giant porticoes and wide arches, but there is certainly a touch of Vanbrugh in their manner.

The expense of the work at Blenheim Palace had meanwhile led to a furious quarrel with the Duchess of Marlborough which ended in Vanbrugh resigning the commission in 1716. But his friendship with the Duke continued, and in the following year it appears that the great general obtained for Vanbrugh the commission of designing buildings for the Board of Ordnance. The resulting buildings have not been established as Vanbrugh's work beyond doubt, though they are certainly strikingly typical of him.

38 *Detail of The Model Room, Royal Arsenal, Woolwich (1719), attributed to Vanbrugh*

The most important buildings are a group in the **Royal Arsenal** at Woolwich, just along the river from Greenwich. They consist of the **Brass Gun Foundry** (1717), **The Model Room** (1719) and the **Gun Bore Factory** (1720s). The buildings demonstrate that, like Hawksmoor, Vanbrugh was no less powerful a designer when working in simple brick.

Apart from the remote possibility that he designed the romantically castellated Water Tower that used to stand on Kensington Palace Green, that completes the London buildings which can be attributed to Vanbrugh.

He continued to build many country houses, and finally, at the age of fifty-five, the confirmed old bachelor got married to Henrietta Yarburgh of Yorkshire in 1719. They had two sons, and after they had been married six years Vanbrugh tried to take her to see Blenheim Palace as completed by Hawksmoor. Sadly, the Duchess refused to allow him even inside the gates. One can imagine Vanbrugh receiving this news with a mixture of uproarious laughter and anger. He died a year later in his own house in Whitehall. His young widow lived for fifty years after him.

Thomas Archer (c.1668-1743)

Thomas Archer, portrait

Thomas Archer, the only English architect who worked in a full-blooded Roman Baroque, is one of the most mysterious figures in English architecture. He came to notice as an architect in 1704 and then gradually disappeared during the 1720s. But during that time, he designed a number of houses as well as three of the most important Baroque churches in England. He was probably born in about 1668 and brought up at Umberslade, Warwickshire. His father was also called Thomas and was apparently fairly wealthy, for he sent his young son to Trinity College Oxford from 1686 and paid for him to travel abroad for four years starting in 1689. Nothing is known of how he spent his time abroad, but it seems probable that he studied architecture in Rome and possibly in Vienna.

He seems to have had few friends or enemies, and extraordinarily little is known about his life. He probably established himself as a country house architect in the late 1690s, and he may have designed Umberslade House for his elder brother in about 1700, but the first thing we know for sure is that he designed and built the north front of Chatsworth in Derbyshire for the Duke of Devonshire in 1704.

In the next year of 1705 Archer was granted the Court post of "groom porter", said to be worth one thousand pounds a year, so one must presume that he had some powerful patrons.

Roehampton House, Roehampton Lane, Roehampton (1710–12) was built as a country house for Thomas Cary. It has a dignified brick exterior, similar to his later Russell House, although it has since been greatly added to and is now part of a hospital.

Archer started work on his first church (St. Philip in Birmingham) in the same year as Roehampton House and two years later he started the first of his two London churches. In 1711, with Wren and a number of others, Archer had been appointed one of the commissioners for the Fifty New Churches, whose job was to supervise the work of the surveyors, Hawksmoor and Sanderson. Archer secured the job of designing two of these churches.

The first was **St. Paul**, Deptford (1712–30) which sits massively in its park-like churchyard off Deptford High Street near Greenwich. The great semi-circular portico rises to a circular Borromini-like tower and a very English spire. The giant rusticated pilasters all round the church make the flanks rather ponderous, though the ambitious double stairways of stone up to each side door (now closed) are well brought off.

The portico contains an almost round lobby without windows, but the feeling of enclosure is gone once inside the door into the main church. The first

39

40

impression is of a very complex plan—there are similarities to contemporary Hawksmoor churches, but the contrasts are even more striking.

The plan is centralized (but not a square), elongated towards the altar. The giant Corinthian columns all around and the rectangular panel ceiling are splendid but rather heavy. There are side galleries and four miniature corner galleries like opera boxes set diagonally to the plan of the church. Behind these, the corners of the church contain rooms with big windows on all sides that let a subtle light into the interior. It is an ambitious Baroque composition, with a personal taste of its architect, though without the flare of inspiration that lit Hawksmoor's churches.

Archer's last church is the nearest thing in London to the Roman Baroque of Borromini. **St. John**, Smith Square, Westminster (1714–28), is tucked away among small streets to the south of Westminster Abbey, where its four towers dominate the low houses, many contemporary, which surround it. These splendid towers, which have brought the church much mockery from Classical purists and are still astonishing, were based on those of Borromini's Sant' Agnese in Rome of 1653–66. Their circular plan, rectangular lantern openings and concave roof line are all adapted from that source. The main windows and porticoes with melodramatically fractured pediments above, are on a giant scale.

The church was burned out during the 1939–45 war and has been restored as a concert hall. Both entrances are at the sides, and the first impression inside is of a clear white lantern. The probable Roman training of the English architect is at once obvious in the way that the whole shape and plan is revealed immediately, just as in a Bernini church and in complete contrast to Hawksmoor whose subtleties reveal themselves only gradually. Here it is clear at once that the plan is a combination of a groin-vaulted square, with an east–west barrel-vaulted nave running through it, emphasised by the two long galleries. The plan of a cross is completed by the giant porticoes outside on north and south. The space is again lined with Archer's beloved giant columns and pilasters.

This was the last of Archer's major works in London. He was a man of forty-six when the building started in 1714 and it may be that he inherited enough family money to make his pursuit of work less keen. He was twice married, but had no children. The names and families of his wives are known but little more than that. In 1715 he bought a manor and estate at Hale, Hampshire, which he rebuilt for himself.

His next London work was the grand town house,

39 *Archer. Russell House, No. 43 King Street, Covent Garden (1716–17)*

40 *Archer. St. Paul, off Deptford High Street, Deptford (1712–30)*

41 *Archer. St. John, Smith Square, Westminster (1714–28)*

Russell House, No. 43 King Street (1716–17), facing the side of the Inigo Jones church in Covent Garden. The strong vertical accents, together with the rather stiff magnificence of the almost cubist composition, are typical of Archer's houses. The house was used as a vegetable warehouse in Covent Garden market until 1974, but its original appearance has now been largely restored.

The design of the **Queen's House**, 16 Cheyne Walk, Chelsea (c. 1720) has been attributed to Archer, as has the surviving façade of **Butterwick House** (interior destroyed) in Queen Caroline Street, off Hammersmith Broadway, also of the 1720s. There is no documentary proof of his involvement in these houses, and a house which he did build in Cavendish Square in 1722 has been demolished.

By the time his two London churches were completed in 1730, Archer was in his sixties and his style was even more unfashionable than Hawksmoor's. His last known London work is the **monument** to a lady called Susannah Thomas, in the south aisle of St. Mary's Parish Church, Hampton, Twickenham, done in about 1731. After that little is known of him. He owned a house in Whitehall and divided his time between London and Hale until his death in 1743, the last survivor of the English Baroque movement.

41

James Gibbs (1682-1754)

James Gibbs, portrait

Gibbs has a peculiar position in the history of London architecture, practising successfully during the fashionable periods of High English Baroque and then of Palladianism, without really belonging to either movement.

He was born in 1682 near Aberdeen. His father, Peter Gibbs, was a fairly wealthy member of the local gentry, and James was brought up as a Roman Catholic and a supporter of the house of Stuart.

His own rather vague memoir survives in manuscript but it tells little until about 1700 when he went "rambling" through Holland, France and Germany, finally arriving at Rome in about 1703. At first he entered Scots College with the intention of becoming a priest, but after a year he started to study architecture under Carlo Fontana. Fontana had been Bernini's pupil and at this late stage in his career was turning away from High Baroque towards a more academic Classicism. Gibbs obtained a very professional training from him, and much of his later reputation was based on the fact that he had worked under the old master.

From contemporary sources and from his own writings, one gets the impression that Gibbs was a rather unpleasant man. His face in portraits is aggressive and a little smug, though obviously intelligent. His family was Tory and understandably he cultivated members of the British aristocracy of the same politics who visited Rome while he was working there.

In 1709 Gibbs returned to Britain when his brother died and then came to London to follow up the contacts he had made in Rome. Business seems to have been thin at first, but it was a well-timed arrival and he had the special patronage of the Earl of Mar. He immediately made friends with Wren, who was then nearly eighty years old, and for a time they saw much of each other. A year later the Whigs at last lost power, and when the Tories took over the government, Gibbs became their favourite architect. Quite soon, he gave up his Catholicism and turned to the Tory High Church for purely practical reasons, though he maintained contacts with Catholic priests.

When the Commission for Fifty New Churches was set up, Hawksmoor and William Dickinson were given the two surveyorships. But in 1713, Dickinson resigned and Gibbs obtained the post. Within a year, he had taken over the designing of one of the churches and started work on it.

This was **St. Mary-le-Strand** (1714–17) which stands on an island site in the middle of the Strand. In this first main frontage and tower, one sees at once the way Gibbs combined elements of the Roman Baroque of, say, Bernini and da Cortona with others more typical of Wren and the English tradition. At the same time, partly because of the available site, the appearance of the church has a very different feeling from the rest of the Fifty New Churches. Instead of rearing up from the ground like a Hawksmoor or Archer church, it sits on its base delicately and charmingly, a small gem.

The steeple and semi-circular porch are clearly derived from Roman models, especially Pietro do Cortona's churches, and when one has climbed the steep steps to the door, the interior is also Roman Baroque in the way that its whole simple space can be taken in at a glance. But around the high windows the walls and ceiling are rich with architectural detail. Sometimes Gibbs's detailing tends to be almost too pretty and lacks sheer architectural vigour. But it is quite understandable that the elegance of the church enchanted the Londoners of 1717, who had never seen anything like it.

The church was finished very quickly but in the meantime Gibbs had suffered a bad setback. In 1714 Queen Anne had died and the Whigs returned to power with the Hanoverians on the throne. The 1715 rebellion in Scotland led to a political purge, and in December Gibbs was discharged from the surveyor-ship as a Scot, a Tory and a Jacobite. Indeed, that was the end of his government appointed career. But it was only the beginning of his professional success, especially among the Tory upper classes who were building country houses.

Gibbs's reputation as an Italianate architect led even Lord Burlington, Whig and Renaissance purist that he was, to employ him for a time on his house in Piccadilly in 1716. The job did not last long, for Colen Campbell soon came along to convert Burlington to Palladian ideals, and Gibbs was dismissed. But when the scaffolding was removed from St. Mary-le-Strand the following year, the acclaim was so great that he had no need to worry about employment. His social standing too was high enough for him to be on visiting terms with several peers. He obviously cared about such things, for he had a great interest in heraldry and adopted the arms of the Gibbs family of Devon, with no sort of justification.

He was able to buy himself a house in Henrietta Street, Covent Garden, and though he never married, he lived there in comfort. He started work on building the palatial Cannons House (it survived only thirty years) at Stanmore, Middlesex (now north London) for the Duke of Chandos and possibly the Italianate **Duke's Mausoleum Chapel** in the nearby church of St. Lawrence, Whitchurch Lane, Little Stanmore (*c*. 1716–20).

Gibbs also developed a new and successful line in designing **church monuments**. He did six of these

42 *Gibbs. St. Mary-le-Strand, Strand (1714–17)*

in Westminster Abbey in the next dozen years, those of **Lady Annandale** (south aisle), **John Smith** (south aisle), **Mathew Prior** (Poet's Corner), the **Duke of Newcastle** (north transept), **Mrs. Bovey** (south aisle) and **Dr. John Freind** (south aisle). These monuments were designed by the architect in considerable detail before the sculptor was called in to execute them.

In 1719 Gibbs designed and built the steeple for **St. Clement Danes**, Wren's church in the Strand. Gibbs's work starts at the level of the clock and rises in playfully varied stages to the topmost cupola. Wren must have driven past it as an old man and would certainly recognise it as the offspring of his own steeples. The windows of the bell stage, incidentally, show an early use of what became known as the "Gibbs surround" (rusticated blocks used as ornaments around the frame of a door or window).

The following year, in 1720, he built one of his most charming buildings, the almost free-standing **Octagon** of Orleans House, Orleans Road, Twickenham, built as an extra room for entertainment. Most of the house was demolished in 1927 and the Octagon now stands remote in this wooded stretch of the Thames riverside. It is of stone-dressed yellow brick, with pilasters at each angle and high windows,

round-topped and with Gibbs surrounds, on the five
detached sides. The interior is ornamented with
marvellous doorways and plaster work carried out by
his favourite Italian plasterers, Artari and Bagutti.
The coved ceiling is crowned by a *trompe l'oeil*
painted lantern in the centre. The Octagon is rarely
open during the day, but is used for occasional
concerts.

St. Peter, Vere Street (1721–24) is a chapel in a
back street off Oxford Street near Cavendish Square.
This is Gibbs in the domestic Wren tradition—the
church was built as a chapel for the Earl of Oxford. It
sits four-square on its island site, built of brown and
orange brick with stone and timber trimmings, and
its double cupola tower is obviously kept in-
tentionally small in proportion to the building's
broad mass. The plan is of the late-Wren type, with
broad nave and narrow aisles, though stained glass
turns what should be a gleaming Baroque interior
into a dim Victorian one. The unexpected frilly nave
plasterwork by Artari and Bagutti survived the
alterations of 1881.

In 1720 Gibbs had submitted designs for the
largest of all his churches. This was **St. Martin-in-
the-Fields**, Trafalgar Square (1722–26), occupying
one of the most prominent positions in London. It is
rather nice to know that when Gibbs submitted his
designs, he arranged for carriages to take the
responsible committee to see a number of Wren's
churches, so that he could point out how tradi-
tionally founded was his design.

The church has a joyous six-columned portico,
like that of Hawksmoor's contemporary St. George
Bloomsbury, although the slightly different proportions change the effect considerably. The way
that the steeple appears to ride on top of the church
was widely copied and has irritated many critics. A
walk around the back of the building is *de rigueur*, for
the walls are marvellously disciplined and taut. Each
elevation is brought firmly to a stop by recessed
coupled columns and every window is enriched by
Gibbs surrounds.

The portico doorway takes one through a circular
lobby and then out into the cream and gold spaces of
the nave. The plan is of the type of Wren's St.
Clement Danes (*q.v.*) but the feeling is distinctly
different—festive in a Roman way, gay plasterwork
on the nave's barrel-vault, swirling in the vaulting
over the aisles, utterly assured and relaxed. The
building is perhaps Gibbs's church masterpiece, a
proudly accomplished design, and certainly his most
influential work—variations of the building, large
and small, can be seen in many parts of the United
States of America and other former British colonies.

His next major work in the London area was a

43

44

45

43 *Gibbs. The Octagon, Orleans House, Orleans Road, Twickenham (1720)*

44 *Gibbs. St. Martin-in-the-Fields, Trafalgar Square (1722–26)*

45 *Gibbs. Interior of the Great Hall, St. Bartholomew's Hospital, Smithfield Market, City (1730–59)*

country house for the Duke of Argyll called **Sudbrook Park** (1726–28) in Petersham Road, south of Richmond. It is now a golf club. The effect is very grand on approaching, brick richly trimmed with stone and a high Corinthian portico. The present entrance to the portico is a later addition which should be removed, but the effect of the big cube room inside is undimmed. It goes from side to side of the house, cutting off the rooms at either end from each other, and the plaster decoration rising to the coved ceiling is flamboyantly Italian Baroque. At the far side of the cube room a door lets one out into another giant portico and then down a double stairway to the garden.

In the year that Sudbrook Park was finished, 1728, Gibbs published a book which was to be even more influential than his buildings. He called it simply *A Book of Architecture*, and it took his designs into architects' offices all over England and North America. Perhaps even more useful to the far-flung members of the profession was another book he published four years later called *Rules for Drawing the Several Parts of Architecture*.

In the late 1720s, apart from a **font** in Dulwich College Chapel (1729), his major London work was **St. Bartholomew's Hospital** (1730–59) at Smithfield, in the City of London. The hospital he built consisted of four linked stone buildings around a main court, though only three of these survive. Gibbs gave the designs as an act of charity—indeed he did so for other buildings too, in striking contrast to frequent references to his stinginess.

The Gibbs court lies immediately beyond the little church inside the seventeenth-century main gatehouse. A Venetian gateway takes you under the first Gibbs block into the courtyard, with a fountain and high plane trees that comfort patients and hot sightseers in summer. Over the years the buildings have lost the urns and statues of their skyline and the big arches that linked the blocks. One cannot help noticing that by 1730 Burlington and the Palladians had influenced Gibbs strongly—there is no sign in these dignified buildings of da Cortona's Baroque massing of columns as in St. Mary-le-Strand sixteen years before.

But a great English Baroque interior lies inside the first of these blocks. This is the Great Hall, whose entrance is to the left inside the courtyard gateway. The immediate impression inside the hall is of a great cream, brown and gold space receding into the distance. The proportions are approximately those of three cubes, with two rows of windows along each side wall, nine bays on each. The ceiling is flat, with swirling white and gold plaster, while the walls are richly decorated with painted brown cartouches and plaques on the creamy background.

Gibbs's final building in London was a **house for the Duchess of Norfolk** at 16 Arlington Street, off Piccadilly, St. James' (1736). All that can be seen of it from Arlington Street is a simple brick house with a massive two-storey gateway, heavily rusticated. This gateway gives some feeling of grandeur, but the other façade of the house, facing onto Green Park, is even simpler than the front. The rusticated gateway gave onto a long narrow courtyard (now kitchens and the like), leading to the much broader area of the house itself. The entrance is now from Park Place, off St. James's Street, through a Victorian house which has been joined onto Gibbs's to form the Royal Overseas League. Despite the alterations, the Gibbs design around a large toplit stairwell can still be made out and many grand interiors survive in the rooms that open off the stairs.

Houses that Gibbs built at about the same time in Leicester Fields and Henrietta Place have now disappeared, and the only other design to be mentioned here is the well-known **monument to Ben Jonson** in Poets' Corner, Westminster Abbey (1737).

By 1740 Gibbs was getting very fat. In spite of his lack of close friends, he had a reputation as a jovial drinking companion. A letter survives written to him by a friend called Patrick Guthrie in 1736 while on a journey with Lord Barnard in France, saying that Barnard "sometimes cites Mr. Gibbs his authority . . . for another bottle" and going on to recommend to Gibbs that long walks "would bring down some of the fat parts".

In the 1740s Gibbs became less active, though his greatest building, the Radcliffe Camera in Oxford, was not complete until 1749. In that year he visited Oxford to receive the degree of Honorary M.A. from the University, but at about the same time, he also had to go to a spa for his health. He suffered badly from gout and gall stone and in 1754 he died, still a bachelor. His last, rather unexpected achievement had been to translate into English the life of a king of Portugal he admired. Gibbs left a fair fortune, and rather touchingly, he bequeathed most of it to Lord Erskine, the son of his patron the Earl of Mar, who had lost a great deal of money.

4
Georgian Palladianism

The English Palladian movement, so named after the late Renaissance Italian architect Andrea Palladio (1508–80), had its roots in the philosophical and aesthetic writings of Anthony Ashley Cooper, third Earl of Shaftesbury, and recognised only Inigo Jones as a true Classicist among earlier English architects. The ideas in Shaftesbury's *Inquiry Concerning Virtue* of 1699 and *Characteristics of Men* of 1711 had been taken up strongly by the powerful Whig aristocrats by the time of his death, aged only forty-two, in 1713. In these books, he wrote that both personal virtue and beauty of all types depended on harmony, balance and proportion. Thus "a man of breeding and politeness is careful to form his judgement of arts and sciences upon right models of perfection"—for example, in the case of architecture, upon the ancient works of Rome. Men should themselves strive to behave with similar balance and avoid excess or "vulgar enthusiasm". "Taste" in behaviour and art was therefore the ideal, and men who behaved in this cultivated way would be rewarded with *virtuoso* status. And it was this quality of "Taste" which came to dominate English Palladian architecture and its typical rules of proportion, rather than the complicated and symbolic mathematics of harmonious proportion which Palladio himself and others had evolved and employed.

In 1712, the year before his death, Lord Shaftesbury in effect initiated the Palladian architectural campaign in a famous letter to Lord Somers from Italy, attacking the Baroque buildings and the

influence of Wren and his protégés. Three years later followed the second Palladian assault, this time by architects. In 1715 Colen Campbell produced the first volume of *Vitruvius Britannicus* (a book of drawings of English Classical buildings with comments on their designs). In the same year the Italian Giacomo Leoni, with Nicholas Dubois, produced the first English translation of Palladio's *Four Books of Architecture*, thus supplying the new movement with architectural examples and with theories. But it was the third wave, led by the *virtuoso* Lord Burlington's energy, social position and political influence, which made Palladianism the dominant English style for nearly half a century.

Burlington re-built the front of his own family house in Piccadilly in the new Palladian manner (the façade was by Colen Campbell, while the Earl himself designed the street screen), with refined and delicate Classicism instead of the power and thrust of Baroque design. He installed a group of protégés there to practise the arts. This Burlington House group consisted of the poet Pope, the composer Handel, the satirist Gay, the draughtsman-architect Flitcroft, the operetta writer John Gay and others, as well as the central figures, the sculptor Guelfi and the painter-turned-architect Kent. Burlington used his own influence with the King, the House of Lords, the Church and all levels of government to obtain commissions for these artists. He denounced the Baroque works of Hawksmoor and Gibbs, and was himself lampooned by artists, such as Hogarth, who opposed his ideas.

His campaign was an extraordinary success within a few years. By 1730 Palladians had effective control of the Royal Office of Works and other key architectural posts. Apart from the architects described in the next few chapters, other Palladians built important London buildings. Henry Flitcroft

46 *One of the grandest Palladian mansions in London, Spencer House, St. James's Place, overlooking Green Park, St. James's (1756–65) by John Vardy. The photograph also shows, on the right, Bridgewater House, designed by Sir Charles Barry, and, on the left, the flats at No. 26 St. James's Place, by Sir Denys Lasdun*

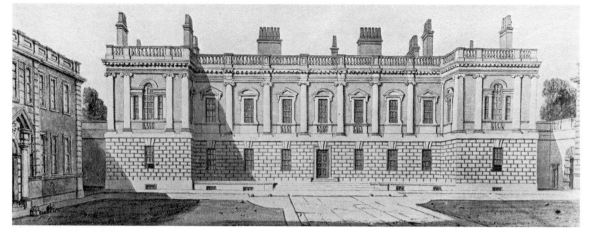

47 *New frontage by Colen Campbell, Burlington House, Piccadilly (1718–19). Much of Campbell's façade for Lord Burlington can still be seen on the main front of the Royal Academy, inside the courtyard, despite the entrance arcade and upper storey added by Sydney Smirke in 1867*

(1697–1769, widely known as Burlington Harry) became Comptroller of the Works, and his buildings include St. Giles-in-the-Fields Church, St. Giles High Street, off Tottenham Court Road (1731–34), Chatham House at No. 10 St. James's Square (1734) and Frognal Grove, Frognal, Hampstead (*c.* 1745, for himself). Isaac Ware (*c.* 1700–1766) became Secretary to the Board of Works; his buildings include Wrotham Hall near Potters Bar in the northern suburbs of London (1754), perhaps the house at No. 1 Greek Street, Soho (*c.* 1750) and the elegant office building for Members of Parliament, Nos. 6 and 7 Old Palace Yard, on the other side of the road from the entrance to the House of Lords. Colen Campbell (?1676–1729), a Scot who was a leader of the Palladian movement, became Surveyor to Greenwich Royal Hospital, and his works included the famous new façade of Burlington House, Piccadilly (1718–19, for the Earl) which can still be seen behind the heavy ground floor colonnade added by the architects Banks and Barry in 1869. Campbell or Roger Morris (1695–1749) were also probably involved in the *virtuoso* Lord Pembroke's design for the villa called Marble Hill (1724–29) in the park overlooking the Thames at Twickenham. Finally, Giacomo Leoni (*c.* 1686–1746) was a Venetian architect favoured by Burlington—Leoni's fine Uxbridge House of 1721 at No. 7 Burlington Gardens, Mayfair, was reconstructed in 1792 with minor alterations only. The house at No. 4 St. James's Square (1725) has also been attributed to Leoni.

During the 1730s and 1740s, William Kent turned from painting to become the most distinguished of the early Palladian architects. Following Kent's death in 1748, a younger generation of Palladian architects became successful. John Vardy (*d.* 1765) executed some of Kent's designs and himself designed the splendid mansion Spencer House, St. James's Place (1756–65) overlooking Green Park. Of the later Palladians not given individual chapters in this book, the most eminent was James Paine (*c.* 1716–89), the contemporary and rival of Sir Robert Taylor. In the London area Paine built many Thames bridges, of which those at Richmond (1774–77) and Chertsey (1780–85) retain some original character despite later widening. Of his many houses in London, only the original inner block of Dover House, Whitehall (1754–58) remains, and that is not visible from outside since Henry Holland added front and rear façades in 1787.

Another successful architect, although he was the object of the strongest disapproval of the Palladians, was George Dance the Elder (1695–1768), Clerk of the City Works for thirty-three years from 1735 onwards. His designs are Classical, but often of a ponderous quality, eccentric without real flair. They include three churches—St. Leonard, Shoreditch (1736–40), St. Matthew, Bethnal Green (1740–46, interior re-built) and St. Botolph, Aldgate (1741–44, interior re-built). Most prominently, Dance designed The Mansion House (the town hall of the City of London) opposite the Bank of England in 1739–52. James "Athenian" Stuart (1713–88) produced much more refined work than the elder Dance did, particularly the first floor rooms (done in 1765) in John Vardy's Spencer House, the elegant Lichfield House at No. 15 St. James's Square (1763–66) and at Greenwich Royal Hospital, the Dreadnought Hospital for inmates (1763) and the new 1779 interior of the Chapel.

Lord Burlington
(1694-1753)

The third Earl of Burlington, portrait

There are now only two surviving buildings designed by Richard Boyle, third Earl of Burlington in London, and so the normal reasons for including architects in this book do not apply to him. But apart from his own considerable achievements as an architect, he was by far the most important single influence in the movement usually called Palladian which uprooted the English Baroque style and established late Italian Renaissance ideals as the only acceptable architecture in England by the second quarter of the eighteenth century.

Very little is known of Burlington's life between his birth in 1694 and his succession to the title at the age of ten. His grandfather, the first Earl, had built up a great fortune as a side line to his political activities, and in 1704 the boy came into extensive Irish and Yorkshire properties, a town mansion in Piccadilly and a Jacobean country house at Chiswick. His mother was a lover of music, and Handel first stayed at Burlington House in 1712, later dedicating his opera *Teseo* to the young Earl.

Burlington was extremely intelligent, perhaps lacking in sense of humour, and he was described at the age of nineteen as being "a good natured pretty gentleman, but in Whig hands". In 1714 he set off on the regular Grand Tour, visiting Germany, Switzerland, most of the major Italian cities (but notably omitting Vicenza on this visit) and Paris. He met William Kent in Rome, starting a friendship which was to become of great importance later.

While he was away, Queen Anne died and George I almost immediately appointed Burlington a Privy Councillor—apparently in error as he was still a minor. Upon his return in 1715 other honours were poured on him, and he was immediately accepted as one of the Whig leaders. But he had no personal political ambition, his passions being directed to all forms of art. At this time he gave Handel a set of rooms in Burlington House and later restored the composer to George I's favour. Within the year he started work with the landscape designer Bridgeman on the gardens at Chiswick, and in 1716 he engaged Gibbs to re-build the façade of Burlington House.

Then he had the revelation which was to develop into the passion of his life. He apparently saw an early volume of *Vitruvius Britannicus* in 1716 and got in touch with its author, Colen Campbell. One can imagine the wily Scottish propagandist selling the young man the idea of the purity of Italian Renaissance architecture, coupled with the English precedent of Inigo Jones whom they misleadingly labelled a Palladian. Burlington's reaction was extraordinarily quick. He drew Campbell into his circle and promoted his cause among likely clients. He dismissed Gibbs and gave Campbell his job at

Burlington House, with instructions to re-build the façade on Palladian principles. Burlington himself designed a small garden pavilion at Chiswick which still survives beside the later villa. It seems possible that he did not like Campbell personally, for their relationship did not last long. Burlington left him to get on with the re-building while he devoted much time to promoting the movement as a whole.

In 1719 he decided that he must study Palladio's buildings at first hand and he set off for Italy by sea, arranging that William Kent and the sculptor Guelfi would meet him in Genoa. This time, he spent almost the whole visit in Vicenza and Venice, where the most important buildings by Palladio are to be seen. He studied the buildings very thoroughly, making copious notes, and buying all the drawings by Palladio to be found. By Christmas Burlington was back in England, bringing Kent and Guelfi with him. He provided them with rooms in Burlington House to act as a core for the miniature court of artists and craftsmen which he proceeded to set up there. For all his protégés he worked hard to obtain employment and preferment. But it was Kent who was the dominant member of the household, where he was known as "the Signior", and who had the most fascinating and unlikely relationship with the Earl.

Burlington did not find it easy to make close friends. The cold face shown in his portrait, with arching brows and a long thin nose, eyes and mouth perhaps a little pinched, is confirmed by all we know about him. William Kent provided a complete opposite in personality and looks and somehow gave Burlington a warmth that few others could. Kent was a jocular little man who adored the frigid Earl and showed a total lack of deference. Their letters to each other make extraordinary reading, but Kent could hardly do wrong at all in Burlington's eyes.

Kent's position in this artists' court was originally that of painter, and Burlington was able to get him the job of decorating the state rooms of Kensington Palace in preference to that very fine painter, Thornhill. Kent was really a very moderate painter indeed but his patron, the great arbiter of Taste, had a completely blind spot about this for many years. He used all his influence to get Kent an extraordinarily high reputation and a great deal of work, which was only to prove justified when the painter turned to landscape design and architecture.

In the architectural field, Campbell and Leoni were now safely established with considerable practices, especially in the great country houses which the Whig nobles were building. Flitcroft, Morris, Ware and other Palladians were soon prospering too, and were gradually taking over the Royal Office of Works. Kent remained only a painter and decorator until 1730 but Burlington himself was already an active architect. He probably designed the courtyard colonnade of Burlington House (demolished) and in about 1721 designed Petersham Lodge near Richmond, a country house which has since been re-built. This was the start of a series of buildings which he designed, earning the disapproval of Lord Chesterfield, who thought it wrong for a nobleman and *virtuoso* to do such work himself.

In 1721, the same year as he designed his first important building, Burlington got married to Lady Dorothy Savile, a good natured girl with a talent for drawing caricatures of her friends. She seems to have had no difficulty in accepting "the Signior" as a necessary part of her new household, and she and Kent liked each other. She had a fine bosom and when Kent heard that another lady of the court was highly praised for the beauty of her neck, he told Lady Burlington that she had nothing to be jealous of as she herself was known as "Cupid's kettle drums".

Later she became a forceful character, and a story of 1727 tells of a fight on the stage between two prima donnas, with Lady Burlington in a stage box verbally supporting one and Lady Pembroke, sitting opposite, supporting the other in a slanging match at the top of their voices. Evenings at Burlington House must have been strange affairs, for Burlington writes in one letter that he is sitting dealing with his correspondence, while a party goes on all around him.

Before he was thirty Burlington had achieved a remarkable success in his campaign for Taste. Apart from his honorary political appointments, he was the principal sponsor of the foundation of the Royal College of Music and was elected Fellow of the Royal Society and of the Society of Antiquaries.

Burlington's earliest surviving London work is the building known as **College** at Westminster School, the residence of the King's (now Queen's) Scholars in Little Dean's Yard, Westminster, though the main façade can only be seen from the private Canons' Garden between the School and the Houses of Parliament. Wren, who was educated at Westminster, had made a design for this building, but Burlington offered to do the job himself. His design was accepted in 1722 though the work was not completed until 1730.

The building consists of one long range of great simplicity and restraint, with no relieving accents in the way of a portico or any decoration of the roof. It is exceptional in Burlington's work in this way, being a simple block of the type which Colen Campbell established as a Palladian norm, rather than having the more elegant advances and retreats of masses and

48 *Lord Burlington. College (residence for the King's Scholars), Westminster School, Little Dean's Yard, facing onto the Canons' Garden, by the cloisters of Westminster Abbey (1722–30)*

49 *Lord Burlington. General Wade's house, Great Burlington Street, Mayfair (1723). Demolished 1935*

roof lines which Burlington and Kent later developed.

When looking at the main façade, it is important to remember that the building consisted originally of an open arcade on the ground floor, with one huge dormitory chamber of two-storey height occupying the entire upper part of the building. In that form, there was of course no glass in the ground floor, and the pedimented window-frames above were blanked in with stone, all the light for the big dormitory coming from the small square upper windows. The interior has now been completely altered, but Burlington's original proportions on the façade remain. They form a very simple exercise in classical harmony. The whole frontage has the proportions of four squares side by side, articulated as fifteen bays plus an extra area of wall at each end. There are many relationships between the various parts of the building which can easily be detected, to demonstrate in a simple form the Renaissance and ancient Classical ideas of harmonious proportions which Burlington got from Scamozzi rather than Palladio himself. One interesting point about this building is that Burlington already used the con-

venient precedent of Inigo Jones's Banqueting House in using the semblance of two storeys (as expressed by the rows of windows outside) to overcome the difficulty of handling the very high room inside.

The next building designed by Burlington, the house for General Wade in Great Burlington Street of 1723 was demolished in 1935. This loss was a disaster in the architectural history of London, though much less than a disaster for potential occupants, since the house was notorious for the discomfort caused by the symmetry imposed on its plan.

The most important of all the Earl's London buildings is of course the villa he built, for his library and for entertaining friends, beside his inherited house at Chiswick. The Jacobean house has now vanished and so it is only Burlington's work that we know today as **Chiswick House**, Burlington Lane, just off the Great West Road out of London. The dates were probably 1723–29, though work of various sorts at Chiswick was too continuous for this to be clear, and the original drawings were burnt. The division of responsibility has still never been clearly proved, but it seems that the design of the building was Burlington's and the rich interiors were Kent's.

From the entrance to the grounds in Burlington

50 *Lord Burlington. Chiswick House, Burlington Lane, off the Great West Road, Chiswick (c. 1723–29)*

Lane, a formal avenue with rusticated gate piers and classical busts leads up to the quadruple stone stairway of the villa. The basic idea came from Palladio's Villa Rotonda outside Vicenza, but Burlington developed it a long way from this prototype. Today the cold but grand proportions of the house sit elegantly and a little stiffly above the softly rising landscape which Kent and others later created. The same type of relationships of proportions referred to in the description, above, of the Westminster Dormitory can be worked out here, but the pattern is much more adventurous. The six-column portico dominates the entrance front, forming an airy relief from the solid walls on either side, and above it rises the octagonal dome which is the Villa's most original feature. The form is truly Italian in its low basement storey and higher *piano nobile* above, while Burlington has ingeniously used obelisks to contain the chimneys so necessary to the English climate. The windows of the *piano nobile* are richly varied, aedicules, simple rectangles, variations on the Venetian window and—in the dome above—three-part lunettes. It is interesting that Burlington felt himself justified in departing so far from symmetry that no two sides of the building reflect each other.

It is unfortunate that at present the visitor has to enter the Villa at basement level (which Burlington reserved for his library and his studies) rather than grandly up the stairway and into the portico. By that proper approach the entrance would pass through a high dark passage and then arrive directly in the breathtaking central saloon with its high octagonal dome. From here the doors radiate out into the other main rooms, while the staircases are restricted to small spirals in each angle of the octagon. It is an ingenious though not convenient plan, and it is curious that the many rooms do not have the strict Classical proportions which one would expect. The gallery, however, was something of a Palladian prototype. Each part is an unexpected shape—a circle, an apsed oblong and a small octagon respectively.

The Earl's other London buildings have all been destroyed. They probably included the Burlington School in Old Burlington Street, Richmond House in Whitehall, and another house in North Audley Street. In addition, it is said that he assisted Kent with the designs for the Royal Mews building at Charing Cross built in 1732 and demolished in 1830. Professor Wittkower's researches have left no doubt that he worked with Kent on several designs and that his influence on his protégé's later buildings remained powerful. Between them they devised the type of Palladian building, with complex advancing and retreating parts, of which the Horse Guards is the most important London example.

It should also be mentioned that Summerson has convincingly shown that the houses which the Earl financed in the streets behind Burlington House (Burlington Gardens, Old Burlington Street, Savile Row *etc.*) saw the birth of the Palladian town house, in both its grand and its simpler forms. Most of the finest houses of the eighteenth century were derived from these models, which were themselves rooted in the Lincoln's Inn Fields houses designed by Inigo Jones. Such London houses are normally of brick, often with stone trimmings, and the type provided the bulk of good quality London houses for the next hundred years (Kent's No. 44 Berkeley Square is a particularly splendid example).

In 1733 Burlington withdrew almost completely from public life. It seems likely that the chief cause of this was his personal financial difficulties stemming from his own building activities around Piccadilly and at Chiswick, though the political spark was the introduction of the Excise Bill by Walpole. In protest, the Earl resigned almost all his honorary posts and ceased to be a Whig. In the following year he closed up most of Burlington House (though his protégés continued to occupy their rooms) and took his favourite pictures and furniture to Chiswick. From then on he spent almost all his time there, though he still frequently visited Yorkshire, and Lady Burlington remained close to the Queen at Court.

He did not stop architectural work altogether, for in 1734 he helped Kent with the design of Holkham Hall in Norfolk and in 1736 he attended the ceremony for the opening of the Assembly Rooms at York, which he himself had designed six years earlier. But most of his time was spent cataloguing and studying in his vast library in the ground floor of Chiswick Villa, or attending to his estates. He wrote to his wife from Yorkshire that he was sending "a doe which I suppose will be more for the Signor's Gola than anyone else" and mentioned that the vicar had complained of his "greatest coldness" of manner.

The last ten years of Burlington's life were spent very quietly, and he died in 1753, before the architectural reaction to his Palladianism set in. He had succeeded in his ambition to change English architecture radically and his name was widely respected throughout Europe. This was especially so in Italy, and the great Piedmontese architect Juvara, among others, dedicated a book to him. He was buried at Londesborough in Yorkshire. Lady Burlington, who had become famous for her rages in later life, died five years later with "curses and blasphemies even on her death bed".

William Kent
(c.1685-1748)

William Kent, portrait

The most successful and distinguished architect of Lord Burlington's Palladian group was William Kent, the son of a working class Yorkshireman. Several of Kent's buildings in London still survive, certainly enough to demonstrate his very personal approach to Palladianism. Characteristics of this approach are his strong feeling for advancing and retreating solid volumes, low pyramid roofs and the rather surprising Baroque touches which appear in his buildings and, most strongly, in his splendid furniture.

Kent was born at Bridlington in Yorkshire and was apprenticed to a coach-painter in Hull in about 1700. His talent was discovered by a group of aristocratic patrons of the arts, who paid for him to go and study painting in Italy. In exchange, he was to send back paintings and sculpture for his patrons.

The young Kent set off for Italy in 1709 or 1710 and studied in Rome in the studio of the painter Benedetto Luti. There, he met many wealthy English travellers doing the Grand Tour and established personal contacts which would last. For a while he helped these visitors with their purchases of works of art. He made them laugh too: Kent was plump and very short, with an impish sense of humour which recognised no social superiors. And by 1713 he had established a fair reputation as a painter in Rome—rather curiously, it seems today, when one considers the poor quality of his surviving paintings. His great talents for architecture, furniture and landscape design were not discovered until a decade later.

Kent probably met Lord Burlington in Rome in 1714 and the two very different Yorkshiremen took to each other at this first brief contact. After travels around Italy with other noblemen, the young painter wrote in 1717 that he wanted to come back to England, but was worried about the popularity in London of "ye French gusto in painting". In 1719 Kent went to meet Lord Burlington in Genoa during the latter's tour to see Palladio's buildings at Vicenza. Burlington brought Kent back to London that Christmas.

On 30th January 1720 Kent wrote to one of his original patrons, Burrell Massingberd, about "ye days being so short and cold to an Italian constitution yt I keep my little room, only twice a week yt I go to ye Operas". Burlington installed the "Signior" in an apartment in Burlington House, and Kent was to live there, in effect as jester to the court of resident artists, until his death.

Lord Burlington immediately started to promote his protégé's interests to the King and to the court, gaining him several commissions for paintings. In 1724, Kent edited a book of Inigo Jones's designs, and in the following year he designed the **interiors** for Burlington's own villa at Chiswick and the picturesque ruined temple at Claremont in Surrey. It seems that Kent may have returned to Italy in 1730 to study architecture at last and his career in building design dates from that time, coinciding with Burlington's withdrawal from fashionable court life.

Kent's White House at Kew Palace of 1731–35 has been demolished, as has his large Royal Mews building of 1732, which stood on the site of the present National Gallery in Trafalgar Square. His **Gothic entrance** of 1732 in the Clock Court of Hampton Court Palace, with the Cumberland Suite, survives, and his painted **Royal Barge** of the same year is in the National Maritime Museum at Greenwich. At this time he also did the **monument to Lord Stanhope** in Westminster Abbey, restored the Rubens ceiling in the Banqueting House and designed fancy dress costumes which could turn a fashionable lady into a "walking Palladio in petticoats".

During the 1730s Kent's practice grew enormously and included some major country houses. In 1733–36 his design for the **Treasury building** was started. The design consisted of a long three storey block with pavilions at each end. Unfor-

51 *Kent. The old Treasury building, Horse Guards Parade, Westminster (1733–36). The flanking wings and pavilions which were part of the original design were never built*

53

52 Kent. No. 44 Berkeley Square, Mayfair (1742–44)

53 Kent. Staircase and screen, No. 44 Berkeley Square

tunately, only the centre of the block was built, omitting three bays at each end as well as the pavilions, and this stands on the south side of the Horse Guards Parade off Whitehall. The building, with its projecting pedimented central section and sophisticated rustication overall, is of great Palladian elegance. But, standing alone without its wings, the height of the elevation makes the proportions appear strange. The interior has been largely re-built as flats for present-day government ministers.

In the same years during which the old Treasury was designed and started, Kent was building Devonshire House in Piccadilly for the third Duke of Devonshire. It was a simple and strong brick mansion with splendid Kent interiors. In 1924 it was demolished and replaced by the office block of the same name.

It was in 1738 that Kent started his revolutionary landscaping of the park at Rousham Hall in Oxfordshire, and at the same time he was working on designs (1732–39) for re-building Westminster Palace, which were never executed. In 1740–42 he designed the famous **monument to Shakespeare** in Westminster Abbey (the statue was carved by Scheemakers) and rooms at No. 10 Downing Street. The much-altered house at **No. 22 Arlington**

Street, beside the Ritz Hotel, dates from the same years. It was built in 1741–50 and is now being restored to its orignal state.

The finest of all Kent's town houses, **No. 44 Berkeley Square** in Mayfair, was built in 1742–44 for Lady Isabella Finch. The glorious frontage on Berkeley Square is of brick with stone detailing of great dignity. The importance of the first floor *piano nobile*, where the great saloon occupies the whole front, is expressed by three tall pedimented windows. Rustication is restricted to the ground floor, where it is used with particular effect around the grand front door. Inside, the entrance hall has a door to a rich but restrained ground floor saloon and, to the right, leads up into the high curving stair well. The stairs start with a single flight, then swing out on both sides. At the turn of the stairs there is a breathtaking sudden view of the great gold and grey screen piling up on the landing above. On the *piano nobile* is a fresh little square room and, in the front of the house, the splendid main saloon of one and one-third cubes, with inset panel paintings and rich gold plasterwork on the coved ceiling. The whole house, now a gambling club, is one of the supreme works of architecture in London.

By this time Kent was established as the leading architect in the capital. He was not a cheap artist to employ. According to the Palladian amateur Sir Thomas Robinson, "The Signior often gave his orders when he was full of Claret, and as he did not

perhaps see the works for several months . . . would order without consulting his employers, three or four hundred pounds worth of work to be directly pulled down." He lived extravagantly, keeping a mistress named Elizabeth Butler in Covent Garden, for whom he later provided in his will, but becoming very fat from "high feeding and life" at Burlington House.

During the 1740s, Kent was at work on designing two major public buildings for London which were not built until after his death. The first, the Courts of Justice beside the Houses of Parliament, stood where the public entrance to the House of Commons is today. The range, erected under the supervision of John Vardy in 1758–70, was a typical Kent design with a pedimented central section facing the east end of Westminster Abbey, wings and corner pavilions with Kent's favourite pyramid roofs. The building was damaged by the 1834 fire at Parliament and was finally demolished in 1850.

His other public building remains as Kent's most famous contribution to the London scene. This is the **Horse Guards** building facing both onto Whitehall, opposite Inigo Jones's Banqueting House, and onto Horse Guards Parade. It was designed in about 1748, the year of Kent's death, and building was again supervised (and perhaps altered) by his disciple

John Vardy in 1750–59. Although the building is English Palladian in its detailing, the overall design is very particular to Kent. The plan advances and retreats, and the skyline is broken and full of incident, almost romantic in its general effect. The texture given by the typically English use of windows recessed in arches, the restrained rustication of the stonework and the pyramid-roofed pavilions provide a suitable last monument to Kent's genius. The central room marked by the Venetian window over the archway on the Horse Guards Parade side was the office of the Commander in Chief of the British Army. It is a fine restrained room with handsome doors and niches, now named after the Duke of Wellington who used it for ten years. This room, the offices around it and the hall which runs up into the octagonal central tower are the only interiors of interest.

In early 1748 Kent made a visit to Paris. In April of that year he got an "inflammation of his bowels and foot" which spread through his body quickly. He died on 12 April, and Lord Burlington had his Signior buried in the Boyle family vault at Chiswick.

Sir Robert Taylor (1714-88)

Sir Robert Taylor, portrait

Sir Robert Taylor was the leading figure of a new generation of Palladian architects in London. By 1750 Burlington, Campbell, Leoni and Kent were dead or no longer practising. Flitcroft was building only outside the capital, and the major survivor of the Wren tradition, Gibbs, was right at the end of his career. During the following decade, according to T. Hardwick in his *Memoir of the Life of Sir William Chambers*, Taylor and James Paine "nearly divided the practice of the profession between them till Mr. Robert Adam entered the lists". And much of Paine's huge practice was outside London.

Taylor was born in Woodford, Essex, the son of a master mason who carved some major monuments and was a prosperous contractor. In about 1728, aged fourteen, young Taylor was apprenticed to a successful sculptor called Henry Cheere, whose clients included the Bank of England. During the 1730s, after completing his apprenticeship, his father paid for the young sculptor to study in Rome. He returned to London when his father died a bankrupt in 1742 and was befriended by the wealthy Godfrey family, who had been involved in founding the Bank of England.

With friends like these, Robert Taylor soon started on his unremittingly prosperous and distinguished career. In 1744, virtually unknown, he was commissioned by Parliament to carve the large **monument to the hero Captain Cornewall** in Westminster Abbey—the spectacular scenic sculpture was later moved to its dark position in the Abbey cloisters and rock formations were substituted for Taylor's architectural features. Also in 1744, he was commissioned to carve the sculpture in the **pediment of the Mansion House**, opposite the Bank of England in the City. It is pedestrian in design and execution, and it was surely Taylor's City connections (his father had been one of the contractors for the building) which secured him the commission despite the competition of the great sculptor Roubiliac for the job.

By 1750 Taylor was giving up sculpture and starting his successful architectural practice. He built a house in Essex for the Godfreys at this time and another for the banker John Gore at No. 112 Bishopsgate in the City (now demolished). In 1752 he designed and carved the **monument to General Guest** in the west aisle of Westminster Abbey, one of his last sculpture commissions. The houses he built at Nos. 35 and 36 Lincoln's Inn Fields in 1754–55 have been destroyed. The Lord Mayor's present **ceremonial coach**, which can usually be seen in the London Museum, was designed by him in about 1758. Taylor's re-building of The Grove, Hemel Hempstead Road, Watford for Lord Clarendon in

55

1756 has been much altered, while his Asgill's Bank of the same year in Lombard Street, City has been demolished. But his other work for the Asgill family survives and has been carefully renovated by a recent wealthy owner.

This building is **Asgill House**, in Old Palace Lane, Richmond (1760–65). It is a notable example both of the long tradition of villas outside central London along that stretch of the Thames and of the polygonal plan for villas which Taylor developed.

In 1757–60 Taylor was at work with the elder George Dance, the Clerk of the City Works, on the re-building of old London Bridge, inserting a wide arch in the centre and removing the buildings on the bridge. This was Taylor's first commission in the field of public building. The next was at the Bank of England in 1765, but in the meantime he built Grafton House in about 1760 at No. 85 Piccadilly, which was demolished in 1966. Taylor's **No. 33 Upper Brook Street** (1767–68) survives, however.

Taylor's rebuilding of the **Bank of England** has been well described by Marcus Binney, who is writing his biography. The Bank, built in 1732 to provide a secure base for England's banking activities, was growing as its role increased. Taylor's buildings, and those by his great successor Soane, were largely destroyed during the reconstruction by Sir Herbert Baker in 1921–37. The famous **Court Room** by Taylor was built in 1766–70 and has

survived in a slightly altered form, losing much of the plasterwork when Baker moved its position. But its glorious Venetian windows and the arcade screens of coupled Corinthian columns at each end can still be enjoyed. Taylor continued work at the Bank of England on and off until his death. In his Reduced Annuity Office of 1782–88 (now destroyed) he introduced the idea of the shallow dome with side lighting, providing a suitable working daylight for the clerks below, which Soane developed so effectively after him.

By the 1770s, Taylor's reputation and fortune were well established. It is hard to get a picture of his personality, but he had a formidable reputation for

55 *Taylor. Asgill House, Old Palace Lane, Richmond (1760–65)*

56 *Taylor. Interior of the Court Room, Bank of England, Threadneedle Street, City (1766–70). Much of the delicate plasterwork was lost when the position of the room was changed in the 1920s*

57 *Taylor. Ely House, No. 37 Dover Street, Mayfair (c. 1772)*

58 *Taylor. Stone Buildings, Lincoln's Inn, off Chancery Lane (1774–80)*

56

57

58

organisation and hard work. It appears that he was always up out of bed by four o'clock in the morning, and he travelled to his country commissions by night coach to save working time. His designs were usually finely realised essays in the English Palladian manner, only the polygonal villas and the banking halls showing real originality.

The grandest of all Taylor's London houses, **Ely House** at No. 37 Dover Street in Mayfair, dates from 1772–76. The frontage is high in proportion to its three-bay width, with a splendid rusticated and vermiculated arched ground floor, and grave pedimented Corinthian aedicule windows on the *piano nobile* above. The cornice perhaps lacks the weight needed for the top of such an ambitious elevation. The interiors were largely re-built by that excellent architectural partnership Smith and Brewer in 1909 and are in harmony with the outside. Taylor's four noble Classical houses at **Nos. 3–6 Grafton Street**, also in Mayfair, of 1771–73, are among the finest examples of strong yet elegant design in brick to be found in London.

During the same decade Robert Taylor started work on his greatest country house, Heveningham Hall in Suffolk, and on his largest surviving building in London. This is **Stone Buildings**, on the east side of Lincoln's Inn, opening off Chancery Lane. Taylor designed and built the first part of this great Palladian block of barristers' offices in 1774–80, the south wing being completed in 1843 long after his death. It is one of the prime examples of restrained Palladian public buildings in London, a long range facing onto the Lincoln's Inn gardens to the west; two rusticated storeys topped by two of plain stonework with a cornice and balustrade above. The ends are accented by advancing pedimented pavilions with giant Corinthian columns running up the two upper storeys. All is calculated for grave dignity without vulgar display, a dignity which is maintained in the best offices within, with their restrained Classical decoration. The Chancery Lane side of the building, with the entrances to the offices, faces onto a narrow courtyard. The range on the other side of this courtyard is also Taylor's work.

During the 1780s Taylor continued his country house practice and Bank of England work. He received many public appointments and was knighted in 1782. In 1788 he caught a chill at the funeral of one of his best clients, Sir Charles Asgill, and died of it. He left a considerable fortune to Oxford University for a foundation for the teaching of modern languages. C. R. Cockerell's great Taylorian Institute building, erected over fifty years later, has given Taylor's name an unexpected immortality.

Sir William Chambers (1723-96)

Sir William Chambers, portrait

Just as Sir Robert Taylor and James Paine dominated English architecture in the years immediately after the middle of the eighteenth century, the 1770s and 1780s were the great period of William Chambers and Robert Adam. The former made his name by his work in the Chinese taste and then became a by-word for late academic Palladianism, while the latter gave his name to a Classical style of his own.

Chambers was from a Scottish family, but he was born in Sweden, where his father was a successful Baltic merchant in Gothenburg. The boy was given an English education at Ripon, where he stayed with a relative. He returned to his family at Gothenburg in 1739 where, although he later said he already had "the strongest inclination for architecture", he was launched into the life of a merchant. He went on three major voyages during the next ten years—two years at sea to Africa, India and Ceylon, over two years to China and then another year to China, returning to Gothenburg in 1749.

During his mercantile travels he studied and drew the Chinese buildings he saw and determined to become an architect. So, at the age of twenty-seven, he went to study for a time under the famous architect Jacques-François Blondel in Paris, after a period in England during which he met the Prince of Wales (later King George III) and his own future wife. There followed five years in Rome living in the same house as Piranesi and building up a considerable reputation as a draughtsman and pundit of the arts. Among others, he met Joshua Reynolds and Robert Adam there; Adam was a great worrier about his architectural competitors and anxiously described Chambers as regarded by the English colony as "a prodigy for Genius, for sense and good taste".

In 1755 Chambers and his wife returned to London where they could at first afford only a "poor mean lodging up a long dark stair". His Italianate design for Harewood House was rejected, and he decided to make his future Classical designs more in the English Palladian tradition. Better times came in 1757 with the publication of Chambers' book *Designs for Chinese Buildings* and his appointment as tutor of architecture to the Prince of Wales.

It was the favour of Princess Augusta, mother of the Prince of Wales, and his own knowledge of China which obtained Chambers' first important commission. The Princess employed him from 1758 until 1763 to lay out the grounds at Kew, now **Kew Gardens**, and to decorate them charmingly with the towering **Pagoda**, **orangery** and a variety of small **temples**. Many of these survive today and Chamber's Pagoda of 1761, with its ten tiers of octagonal Chinoiserie roofs, is one of the two most famous buildings by the great Palladian architect.

59 *Chambers. The Pagoda, Kew Gardens (Royal Botanic Gardens), Kew, south-west London (1758-63). The largest of many temples in oriental and European styles which Chambers built in the gardens*

Sadly, the Chinese temple, the Mosque, the Alhambra and some of the other temples which he built at Kew have been demolished. But the delights of the Gardens today still owe much to his surviving temples.

From that time on, Chambers' royal patronage was as much at the core of his success as his own considerable talent. His former pupil and patron became King George III in 1760, and when the Royal Academy was founded in 1768, Chambers was appointed Treasurer. He so dominated the proceedings of the Academy until his death that the President, Sir Joshua Reynolds, complained half jokingly that "Sir Wm. was Viceroy over him". In 1769 Chambers became Comptroller of the Works upon the death of Henry Flitcroft, the last of Lord Burlington's own Palladian group, and in 1782 he was appointed Surveyor-General by the King.

In the meantime Chambers developed a flourishing practice in and outside London. Many of his London buildings have been demolished, including the Society for the Encouragement of the Arts (1759), the work he did at Buckingham House when the King made it his palace in 1762, several houses in Berners Street, the German Lutheran Church of the 1760s on Savoy Hill and Carrington House in Whitehall (c. 1769).

Three works by Chambers, however, can still be seen in south-west outskirts of London. **Manresa House** (originally called Parkstead) in Roehampton Lane, Roehampton was built in 1760–68 and is a splendid example of his early work. The chaste Palladian block, lightly rusticated on the bottom storey, has a great Ionic portico approached by steps which curve up on both sides. It is now a Jesuit college. Chambers' **Observatory** building in the Old Deer Park at Richmond dates from about 1768–69 and has an unusual plan, with two octagonal rooms which protrude in the central bay on both sides of the block. The working observatory itself emerges as a sort of cupola on the roof.

The famous villa built for Sir Joshua Reynolds, **Wick House** of 1771–72 on Richmond Hill, has been sadly altered though it still has much the same lovely view over the Thames that Reynolds painted.

In 1770–74 Chambers was also at work on a house right in the middle of London. This was built as Melbourne House, set back a few yards from Piccadilly itself, near the Royal Academy. It has a handsome seven-bay brick frontage, trimmed with stone, and the pedimented three-bay centre behind the Doric porch is brought forward just enough to give it a dignified accentuation. This is **Albany**, the best-known apartments in central London, homes for Prime Ministers and the wealthy. The interior is

60 Chambers. Manresa House, off Roehampton Lane, Roehampton (1760–68). Now a Jesuit College

now little to do with Chambers, for Henry Holland re-built and extended the house to form "residential chambers" in 1803–04. Another house in Piccadilly by Chambers for Lord Fitzwilliam has been demolished, while his Warwick House in Cleveland Row, St. James's, of 1770–71 was re-built beyond recognition in 1890.

It can be seen that Chambers had a vast practice in London alone. His standing was expressed in what one Swedish visitor described as a "princely manner". We get a glimpse of his outward personality from another piece of description by Adam. "His appearance is gentell and his person good. . . . He despises others as much as he admires his own talents which he shows with a slow and dignified air, conveying an idea of great wisdom."

Chambers was certainly conscientious, too. In 1774 the decision was made to build the palatial government office building of **Somerset House** between the Strand and the Embankment of the River Thames, now beside Waterloo Bridge. When he was appointed to do the design, Chambers went off to Paris to study the planning and design of the great government offices recently built there. The resulting building, the first part built in 1776–86, is one of the most splendid pieces of architecture in London. Approaching from the Strand, three deep arches penetrate the dignified Palladian block on that side and open out into the grand central courtyard. Fine rooms in the building were originally occupied by artistic and learned bodies under the King's

patronage, and some of these have recently been reopened to the public. Most famous of all is the long, long river frontage opposite the National Theatre. Here Chambers' English Palladianism is mixed with deep voids, screens of giant columns and vast dramatic arches on the lower levels, echoing the imaginative spatial effects in the engravings of his old acquaintance Piranesi.

Although the first stage of Somerset House was finished in 1786, work continued long after that and the side wings were designed (in respectful harmony with Chambers) by other architects after his death. In the 1780s, Chambers continued to work hard but suffered severely from gout and asthma. In 1795 he requested the King to relieve him of responsibility for the works at Somerset House, writing of "infirmities incident to old age, which of late have come fast and severely upon me. I am now rendered totally unable to manage such a work." A year later, in March 1796, he went into a gradual decline and died peacefully enough.

Chambers was a strict and straight-laced father to his children, but one letter to his favourite daughter has much appeal. Considering his life's work, he wrote "I feel such pleasure as no General ever felt in War . . . His business is to destroy . . . mine is to enrich, to beautify it [the world] and to supply its inhabitants with every comfort."

61

62

61 *Chambers. Albany, frontage on Piccadilly, Mayfair (1770–74). Built as Melbourne House, converted into apartments 1803*

62 *Chambers. Somerset House, Strand and the Embankment, by Waterloo Bridge (first part 1776–86, east and west wings built over the following seventy years)*

71

5
Adam, Neo-Classicism and the Regency

Neo-Classicism in British and European architecture is not a phase that can be defined clearly. With increasing travel by European architects to see the buildings of Greek and Roman antiquity, and increasing publication of books illustrating ancient sites, the inspiration for buildings of the late eighteenth century relied more and more directly upon these Classical sources rather than upon their reinterpretation during the Italian Renaissance. Sir John Summerson has analysed three prime elements in Neo-Classical architecture—"the concept of art through archaeology", "the power to choose between styles or to combine elements from different styles" and "the concept of a modern style, a style uniquely of the present." The work of the architects described in the following chapters will show how very diverse the interpretation of Neo-Classisicm could be, depending on which of these three elements was given priority. The element of Greek archaeology may be seen in many of them, but most typically in Smirke's designs. The element of power to combine styles may be seen dramatically in Soane's work. The element of a style uniquely of the present can be exemplified not only by Soane but by Adam's very individualistic revolt against Palladianism.

In Europe, Neo-Classical architecture can be seen in great sections of Helsinki, St. Petersburg, Berlin, Vienna, Paris, Rome and elsewhere. Adam's designs are part of this European Neo-Classicism, but he also employed two concepts of his own. The first was that of "Movement" in architecture—the rise and fall of rooflines, the advance and retreat of frontages. He complained about its absence from most Palladian

work and mentioned its importance frequently, giving Kent's Horse Guards and Vanbrugh's mansions as good examples of it. It is a quality difficult to find in his own London works, though it is more evident in his country houses. The other Adam innovation was his reinterpretation of ancient Classical domestic interiors, which he pointed out were quite different from the interiors of temple and public building architecture. It was in this field that he made his lasting contribution to European architecture.

All the same, it was George Dance the Younger who pointed the way, in his later and lesser known works, to the subsequent development of Neo-Classicism in English architecture. These designs contain the seeds of Soane's great achievements with free use of Greek elements and of Smirke's rather arid Neo-Greek manner which was so widely taken up by others in the 1820s and 1830s.

Neo-Classicism was, however, complicated by the development of another movement after about 1800. This may be dubbed Picturesque Romanticism, a manner which developed in part from the freely lyrical style of English garden and landscaping originated by William Kent in his gardens at Rousham in Oxfordshire. This movement concentrated on the evocatively romantic effects which could be obtained by charming or dramatic treatments of landscapes around buildings and by the position of buildings within the landscape. Architectural *style* was of interest only in as much as it heightened the desired effect. In the London area, the key early building in this movement was the *virtuoso* Horace Walpole's Gothic house, Strawberry Hill, off Waldgrave Road, Twickenham, built in 1749–76 to designs superintended by a "Committee of Taste". But the growth of Romanticism in Europe followed strange and conflicting courses. Walpole's Gothic seemed out-

63 *The Pantheon (an entertainment centre), Oxford Street near Tottenham Court Road (1770–72) by James Wyatt. Demolished 1937*

dated to protagonists of the Picturesque by the end of the century, while Lancelot "Capability" Brown's development of Kent's landscaping ideas was denounced by Richard Payne Knight, Uvedale Price and Humphry Repton, who all published books on picturesque landscaping during the 1790s. As far as buildings were concerned, the Romantic Picturesque could digest Gothic, Classical or Oriental styles with equal ease as long as they fitted the requirements of visual charm and a suitable relationship between landscape and structure. Since the movement almost coincided in time with the Neo-Classicism already described, there are many cases, even in London, where Neo-Classical buildings are sited according to Picturesque Romantic principles—Cumberland Terrace in Regent's Park being a good example.

In the context of Romantic Picturesque ideology, John Nash becomes one of the major European designers of the period, rather than the lightweight which stern Neo-Classicists considered him. His Regent's Park terraces are certainly one of the great achievements of the movement, and the garden front of Buckingham Palace increases in stature if seen in Picturesque terms. The impurity of style from a Classical point of view is a secondary or irrelevant consideration compared with the pleasure available to the unprejudiced eye. Soane remains the greater architect of the two (he too had his Picturesque facets), but the often opposing values and characters of the two men become understandable if considered in the light of Soane's free Neo-Classicism and Nash's Romanticism.

There were other architects of this period whose London work must be mentioned. James Wyatt (1746–1813) was Adam's great competitor in country houses and interiors during the 1770–90 period. In London his few remaining works include the houses at Nos. 11–15 Portman Square (1773–84) and the gem at No. 9 Conduit Street, Mayfair (1779), as well as the staircase building of 1798 for Inigo Jones's Banqueting House in Whitehall. Wyatt's Pantheon of 1770–72, for public entertainments, first made him famous—its interior was loosely modelled on the Pantheon in Rome and it stood near the present Tottenham Court Road underground station in Oxford Street until it was demolished in 1937. Henry Holland (1745–1806) was the architect of the Prince of Wales' (later Prince Regent's) residence, Carlton House (1783–95, demolished 1826) which stood on the present site of Waterloo Place. His existing buildings include Brooks's Club, No. 60 St. James's Street (1776–78), the frontage and rear façade of Dover House, Whitehall (1787), the rear buildings and conversion

work to make Sir William Chambers' Albany in Piccadilly into residential apartments (1803–04) and parts of his big development called Hans Town (1771–c. 1790) around Hans Place, Cadogan Place, Sloane Place and Sloane Street, Knightsbridge.

Samuel Pepys Cockerell (c. 1754–1827), father of the great C. R. Cockerell, was the designer of the First Lord of the Admiralty's house, on the left of the Admiralty itself, in Whitehall (1786–91) and of the extraordinary steeple (1802–06) which is all that remains of St. Anne's Church, Wardour Street, Soho. The new St. Pancras Parish Church, with its Neo-Greek style and Erecteon caryatids, on the corner of Euston Road and Upper Woburn Place, Euston was built in 1819–22 by William (c. 1771–1843) and Henry (1794–1843) Inwood. Thomas Hardwick (1752–1859) was the architect of the new St. Marylebone Parish Church in Marylebone Road, facing the entrance to Regent's Park (1813–17), of St. John's Wood Church on the roundabout by Lord's Cricket Ground, St. John's Wood (1814) and of the re-built St. Bartholomew-the-Less, within St. Bartholomew's Hospital, Smithfield Market, City (1823–25).

Hardwick's more famous son, Philip Hardwick (1792–1870) designed Christ Church, Cosway Street, near Marylebone Station (1824–25), the central warehouse of St. Katherine's Dock, Tower Bridge (1825–28), the Goldsmiths' Hall, Foster Lane, City (1829–35), the City Club, No. 19 Old Broad Street, City (1833–37), the Tudor style new Hall and Library, Lincoln's Inn (1842–45 with his son P. C. Hardwick) and the demolished and much lamented front buildings and great Arch of Euston Station (1836–40, destroyed by British Rail 1964). Of other prominent buildings of this period, Lewis Vulliamy (1791–1871) built many early Neo-Gothic churches as well as the Classical Law Society building in Chancery Lane (1830–32) and the Royal Institution's frontage of giant columns in Albemarle Street, Mayfair (1838). George Basevi (1794–1845, who fell to his death off Ely Cathedral) designed the four side elevations of Belgrave Square (1825–40) and the former Conservative Club in St. James's Street (1843–45, with Sydney Smirke, who also designed the domed Reading Room of the British Museum). The east range which filled in the open fourth side of Nash's Buckingham Palace, and other work there, was erected in 1846–47 by Edward Blore (1781–1879), but the public façade was re-built by Sir Aston Webb in 1913.

Right at the end of the Regency period, and running on into the Victorian age, the extensive housing estates built by the master builder-developer, Thomas Cubitt (1788–1855) must be mentioned. Countless acres of attractive residential London streets were built or sub-contracted by this remarkable man. His many developments include much of Bloomsbury (1820–60), most of Belgravia (1826–c. 1865) and the 229 acres of Clapham Park east and south-east of Clapham Common (1830–

c. 1855). Some of Cubitt's terraces and houses have been demolished, especially by the University of London, but a great deal remains.

64 *The Great Arch of Euston Station (1836–40) by Philip Hardwick, demolished by British Rail 1964*

Robert Adam (1728-92)

Robert Adam, portrait

The influence of Robert Adam's work between 1760 and his death in 1792 has been as strong on subsequent British architecture, and especially on domestic interiors, as that of any other Classical architect. Adam added a rich variety of ancient Roman decorative features to the vocabulary of English Palladianism and created a classical manner which is still in use and still known as "Adam Style" (or often as the corrupted term "Adams").

His father, William Adam, was one of the first purely Classical architects of Scotland and designed many notable buildings. William had a large family including four sons. All became architects, but Robert, the second son, was acknowledged as their leading talent from an early age. Born at Kirkcaldy in Fife, Robert was educated at Edinburgh High School and University, where he matriculated at the age of fifteen. In 1754 he travelled through France to Italy, where he worked in Rome with his brother James for three years, meeting Chambers and Piranesi there. He was an earnest and very hard-working young man, though he liked his amusements too. "The forenoon I devote to Study and Drawing," he wrote in 1755. "Ever after dinner I ride out to see places and draw on the spot and after returning I pay some English visits until 9 o'clock and from that go among my Italians where I stay till 11 or 12 and then I go home and to bed." He adored Parmesan cheese and dancing—in a letter about the Rome Carnival to his sister he wrote "I danced with all the greatest Quality and with some of the greatest Whores, and with the handsomest of both kinds."

In 1758, after visiting and drawing in detail the ancient palace of Diocletian at Split, he returned to Britain. Adam set up in practice with his brother James in London, taking care to "pay his respects to the great" and worrying about the rivalry of Chambers. His early patron was a fellow Scot, the King's first minister Lord Bute, and in 1759 Adam was given his first major commission. **The Admiralty Screen** of 1759–61 forms an elegant wall between the street and the courtyard of the old Admiralty in Whitehall. The central gateway, capped by two sea-horses, has flanking Tuscan colonnades ending in dignified pavilions with blank niches in their walls. There is no sign yet of Adam's reaction against English Palladianism. But the new manner was to appear very soon on the outskirts of London in a major country house started in 1761, the year that Adam and Chambers were both appointed as Architects of the King's Works.

This great house is **Osterley Park**—it and the contemporary Syon House are regularly open to the public. Osterley is entered from Jersey Road in Isleworth. Adam worked there from 1761 until 1780,

65 *Adam. Admiralty Screen Wall between street and courtyard, The Admiralty, Whitehall, Westminster (1759–61)*

66 *Adam. Osterley Park, off Jersey Road, Isleworth, western London (1761–80)*

largely re-building an older house. The great mansion runs around three sides of a courtyard, the fourth side being partly occupied by the superb Ionic entrance portico (*c.* 1763). Of the famous interiors, the entrance hall (*c.* 1766) has a breathtaking cool whiteness, while the white Classical detailing of the bookcases which line the library (*c.* 1767) are a particular delight. The long gallery which runs the length of one side of the house had already been built in about 1720 and Adam altered it little. Of Adam's later work here, the so-called Etruscan Room (1775) is the most notable. Its decoration is derived from ancient Pompeian houses and shows the architect's interest in deploying a wide range of Roman detailing.

In 1762–68 Adam was also employed to remodel the Duke of Northumberland's mansion **Syon House**, entered from London Road in Brentford (the 1773 entrance with its lion is Adam's). Behind a very simple exterior, castellated and rendered with Adam's "Roman cement" or stucco (see Appendix Three), are some ambitious rooms. From a large white apsed entrance hall, stairs run up behind a screen of columns into the tremendous ante-room with pale green walls and giant free-standing columns of grey-green and gold supporting classical statues. This opens into a long apsed dining room and beyond that lie the splendid coved ceiling of the red drawing room and a gallery of more delicacy.

At Osterley and Syon we can see the width of Classical sources from which Adam drew. In 1764 he greatly enhanced his reputation with the publication

of a volume on the *Ruins of the Palace of the Emperor Diocletian at Spalatro* (Split). Sir John Summerson, in his book *Architecture in Britain 1530–1830* analysed Adam's sources in the new manner which he introduced: an adaptation of Kent's Palladianism; some French influence; archaeological influence from recently published works on Palmyra, Baalbec, Athens, Pompeii and what was then thought to be Etruscan work, as well as his own findings at Split; finally, the interior designs of early Italian Renaissance masters who he supposed had seen antique interiors subsequently destroyed. And Adam used all these ingredients with a flexible attitude towards precise Classical rules, which infuriated Palladians although Piranesi had demonstrated that the Orders were endlessly varied in ancient Rome. Adam thus made a very particular contribution to the general Neo-Classical movement in Europe as a whole.

This eclecticism may have caused the enmity which impelled Chambers to bar Adam from membership of the Royal Academy, but wealthy clients adored the new decorative style, and the Adam practice became the largest of its time with nearly one hundred commissions in the two decades after 1760. In central London, Lord Bute employed him to build the house later well known as **Lansdowne House** (1762–68), in Fitzmaurice Place off Berkeley Square in Mayfair. Originally a freestanding town mansion, the house was re-built as the Lansdowne Club in 1936. The present stone façade is Adam's, altered and moved forty feet back. Of the Adam interiors, the club's Card Room is part of the old Entrance Hall, the Round Room survives (with George Dance's Sculpture Gallery as the Ballroom beside it), and the main Drawing Room is in a museum in Philadelphia.

Apart from many interiors for houses, some of them surviving, several of Adam's London works deserve particular attention. In 1766 he designed a Gothic ceiling for the round room at Horace Walpole's **Strawberry Hill**, Waldegrave Road, Twickenham. In 1767–69 he re-modelled **Kenwood House** on Hampstead Heath for Lord Mansfield. The house, approached from Hampstead Lane, shows clearly the alterations and additions by Adam on the entrance front, while the garden front's central façade and side pavilions of stucco or "Roman cement" are an almost make-believe example of an Adam exterior. Within, he designed several rooms, but the library's architectural detailing and colour scheme provide one of the most

67 *Adam. Interior of library, Kenwood House, Hampstead Lane, Hampstead Heath (1767–69)*

extreme examples of the Adam style.

The Adam family remained a close-knit unit throughout Robert's life. He never married, and the brothers' London household (the eldest brother led the life of a country gentleman in Scotland) was looked after by their sisters, who entertained their friends at dancing parties from time to time. They all seem to have felt frustrated by their failure to attract commissions for the large London public buildings of their time, and it was partly the ambition to build "in the monumental manner" that tempted them to speculate financially in a large housing development in 1768.

In that year the Adam brothers bought a large piece of land off the Strand overlooking the Thames and during the next six years built twenty-four terraced houses to their own designs. This famous work was called **The Adelphi**, and the remains of it can still be seen near Charing Cross. The centre of the composition on the terrace above the river was unforgivably demolished in 1936 and replaced with a regrettable building. Around it, several Adam houses survive—Nos. 6–10 and No. 18 Adam Street, Nos. 4 and 6 John Street and Nos. 1–3 and No. 9 Robert Street. Part of the Adam substructure to the terraces survives in Lower Robert Street. The survivors give a dim idea of the whole design. The houses are of dark brick with stucco detailing—some have stuccoed rusticated ground floors with prettily decorated pilasters running up the next two storeys to a cornice and attic. Nearby is another important Adam building, the **Royal Society of Arts** at No. 8 John Street (1772–74), one of their most handsome London street frontages, with some fine interiors. It remains to be said that the Adelphi was a financial disaster for the Adam family. Costs had risen during building work and buyers for speculative houses of this comparative grandeur proved difficult to find. Only a public lottery of the unsold houses enabled them to extricate themselves.

In 1770–71 Adam was also at work on **Chandos House** (for the Duke of Chandos) in Chandos Place off Portland Place, and on the sizeable **town houses in Mansfield Street** beside it. Of Mansfield Street, Nos. 5–15, 20–22 and perhaps No. 18 survive. Chandos House itself has a stone frontage of unusual severity for Adam. Inside are some sumptuous interiors with a charming mulberry motif prevalent in the decoration. Behind the main block is a courtyard and beyond that a striking stucco stable building by Adam—its elevation onto Duchess Street is one of the architect's boldest compositions.

Another of Adam's classic town houses, **No. 20 St. James's Square**, was built in 1772–74. No. 21 beside it was built as a replica of its neighbour in 1937

68

69

68 *Adam. Royal Society of Arts, No. 8 John Adam Street, the Adelphi, off Strand, Charing Cross (1772–74)*

69 *Adam. South side, Fitzroy Square, off Tottenham Court Road (c. 1790–1800)*

when it was transformed into a company headquarters. Of the other individual Adam houses in London, **Nos. 20 and 21 Portman Square** (1775–77) in Marylebone survive in good order. Of his work at **Apsley House**, Hyde Park Corner in 1775–78, only the staircase, drawing room and portico room remain, while his Drury Lane Theatre of 1775 was burned down and re-built again in 1792 by another architect. The Adam style was being copied by others by this time; for example in Boodle's Club, St. James's Street of 1775 by John Crunden. Apart from a number of monuments in Westminster Abbey and the remodelling of the Council Chamber at Chelsea Hospital in 1776, the only later works by Adam remaining in London are two fragments of ambitious projects. **Portland Place**, running up to Regent's Park, was another housing speculation by the brothers. Originally, in 1773, the houses were to be detached mansions of some grandeur. But the crisis caused by the American War of Independence led to the abandonment of that design. Terraces of brick houses were built in 1776–80, following noble integrated designs by Robert and James for blocks of houses. But nothing was done later to preserve the overall design and today only strange remnants can be seen—one block is almost complete, but otherwise fine pediments and pilasters are jostled by their intruding neighbours. When Regent Street was built from Pall Mall to Regent's Park, Nash used Portland Place without alteration to provide the northern part of his triumphal way. More of Adam's work has survived than Nash's here, but that is cold comfort.

In later life, Robert Adam's practice developed largely in Scotland. In London, his final monument is again incomplete. The houses around **Fitzroy Square**, near the northern end of Tottenham Court Road were designed in about 1790. The designs are typical Adam, light and elegant, with protruding accents at the centre and the ends. Rusticated ground floors and recessed columns in each of these accents give a contrast of texture. But only the south and east sides of the square were built to Adam designs. They were completed in 1800.

In 1792 Robert Adam had over thirty commissions in hand. The peak of his style's fashion had passed for the time being, but he was healthy and working as hard as ever. On 3rd March 1792, aged only 63, he had a sudden haemorrhage of the stomach. His sisters and his brother William put him to bed and hoped for recovery for a time. But, as William wrote later that day, he was seized with pain in the night "till 2 o'clock when he became quiet and went off very easily". He was buried in Westminster Abbey.

George Dance the Younger (1741-1825)

George Dance the Younger, portrait

The younger George Dance, architect of distinction and a notable town planner, was the fifth son of the Clerk of the City Works. His father, George Dance the Elder (1695–1768) designed churches such as St. Leonard in Shoreditch (1736–40), St. Matthew in Bethnal Green (1740–46) and St. Botolph in Aldgate (1741–44) as well as the Mansion House of the City of London (1739–52) opposite the Bank of England—all of the buildings mentioned survive in altered form. Their Classicism is somewhat provincial, with proportions that are often ungainly and detailing of patchy quality.

George Dance junior was the youngest of the sons. His talent was for architecture, while his brother Nathaniel was an accomplished painter. Aged seventeen, George set off to study in Rome with Nathaniel, arriving in May 1759. There the brothers lived near Robert and James Adam, apparently having no contact with them, although they too knew Piranesi. Dance's letters to his father are not revealing about his nature, but tell much of his hardworking studies and archaeological interest in the excavations being carried out in the Forum of ancient Rome. In 1761 he met the Duke of Bridgewater and a nephew of William Pitt, who commissioned a drawing from him—"His friendship may be of great service to me in England", Dance wrote to his father, showing an important aspect of an Italian architectural education in the age of the Grand Tour for wealthy young men. In May 1762 there is an appealing sense of wonder in another of Dance's letters. "Behold your son George placed on a couch with a Cardinal on one side and a Prince on the other. . . . I felt a little awkward."

In December 1764 George Dance the Younger was back in London and became his father's assistant. Such was the older Dance's influence that, as soon as he returned in 1765, his son was commissioned to design **All Hallows Church**, London Wall, in the City of London. The church, opened in 1767, survives today and is used for exhibitions. The charming Italianate tower is of stone, the body of the church of brick, with external side arches which are blank except for high lunette windows. The interior has great charm, too, with delicate plaster-work and a boldly free treatment of Classical rules. For example, the shallow cornice above the Ionic columns appalled the young John Soane, but such freedom from convention doubtless contributed to the even greater inventiveness of Soane in later life.

In about 1765 Dance designed the **monument to S. and A. Duroure** in the cloisters of Westminster Abbey and laid out the Vine Street housing development to the north of the Tower of London—a

70 *Dance. All Hallows Church, London Wall, City (1765–67)*

71 *Dance. Houses in The Crescent, off The Minories, north of the Tower of London, City (1765–70)*

handsome curving terrace of his houses in **The Crescent** (1765–70), off The Minories, survives from this large scheme. In 1768–69 he designed the road pattern of Southwark, with streets radiating from St. George's Circus to the Thames bridges (executed 1785–1820), and in 1770 he built Pitzhanger Manor in Ealing (later re-built by his ex-pupil Soane for himself).

In 1768 Dance accepted the post of unpaid deputy to his father to supervise the re-building of Newgate Prison. His father died shortly afterwards and the young man became responsible for the design of what was to be his masterpiece and arguably the greatest Classical building in London. Newgate Prison, built in the Old Bailey in 1770–78, consisted of three magnificent rusticated blocks, with the governor's house standing between two windowless ranges punctuated by strong recessed blank aedicules. The building was severe, as befitted an eighteenth-century prison, but it displayed an intensely imaginative use of space reminiscent of the Prison engravings of Dance's acquaintance Piranesi. The building was demolished in 1902, despite a public outcry, to make way for Mountford's Central Criminal Courts.

Dance built several other important buildings for the City which are now demolished, notably the top-lit Council Chamber for the Guildhall (1777, destroyed 1906) and St. Luke's Hospital for the mentally deranged in Old Street, Finsbury (1782–84, destroyed *c.* 1961). In 1788–89 he built the controversial new **Gothic frontage** for the old **Guildhall** in Guildhall Yard, City of London. Dorothy Stroud, the biographer of Dance, has suggested that in designing this façade he picked up a contemporary theory that the Gothic style had its source in India, spread to Persia and was then taken to Spain by the Mohammedans and so imported into Western Europe. In 1786 Sir Joshua Reynolds had commented that "the Barbaric Splendour of those Asiatic buildings . . . furnish an architect, not with models to copy, but with hints of composition and general effect." The use of the Gothic style on the front of the Guildhall is certainly one of the most exotic and eccentric examples in London.

The King had invited Dance to become one of the foundation members of the Royal Academy in 1768 and he was active in its affairs, though he rarely exhibited there. Dance was a widely respected professional man and many of his town planning patterns such as Finsbury Square (1777), Alfred Place off Gower Street (1790) and Snow Hill at Smithfield (*c.* 1790) remain today with buildings of later dates. His other interests included a passion for music. He adored Handel's works and became very

72 *Dance. Newgate Prison, Old Bailey, City (1770–78).*
Demolished 1902 and replaced by the Central Criminal
Courts, Old Bailey (see Plate 150)

friendly with Haydn during the great composer's
visit to London in 1794. Dance was also a strong
patriot and wrote a highly successful pamphlet called
Address to the People in 1798, denouncing the horrors
of the French Emperor's activities after the outbreak
of the Napoleonic Wars.

Dance's design of *c.* 1792 for the **Sculpture
Gallery** (now Ballroom) in the **Lansdowne Club**,
Mayfair, has been retained. In 1795–96 he built the
present tunnel vault roof above the giant columns of
his father's astonishing **Egyptian Hall** in the City of
London's **Mansion House**. Of his building for the
Royal College of Surgeons in Lincoln's Inn Fields
(1806–13), only the big **portico** has survived Barry's
re-building of 1835.

By 1815 Dance had largely retired. He had a series
of quarrels and reconciliations with his fiery former
pupil Sir John Soane. His wife had died relatively
early, and his children had troubled private lives. In
1817 his son Charles, a colonel and veteran of the
battle of Waterloo, married for a second time. This
daughter-in-law, Isabella Cooper, was a charming
lady and gave Dance much pleasure in his old age—
he wrote to her as his "dearest and most beloved
daughter". Finally, in 1825, he died quietly at home
with his family around him. He was buried near Sir
Christopher Wren's tomb in St. Paul's Cathedral.

73 *Dance. Gothic façade of the Guildhall, Guildhall Yard,*
off Gresham Street, City (1788–89)

83

Sir John Soane
(1753-1837)

Sir John Soane, portrait

Soane ranks with a few others among the great designers of originality in the history of British architecture. Of all such masters represented in this book, Soane has suffered worst at the hands of the demolishers.

Soane's work is very much part of the Neo-Classical revival and of the interest in ancient Greek, rather than Roman, architectural forms which swept through Europe at the end of the eighteenth century. He used these forms with a brilliant inventiveness which has ever since fascinated those interested in the penetration of solid forms by space, the enclosure of space in interiors and the use of subtle daylighting.

The Soan family (he added an 'e' when he married) came from the Reading area. The father was a fairly humble builder, living at Goring-on-Thames, when John was born. Eight years later they moved to Reading itself, and John, the youngest of seven children, went to school there. The boy met one of George Dance's assistants and at the age of fifteen went to work in Dance's London office. This was the year in which Dance inherited his father's practice and became preoccupied with the design of Newgate Gaol. After two years, Soane felt he needed wider experience and went to work with Henry Holland (1745–1806), the architect of Brooks's Club of 1776 at No. 60 St. James's Street and partner of "Capability" Brown. Soane also attended the Royal Academy Schools and after winning the Academy's Gold Medal in 1776, the young man was presented to the King by Sir William Chambers. "This was the most fortunate event of my life," Soane wrote later, for the King awarded him a travelling studentship which enabled him to study and travel in Italy and Sicily from 1778 until 1780. In Rome, like Dance, Adam and Chambers before him, Soane met the great engraver Piranesi and numerous wealthy travelling Englishmen who were to give him work later.

One of these noblemen persuaded Soane to come back to England early and, because his promises of employment failed to materialise, probably started in the young architect the almost paranoid suspicion of plots against himself from which he suffered all his life. "I know your constitution, it is too eager for stormy weather and easily becomes feverish," a friend wrote to Soane later.

In the following year, 1781, Soane's luck changed, and he started to build up a good practice in designing country houses. His few London works of the 1780s have been demolished, and his importance to London starts dramatically with his appointment as Architect to the Bank of England in succession to Sir Robert Taylor. The appointment was made by the Prime Minister, William Pitt, to whom Soane

74 Soane. Interior of one of the many banking halls, Bank of England, Threadneedle Street, City (1788–1833). This great masterpiece was destroyed during the re-building in 1921–37, with the exception of the outer wall

75

76

77

had been introduced by one of his Roman acquaintances, Thomas Pitt.

Dorothy Stroud, who has written much about Soane, has divided the great architect's work into four main phases—the formative years up to 1790, the development of his own characteristic style and favourite features in 1790–1810, the experimental deployment of these typical Soanian features in various ways during the following decade and the period after 1820 of major public buildings.

Soane's work at the **Bank of England** in the centre of the City of London continued almost throughout his life. Today only the fine outer screen wall which surrounds the Bank survives, and even that was re-built at Tivoli Corner, its most spectacular point. Inside, the series of marvellous top-lit banking halls can only be seen in the distorted form in which they were re-built by Sir Herbert Baker in 1921–37, though it is worth seeking the necessary special permission to visit them.

The building of the Bank of England in 1791–1833 in turn involved the replacement of some of Taylor's work, though the Court Room and its surroundings were intact until Baker moved its position and destroyed most of the plasterwork. Soane's Bank Stock Office of 1791–92 was the prototype of the classic Soane interior, with simplified Greek detailing, shallow arches and vaults of great lightness and indirect daylighting developed from Taylor's earlier experiments. During the next six years up to 1798, the Consols Office, the 4% and 5% Office and others added a series of brilliant interiors grouped around the great Rotunda (1794–95). The Screen Wall was started in 1795 and built in stages around the site until 1826. Accounts of the progress of the building up to 1833 will be found in Sir John Summerson's and Dorothy Stroud's books on Soane, and it is at least fortunate that good photographs were taken of the ten or so great banking halls and the other offices and courtyards which made up the huge building. An intense impression of Soane's mastery of lighting and space emerges from this series of pictures and a clear vision of the particular contrast between his pleasure in bold solid forms and his liking elsewhere

75 Soane. *Pitzhanger Place, in Walpole Park, Ealing, west London (1801–03), built for himself and now a public library.*

76 Soane. *Sir John Soane Museum, No. 13 Lincoln's Inn Fields, off Holborn (1812–14, built as Soane's own house, extended later to make room for his collection of antiquities)*

77 Soane. *Mausoleum and Dulwich Picture Gallery, College Road and Gallery Road, Dulwich, south London (1811–14)*

for making thick arches appear almost as thin as paper.

Of Soane's country houses of the 1790s, Bentley Priory at Stanmore (1789–99—only some distinguished interiors remain of this work) and Tyringham Hall near Newport Pagnell are not far from London. His London houses of this decade have all gone, with the exception of the interiors he built for himself in Lincoln's Inn Fields.

In 1784 Soane married Eliza Smith. It was a close and happy marriage, which was just as well for a creative man of a headstrong and neurotic nature. Moreover, his wife's wealthy uncle left Soane his fortune upon his death in 1790. The security of the money may well have freed Soane's boldness in architecture, and it certainly enabled him to buy a house for the family at **No. 12 Lincoln's Inn Fields**. Some interiors are still Soane's, done before he moved into his famous house next door. In this house Mr. and Mrs. Soane would hold dinner parties, one of the few relaxations the architect allowed himself from an obsessively hard-working life. Occasionally he liked to go to the theatre or to take a day off to go fishing. The rest of his life was work, and travel for work, all over England.

In about 1795 Soane was in charge of the division into two parts and the present porch of what is now **Nos. 57 and 58 Lincoln's Inn Fields**, on another side of the square from his own house. In 1800 he bought what was then a country house called **Pitzhanger Place**, now the public library in Walpole Park, south of the Broadway, Ealing in west London. The house had been designed by his old teacher, George Dance, but Soane re-built it inside and outside in 1801–03. The façade is nobly Classical, but wholly typical of Soane. Four free-standing Ionic columns, supporting statues, punctuate a strongly quadrilateral composition with only two windows in the walls. The entrance hall and two other rooms on the ground floor are excellent examples of Soane's developing talent for strange effects with space and lighting even on the smallest site. The former front parlour has a typical low dome supported by caryatids at the corners.

Praed's Bank (1801) in Fleet Street and many other London works by Soane have disappeared. Of his work in **Chelsea Royal Hospital** (where he was appointed Surveyor), the Infirmary was bombed in the Second World War and demolished; but the **Clerk of Works' house** and **Stables** (1809–17, on either side of Wren's main building in Royal Hospital Road) are full of unmistakable Soanian features. The arches of the Stables, in particular, show what can be achieved by concentric layered arches of common brickwork.

The next major work in London by Soane also survives. This is the **Dulwich Picture Gallery** and the famous adjoining **Mausoleum**, built for Dulwich College in south London in 1811–14 to house the collection of paintings donated by the Bourgeois family. The building, of yellowish London stock brick with stone detailing, stands between College Road and Gallery Road. The picture gallery is a long range divided into five main spaces. It is top-lit, and the walls are thickly encrusted with the wide-ranging collection of paintings. The Mausoleum in memory of the donor opens off one side of the gallery, a marvellous little Soane temple composed predominantly of Greek elements. The inside is dim and cool, the light entering subtly and indirectly. Outside, it is a complex design of stepped masses on a miniature scale, the solids penetrated by windows and slits of space in many places.

In 1812 the Soanes decided to move into the house next door at Lincoln's Inn. Their new house, now the **Sir John Soane Museum**, stands at No. 13 Lincoln's Inn Fields, near Holborn. After rebuilding it in 1812–14, Soane went on adding to it and altering it over the years to hold the growing collection of antiquities, drawings and books which he finally left to the nation, spreading into No. 14 in 1824.

The front of the house is an astonishing contrast to the good but conventional brick Georgian row in which it stands. Soane's elevation is of stone and it thrusts forward from its neighbours with a boldness which is echoed in the strong round-topped voids of the windows. On the other hand the decoration is equally typical of Soane—delicately rectangular Grecian patterns barely scratching into the surface and giving that typical illusion that the solid wall is of no thickness. Inside, much of the museum is still furnished with Soane's furniture. The dining room and domed breakfast room on the entrance floor show all the architect's genius in playing with lighting and with the boundaries and division of spaces. These domestic rooms lead through into the almost bewildering complexities of the rooms holding Soane's private museum at the back of the house. Walls of pictures swing back to reveal another space beyond. Galleries crowded with ancient works of carved stone pass from dark to light and back again as the levels are penetrated by spaces running up to the glass domes above. It is a tiny area packed with architectural magic.

At this time, Soane had many personal troubles. He was a difficult friend, with frequent quarrels punctuating his warm relationships. Of his contemporary architect rivals, he disliked his former pupil Smirke intensely and despised Nash as an

78

architectural charlatan. He was an autocratic father and his children rebelled; it was due to his sons' disinterest in Pitzhanger that Soane decided to sell it in 1810. His son George finally attacked his father's work in a London magazine in 1815. The article was anonymous but Mrs. Soane recognized her son's style. To Soane's despair she died of severe gallstones only two weeks later, and he could not believe that the events were unconnected.

Yet his professional life prospered. Apart from the continuing work at the Bank of England he held official appointments, and commissions poured in during the building boom after the end of the Napoleonic wars. Most of these have now disappeared. His National Debt Redemption Office (built to cope with the debt amassed during the wars) in Old Jewry (1818–19), was demolished in 1900. His new range of the Law Courts (1820–24) by the Palace of Westminster was pulled down in 1883, while his extensive work in the House of Lords and the Commons was burned in 1834. His **dining rooms** (1825) are still there in Nos. 10 and 11 Downing

'9

Io

78 *Soane. Holy Trinity Church, Marylebone Road and Albany Street, beside Regent's Park (1824–28)*

79 *Soane. St. John's Church, Cambridge Heath Road, Bethnal Green (1825–28)*

80 *Soane. Tomb of Sir John Soane and his wife, Old St. Pancras Churchyard (now a park), Pancras Road. Designed by Soane in 1816*

Street. The new Treasury Building of 1824–27 in Whitehall (now the Cabinet Office) was re-built by Barry only seventeen years later, although Soane's **entrance hall** and other interiors remain. His final government building, the State Paper Office off Whitehall, of 1829–33, was knocked down for other government offices as early as 1862.

Of his work in London after 1820, the principal survivors are three scattered churches. The most central of these is **Holy Trinity Church** (1824–28) on the corner of Marylebone Road and Albany Street, near Regent's Park. The exterior is a fine compact design with a two-stage tower whose

proportions seem to be stretched upwards. Little can be seen of the interior, for it has been largely filled in with offices for the Church of England publishing house.

St. John's Church (1825–28), Cambridge Heath Road, at Bethnal Green in the East End of London is very different. Its massively rectangular entrance, front and tower (originally intended to be higher) are a typically Soanian play with solid volumes and their penetration by space. The brilliant game is carried on inside the entrance, but there it ends. The interior was burned out in 1870 and re-built quite differently.

It is only at **St. Peter's Church** (1823–25), Liverpool Grove, at Walworth in south London that we can see a complete Soane church in London. The exterior is generally like that of Holy Trinity, rather than the more vigorous St. John, with another vertically stretched tower above a brick block and strong arches along both sides. The interior here is still Soane's, a cool space of no intensity, with flat ceilings separated by arches which the architect has remorselessly made to look as thin and un-solid as possible. They are typical of one aspect of Soane's manner which make one wonder what he was trying to express.

Soane lived to a great age deprived of family companionship but comforted by many friends and young pupils who loved "the dear old tyrant" in his mellow periods and could put up with the irascible and neurotic side of his temperament. His leadership of the architectural profession was acknowledged by a knighthood in 1831, but his style was not carried on by any successors. He had always been as thin as an arrow and "taller than common". A pupil named George Wightwick wrote of him in old age dressed always in black with a high brown wig, red-eyed as his sight gradually failed, his face extensive in profile but seen from the front "something of the invisible".

In 1835 Soane was presented with a gold medal by his fellow architects, which gave him great pleasure. Two years later, after only a few hours of illness, he died at home in Lincoln's Inn Fields. He is buried with his wife in the **Soane Mausoleum** which he had designed for her in 1816 and which remains a notable example of his mastery of three-dimensional design in the churchyard of Old St. Pancras Parish Church, Pancras Road, behind St. Pancras Station. In 1834 the Institute of British Architects had been established, and Soane took a keen interest in its foundation. Its royal charter was granted in the year of his death. The money he gave the new organisation still provides pensions for widows of architects and an annual medallion with a travelling studentship so that young architects may enjoy the experience of seeing buildings abroad.

John Nash
(1752-1835)

John Nash, portrait

Londoners and lovers of London's scenery owe as much pleasure to John Nash as to any other architect in the city's history. Carlton House Terrace in The Mall, All Souls' Church in Regent Street, the Theatre Royal in Haymarket, the original part of Buckingham Palace, the Marble Arch, the lay-out of the whole length of Regent Street and Regent's Park, with its famous Classical white terraces, are all among Nash's London designs. It is not for any purist architectural qualities that his work is admired and loved. Nash was the great English exponent of the Romantic Picturesque movement in building. His works are often open to much criticism on grounds of impure style, but as large-scale urban design they often achieve sublime picturesque splendour.

Nash was brought up in Lambeth, the son of a mill-wright, who died when the boy was aged eight, and of a Welsh mother. From the age of fifteen until he was twenty-six, Nash worked for the eminent Palladian architect Sir Robert Taylor. It was a distinguished schooling, but Nash reacted strongly against his master's strict Classical rules, which he later said he found extremely dull.

In 1778 a rich uncle left Nash £1,000, with which he bought and re-built five **houses in Great Russell Street**, Bloomsbury. The houses, his first building designs, are still there as Nos. 66–71, as well as **No. 17 Bloomsbury Square** on the corner, which was later reconstructed magnificently as the Pharmaceutical Society of Great Britain. But the speculation failed, as had so many others before it; Nash was bankrupted in 1783 (partly as the result of the extravagant milliners' debts of his first wife) and he disappeared from London for the next twelve years. Sir John Summerson has recently discovered evidence of Nash's scandalous attempts to be rid of his first wife, who eventually died of natural causes.

After this financial ruin Nash went to ground in Wales, where his mother originated. But his irrepressible energy soon involved him in a growing practice in Carmarthen, where he designed the gaol and other buildings. He became involved in Whig politics and also made friends with an artistic group who filled him with the ideas of the Romantic Movement. More important still, he met and employed a refugee from the French revolution who was a brilliant draughtsman; this was Auguste Charles de Pugin, father of the great Pugin.

Almost everyone he met seems to have found Nash an irresistible companion. Later, a London diarist, Mrs. Arbuthnot, wrote of him as "a very clever, odd, amusing man with a face like a monkey's". He was very small, talkative, totally uninhibited even in the grandest company and had a passion for amateur theatricals.

By 1795 Nash had met, among others, the politician Charles James Fox and the London architect Samuel Pepys Cockerell. Such contacts helped him to re-establish himself in London by March of that year and he was soon in partnership with Humphrey Repton designing romantic Gothic or Italianate country houses and gardens. Then, in 1798, Nash married Mary Ann Bradley who was, or apparently soon became, a mistress of the Prince Regent. Despite a burning of her papers, the evidence all points to the existence of this relationship for many years. There is a possibility, but no more than that, that Mary Ann Nash's five children, said to be adopted, were the Prince's. There is no record of what Nash thought of his young wife's situation, nor is there evidence that it brought him income, but certainly the Nash household and way of life showed otherwise inexplicable prosperity from 1798 on.

Of Nash's many country houses built in the 1795–1810 period, three survive in outer London. **Grovelands**, at The Bourne, Southgate (c. 1797) in the northern suburbs is perhaps the finest. Now a convalescent home, the Classical villa stands in extensive grounds which are today a public park. The other two are **Sundridge Park** of 1799, off Plaistow Lane, near Bromley (now a hotel) and **Southborough Place** of 1808 in Ashcombe Avenue, Surbiton. Except for his own house in Dover Street, now vanished, he built nothing in central London for thirty years after 1782. Then his great works followed rapidly.

In 1806, perhaps through the Prince Regent's patronage, Nash was appointed Architect to the Chief Commissioner of Woods and Forests, and in 1811 his chance came with the decision to develop the Crown property which is now **Regent's Park**. Two other architects submitted conventional plans of streets and squares. Nash's first plan included straight streets of houses within the park, but some garden land and water. This was accepted in July 1811, but Nash later developed it into a fully flowering product of romantic picturesque ideas— landscaped parkland with grand terraces of houses around the edges, curving roads and lakes and some free-standing villas in the centre. As it is today, the development follows his revised plan closely. At much the same time Nash put forward a plan for cutting a wide *Via Triumphalis*, a triumphal way, from the Prince Regent's new Carlton House in Pall Mall all the way north-westwards to Regent's Park, where the Prince planned to have a villa. Work started on Regent's Park and its buildings in 1812, and the buildings of this period were finished in

about 1828. The triumphal way, **Regent Street**, needed a Bill in Parliament in 1813; work started in 1818 and the original buildings (by many architects, including Nash) were largely completed by the middle 1820s.

As far as the buildings are concerned, the imagination must nowadays be used to appreciate the grandeur of Nash's overall plan for the Prince Regent. Carlton House, re-built palatially for the Prince in 1783 on the present site of Waterloo Place and Carlton House Terrace, was knocked down as early as 1827. From there, Lower Regent Street runs up the hill to Piccadilly Circus. The way then turns along the curve of Nash's famous Quadrant and straightens out to go across Oxford Circus and up to the circular portico and high spire of Nash's **All Souls' Church**, Langham Place (1822–25, the interior, with its circular entrance hall and quadrangular main space, was well restored in 1976). In all that length of Regent Street, before the church, not a single building by Nash or his contemporaries survives. Originally, the Regency buildings were about four storeys high, giving the street a spacious visual width which disappeared with the higher rebuilding of the two decades up to 1927. Even now, however, Regent Street remains one of the finest thoroughfares in London.

North of the church, which acts as an ingenious accent for a necessary turn of direction, Nash's triumphant way bends into Portland Place, where the fragments of the Adam buildings, which Nash incorporated in his scheme, can still be seen. At the northern end of Portland Place the park is reached, and the buildings swing out on either side into the curving colonnade of Nash's white Neo-Classical **Park Crescent** (1812–22). Beyond the Crescent, the famous Terraces themselves begin—not all of these are by Nash, and some later buildings have been inserted.

To the left hand, or west, of the Crescent, the buildings designed by Nash's office are one side of **Park Square** (1823–25), probably **Ulster Terrace** and **York Terrace** with **Upper Harley Street** (all 1824–26), possibly **Clarence Terrace** (1821–23), certainly **Sussex Place** and **Hanover Terrace** (both 1822–23). Cornwall Terrace (1821–23) was designed by Decimus Burton and Clarence Terrace may have been too.

To the right hand, or north-east, of Park Crescent, Nash designed that side of **Park Square**, the Regency parts of **St. Andrew's Place** (1826) and of **Cambridge Terrace** (1825–27). Beyond that lie his **Chester Terrace** (1825–27), and his glorious **Cumberland Terrace** (1826–28) and **Gloucester Gate** (1827–28). The detached villas in the centre of the park were built by other architects, with the exception of Nash's pretty **Hanover Lodge** of 1827, but Nash and his step-son James Pennethorne built the picturesque smaller villas just east of the park, called **Park Village East** and **Park Village West**, from 1824 onwards. Most of the terraces have had their interiors completely re-built, but it is the romantic classicism of their exteriors that matters.

In 1826 a Prince Pückler-Muskau, visiting London, wrote "it cannot be denied that his buildings are a jumble of every sort of style, the result of which is rather 'baroque' than original—yet the country is in my opinion much indebted to him for conceiving and executing such gigantic designs for the improvement of the metropolis . . ." Few would disagree with this judgement of the lovely white stucco buildings in their rich parkland.

Other famous places in London also owe their existence to Nash and the Prince Regent (King George IV after 1821). Traces of the outlying parts of Nash's triumphal way can be seen in his **Royal Opera House Arcade** off Pall Mall (1816, all that remains of his opera house in Haymarket, which was burned down in 1867). In the Haymarket, Nash's **Theatre Royal** (1820–21) is still outwardly his design, and behind it can be seen his **houses in Suffolk Place and Suffolk Street** (1820–23). **Clarence House** (1825), one of the royal residences beside St. James's Palace, was designed by Nash, although an unfortunate top storey was added fifty years later. Again, it was Nash who, in the middle 1820s, designed the large triangular block of the **West Strand Improvement**, whose pepperpot towers add so much charm to the area around William IV Street at Charing Cross; the design was executed by William Herbert in 1830. The original layouts of **Trafalgar Square** and the formal landscaping of **St. James's Park** were Nash plans of the same time, although their appearance has since been dramatically altered. Nash also designed the **United Services Club** (1827) in Waterloo Place, but the exterior was altered in 1842 by Burton. His other major London building, however, is **Buckingham Palace**.

81

82

Buckingham House had been purchased by King George III and improved for him in 1762 by Sir William Chambers. In 1825–30 George IV, the former Prince Regent, commissioned Nash to rebuild it on a far grander scale: the architect had already done the Prince's famous Royal Pavilion at Brighton in 1815–23. Nash's Buckingham Palace was built to a large U-plan, the open courtyard facing down The Mall. The free-standing triumphal arch forming the main gateway on the entrance of this courtyard was built in 1828—it was removed when

83

84

81 *Nash. Royal Opera House Arcade, off Pall Mall, near the Haymarket (1816)*

82 *Nash. The Theatre Royal, Haymarket (1820–21)*

83 *Nash. All Souls' Church, Langham Place, Regent Street (1822–25)*

84 *Nash. Park Crescent (1812–22), which opens the northern end of Nash's 'Via Triumphalis' into the spaces of Regent's Park*

85 *Nash. Buckingham Palace east front as built in 1825–30. The open side of the courtyard was closed off by an east range built by Edward Blore in 1847 (façade re-built by Sir Aston Webb in 1913) and the Nash gateway was then removed to the north side of Hyde Park, where it is now known as the Marble Arch*

86 *Nash. Cumberland Terrace, Regent's Park east side (1826–28). Perhaps the grandest of the eleven terraces built around the perimeter of the park*

85

86

another architect built a further range closing off the open side in 1847 and was reassembled as **The Marble Arch** on the north side of Hyde Park. The garden front of the palace, with its curiously over-enlarged Neo-Classical architecture, is nearer to the state in which Nash left it. Most of the interiors have had their decoration altered over the years.

Nash's last great design was **Carlton House Terrace**, built in The Mall in 1827–33 after the demolition of the King's old residence, Carlton House. It is one of Nash's most cool and distinguished works.

The cost of Buckingham Palace grew wildly as building progressed, and in 1828 Nash was summoned before a Select Committee of the House of Commons to account for the extravagance. It was whispered that he had made a personal fortune out of the work, though the truth is that he never became really rich, considering that he was such a successful architect. The Committee found that there was little that they could blame Nash for, but the ill-founded rumours of corruption continued in broadsheets distributed in the streets and in higher places too. For example, Sir John Soane was infuriated by what he saw as royal favouritism. The three official

87 Nash. Carlton House Terrace, The Mall (1827–33)

architects to the Board of Works since 1813 were Nash, Soane and Sir Robert Smirke. A very funny letter of 1822 survives in which Nash told Soane that he himself provides for the King, Soane for the Lords and Smirke—whom both of them disliked—for the Commons, but teased the neurotic old genius with wanting to steal the royal share as well as his own.

After the Commons Committee had reported, the King quarrelled with the Duke of Wellington in 1829 because the Duke refused to make Nash a baronet. A year later the King was dead. Nash's protector and practice had gone and he retired to his house in the Isle of Wight. For the first time in his life Nash became ill, and he suffered a stroke within a year. In 1834 he wrote to the Office of Woods and Forests that "I have quitted London and resigned my Professional practice to Mr. Pennethorne".

In 1835 Nash's health deteriorated rapidly and he died quietly at home. He was buried at Cowes. Mrs. Nash and her family received a handsome enough pension from unrecorded sources for many years, which ceased abruptly upon her death in 1851.

Sir Robert Smirke
(1781-1867)

Robert Smirke, portrait

The Greek Classical revival of the early nineteenth century had no stronger advocate than Robert Smirke. Architect of the Royal Mint at Tower Hill, of the British Museum and of Canada House, Smirke has been dubbed "architect of the rectangular" by a leading architectural historian of the period, J. Mordaunt Crook. The great Gothic revivalist Pugin described his vast number of buildings more insultingly as "the new Square Style of Mr. Smirke".

Smirke was born in London, the second son of a successful painter and Royal Academician. The boy went to school in Bedford and in 1796 became a pupil of Sir John Soane. Soane loathed him and Smirke was miserable. He left a few months later to work with a surveyor. His architectural education was gained in two years' private tuition from George Dance the Younger and at the Royal Academy Schools, where he won the gold medal in 1799. He then spent five years travelling with his brother and studying in France, Germany, Italy and Greece. This was the time of the Napoleonic Wars and, rather appealingly, Smirke tried to visit Paris by pretending to be an American; he was discovered and turned away.

In 1805 he returned and set up practice in London. His father's contacts provided some good clients and his own politics soon established him as the architect of the Tory party. As to his theories of design, his manuscript treatise of about 1815 in the RIBA gives firm views. He found the Grecian style "certainly the noblest ... it has a kind of primal simplicity ... excess of ornament is in all cases a symptom of vulgar or degenerate taste." He found Piranesi and his type of Italian Classicism "a monument ... of corrupt taste." His mission was "to rediscover pure classical forms and to adapt them to new circumstances". He disliked the Baroque and the Palladian styles equally.

Physically, Smirke was a tiny man. Lord Lonsdale, a Tory magnate, described him as "ingenious, modest and gentlemanly in his manners". It was Lonsdale who gave him his first major commission in 1806, for Lowther Castle in Westmorland, but the romantic medieval manner of this mansion contrasts sharply with Smirke's Neo-Greek ideals.

In 1807 another Tory aristocrat, Lord Bathurst, obtained for Smirke the job of completing the **Royal Mint** (already started by James Johnson), beside the Tower of London, to revised designs. He also rebuilt the interior after a fire in 1815. The Mint itself moved out of London in the 1960s but Smirke's 1807–09 work survives, a fine Classical façade and a garden with two austere entrance lodges on either side. The interior has some good rooms in the front, but the rest was a factory for making money and was altered as new machinery was introduced over the years.

It was the re-building of Covent Garden Theatre in Drury Lane in 1809–10 which made Smirke famous. The modernised Grecian design was controversial and Smirke protested strongly when his former master, Sir John Soane, criticised it in the course of a lecture. The commission was obtained through the patronage of J. P. Kemble, another leading Tory. Smirke's theatre was burned down in 1857 and only the frieze by Flaxman under the portico survives in the present mid-Victorian Classical building by E. M. Barry which is the Royal Opera House, Covent Garden.

Smirke soon capitalised on the celebrity brought by the theatre. In London, he did much work for the barristers of the Inner Temple, of which **Nos. 9–13 King's Bench Walk** (1829) and the much later **Paper Buildings** (1838–39) survive as good examples of his severely simplified style for office buildings. In 1815 he was appointed through Tory patronage as one of the official architects to the Board of Works—the other two were Soane and Nash, both now in their sixties while Smirke was aged thirty-four. In that capacity, one of his first jobs was the completion of the huge General Penitentiary at Millbank in 1816, demolished to make way for the Tate Gallery in 1898.

In the years following 1820 Smirke built a number of Neo-Greek churches. **St. Anne** in St. Anne's Crescent, Wandsworth (1820–22) has a round tower which is curiously ill-proportioned work for a would-be purist of Neo-Classicism. But then J. Mordaunt Crook has pointed out that Smirke's designs rarely implemented the Greek purity of his theories.

St. James's Church, West Hackney (1822–24) was bombed in 1940, but another of Smirke's churches can still be seen nearer the centre of London. This is **St. Mary**, Wyndham Place, in Marylebone. The church was built in 1821–24 and its slim round tower is positioned to provide an effective climax to the view northwards up Bryanston Square. The interior is a fine space, typical of Smirke's handling of the Neo-Greek manner, with high Doric columns above the gallery which are really Roman in their detailing. At about this time Smirke was also adding the present **bell-tower** and south wall of the old Savoy Chapel, off the Strand. It may well have been his extensive Grecian church work which attracted the particular fury of Pugin at the beginning of Queen Victoria's reign, for Pugin held passionately that only Gothic was a Christian style.

The opportunity for Smirke's most famous work

and grandest Grecian design came with the commission for the **British Museum** in Great Russell Street, Bloomsbury. Built in 1823–47, this first part of the great museum is perhaps Smirke's finest achievement. The central section, with its giant Ionic colonnade spreading from the pedimented portico out around the two wings, contains nobly spacious, if impersonal, halls and galleries for exhibiting the collection of antiquities. The outer wings of the front courtyard show Smirke at his most rectangular, strip pilasters replacing the columns of the middle section. The huge domed library Reading Room in the centre of the complex was added by Smirke's brother Sydney in 1854 and the buildings spread even further to the north at the end of the century.

It must be mentioned here that although Smirke's designs were aesthetically unadventurous, he was a pioneer on the structural side of architecture. He was the first architect to use quantity surveying rationally and in his buildings employed concrete foundations and load-bearing cast-iron girders imaginatively; in the British Museum, these girders reached unprecedented lengths of fifty feet. His practice was huge, his staff of draughtsmen and clerks large, and he would by this stage in his career refuse commissions for work costing under £10,000. He was knighted in 1832 in recognition of his services to the Board of Works.

In 1824–27 Smirke built the large block that fills the west side of Trafalgar Square. Now **Canada House**, the southern end was originally the Royal College of Physicians, with the Union Club at the other end. Smirke's dignified design, with advancing Ionic porticos at both ends and a recessed portico in the flank, can still be appreciated under the later alterations and additions piled up above.

His General Post Office of 1824–29 at St. Martin's-le-Grand in the City was demolished in 1912, but his 1825 river frontage and Long Room for the **Custom House** in Lower Thames Street (added to D. Laing's building of 1813–17) can still be seen. Few traces remain of the façades he did in 1825 for the north and south approaches to London Bridge.

88 *Smirke. The Royal Mint, Tower Hill, City (1807–09)*

89 *Smirke. The British Museum, Great Russell Street, Bloomsbury (1823–47). Main frontage*

90 *Smirke. St. Mary's Church, Wyndham Place, Bryanston Square, Marylebone (1821–24)*

91 *Smirke. Canada House, Trafalgar Square, Westminster (1824–27). Built as the Royal College of Physicians and the Union Club buildings*

88

89

90

91

The next major commission was the large building to house **King's College** of the University of London (1830–35), the religious establishment's response to the secular University College. King's College forms the east wing of Chambers' Somerset House, running from the Embankment through to the Strand. It is reasonably respectful in its manner to its great Palladian neighbour. The section containing the Strand gateway which Pugin ridiculed in his book *Contrasts* was replaced by a massive modern block in the 1960s. And Pugin would have been glad to know that Smirke's chapel was replaced by Sir Gilbert Scott's Gothic one in 1861.

Smirke had a tremendous reputation for structural soundness, and he was often called to the rescue in cases of difficulty with historic buildings. It was he who refaced the stone interior of Westminster Hall after the fire which destroyed the Houses of Parliament in 1834. In 1836–37 he built the present steps up to the portico of the Mansion House in the City, and restored the Chapel Royal at St. James's Palace and the interior of the Inigo Jones Banqueting House in Whitehall.

In 1835 Smirke built the Carlton Club, the social gathering place of the Tory party, but this was re-built in 1847. The **Oxford and Cambridge Club** of 1836–37 which he and his brother Sydney designed further along Pall Mall at No. 71, is noticeably less chaste than is typical of Robert's work. It is a distinguished building, but its general character is that of anti-scholarly early Victorian Classicism. The

92 *Smirke. Earl Brownlow's house, No. 12 Belgrave Square, Belgravia (c. 1836). The fine terraces of houses around the four sides of the square were designed by George Basevi and built in 1825–40*

rooms are good but some, including the sweeping staircase, date from a re-building in 1910.

After 1840 Robert Smirke took on less work in London. A few of the many houses he built about that year in Moorgate in the City can still be seen, as can the tall stuccoed **mansion** which he designed in about 1836 for Lord Brownlow in the north-west corner of Belgrave Square. He gradually handed over his work to his adored younger brother Sydney, and in 1845 he retired from architecture altogether when Sir Robert Peel appointed him a member of the Commission for London Improvements. (The Commission supervised the construction of such major new thoroughfares as Victoria Street, the Victoria Embankment and Queen Victoria Street.) By now Smirke was aged 64 but he had twenty-three more years of prosperous old age left to him before his death at his house in Cheltenham.

It is difficult to be enthusiastic about Smirke's architecture. He had neither the spatial genius and originality of Soane nor the picturesque brilliance on a large scale of Nash, his two great rivals of the Regency period. But Smirke's buildings should not be underrated, even if we cannot love most of them, for they have a cool dignity and probity which reflects the virtues and shortcomings of his own personality.

Benjamin Wyatt (1775-c.1850)

Benjamin Wyatt, portrait

Benjamin Dean Wyatt, the eldest son of the great architect James Wyatt (1746–1813), was a bit of a wastrel among architects. He is of little importance artistically or historically, except that he did leave four or five major London buildings, such as Drury Lane Theatre and Apsley House, as a legacy from his brief career.

The building which made his father James Wyatt famous, the Pantheon in Oxford Street of 1770–72, has disappeared—as have most of his other London works with very few notable exceptions such as the house at No. 9 Conduit Street, Mayfair (1779). James was immensely hard-working and built up a big practice all over England. He was devoted to his four sons and did all he could to forward their careers. But they did not inherit his liking for work. Indeed, a comparison of Ben's life of flashing success and disastrous debts with the solid virtues of his contemporary Sir Robert Smirke, would provide a neat Victorian moral tale.

Benjamin, known to everyone as Ben, was born and brought up in London. He was given an expensive education at Westminster School and Christ Church, Oxford. After two years at university he got into severe debt and left without a degree. His father obtained posts for him and his brother as Writers to the East India Company. In India between 1798 and 1802 they worked on the staff of the Governor-General, a brother of Sir Arthur Wellesley. Ben, after writing a memorandum of seventy items to his father dismissing the prospects of a career in India, returned to London with an introduction to the great general. Wellesley, later the Duke of Wellington, took Wyatt with him as his private secretary when appointed to govern Ireland in 1807–09.

Back in London, Ben took it into his head to follow his father's career. The Drury Lane Theatre was burned down that year and, amazingly, Ben submitted designs for re-building it. At this time he seems to have had no architectural training at all. James Wyatt's other son Philip, who was in debt in his turn, also sent in plans, and James hoped to start him on an architectural career in this way. In 1811 James Wyatt wrote to another son that the Prince Regent, interceding for Philip, had told him that he had "said and done all he could without absolutely quarrelling with that pig W———d." This referred to Samuel Whitbread, in whose gift the commission lay. Whitbread gave the job to Ben, and James Wyatt was so furious that he never spoke to his eldest son again before his death two years later.

The present main building of the **Theatre Royal**, Drury Lane is still Benjamin Wyatt's structure of 1811–12. It is in effect a huge brick box with

93

conventional Classical detailing of the Regency period in stucco on the main entrance side. The portico and colonnade are the work of other architects in 1820 and 1831, while Wyatt's interior was re-built in 1822 and altered again later.

When James Wyatt died in 1813, he left a disappointingly small estate. What he had was given up by his widow Rachel in favour of Benjamin, the oldest son, while she survived on a small pension from Lord Liverpool. Ben's practice flourished during the next few years and he succeeded his father as Surveyor of Westminster Abbey until 1827.

In 1814 Benjamin restored the rose window in the south transept of Westminster Abbey and in the same year he re-built "**School**", the great hall of Westminster School, Little Dean's Yard, where he himself had been educated. The huge room remained in the form in which he left it until it was bombed in 1941; it has since been restored with a different roof and walls, but some of his work is incorporated.

A strange paradox about Benjamin Wyatt is that he had little known architectural training, yet built extremely soundly. Equally, everything suggests that he was an unstable character, yet he was able to convince men of the establishment that he himself was sound enough for them to entrust major buildings to him. It seems likely that his was a convincing manner and that he possessed powerful charm.

In 1825 one of the King's brothers, the Duke of York, was building himself a mansion near Buckingham Palace. When the building's foundations reached ground level the Duke dismissed his architect, Robert Smirke, and commissioned Benjamin Wyatt to re-design and build the house. Wyatt worked on the project with his brother Philip, and the stone mansion was completed in 1839. It lies at the corner where houses along the edge of Green Park reach The Mall and, now called **Lancaster House**, it is used for government receptions. Wyatt's exterior was one of his best, a simple Classical block relieved by advancing accents and porticos. The interior retains some of his fine rooms, but the core of the house with its great staircase was re-built in 1843 for the Duke of Sutherland by Sir Charles Barry, who also added the attic storey.

This building marked the start of Wyatt's most successful six years of practice. In 1825–28 he re-built Londonderry House at No. 19 Park Lane, a fine mansion unforgivably destroyed in 1964. This was designed with Philip Wyatt, as was the surviving **Devonshire Club** of 1827 at No. 50 St. James's Street, the finest and most complete example of his buildings in London. The building was originally Crockford's, the famous gambling club of the period.

Wyatt's Oriental Club of 1827–28 at No. 18 Hanover Square, Mayfair, was demolished in 1964 when the club moved to its present premises. In 1828–29 Benjamin and Philip Wyatt received one of their most famous commissions when the Duke of

94

95

93 Benjamin Wyatt. Drury Lane Theatre, Catherine Street and Drury Lane, Covent Garden (1810–12). Portico, colonnade and interior have been altered and re-built over the subsequent years

94 Benjamin Wyatt. Apsley House, Hyde Park Corner (1828–29). Built for the Duke of Wellington, preserving several of the Adam interiors of the earlier house

95 Benjamin Wyatt. The Duke of York Column, Waterloo Place, Pall Mall and The Mall (1831–34)

Wellington, Ben's former employer before he became an architect, decided to alter and extend **Apsley House** at Hyde Park Corner. Known as No. 1 London, the house was basically by Robert Adam. Benjamin Wyatt kept many of the Adam interiors, but the exterior is now a Wyatt design (the east side was copied from the west when the adjoining buildings were demolished in the 1960s). The house is open to the public and, apart from Adam's work, the highlight is Wyatt's Waterloo Gallery where the Duke used to hold banquets. The work seems coarse in comparison to Adam's, but it has a suitably military vigour.

Apart from an unidentified house for the Marquess of Tavistock in Carlton House Terrace, following Nash's external design, Benjamin Wyatt's last London work is the **Duke of York Column** of 1831–34, erected at the end of Waterloo Place and at the top of the steps down to The Mall. Wyatt's memorial is a great Tuscan column of heavy entasis, with a balcony and drum above it, bearing the statue of the Duke by Westmacott. It makes a good enough starting point for Nash's triumphal way up Regent Street, though the Duke of York himself faces in the opposite direction.

After this work, Wyatt's career ended abruptly. The reason for this fall is not known, but recurrent debts from high living is the most likely cause. It is known that Ben was in debt again in 1841 and was imprisoned for it. He died in Camden Town, apparently in poverty, in about 1850.

William Wilkins
(1778-1839)

William Wilkins, portrait

The buildings of William Wilkins are a central part of the achievement of the early nineteenth century Greek revival in northern Europe, for he was the pre-eminent English scholar of that style. "Perhaps the best educated classic that has honoured the profession of architecture since Sir Christopher Wren," wrote James Elmes in 1847. "No liberty would he give or take, no line or member would he use, for which he could not find a precedent in some ancient Greek building . . ." But Elmes felt that Wilkins lacked "the architect's greatest qualities, invention and freedom from pedantry." In Cambridge, where he built more than anywhere else, Wilkins in fact designed buildings in the Gothic and Tudor styles as well as in the Grecian manner. In London there remain three major Neo-Greek buildings of his.

Wilkins was born in Norwich, the son of a successful designer-builder there. After a schooling at Norwich Grammar School, he won a scholarship to Caius College, Cambridge. He had a brilliant academic career and, during his four years after 1801 on a travelling scholarship to Greece and other Mediterranean countries, was elected a Fellow of his old college. His first major commission, for Downing College in Cambridge, was won in 1807 largely because of the Neo-Classical campaign for the Greek style. He designed many buildings in Cambridge and elsewhere before building his first work in London, the United University Club of 1822. It was demolished in 1902.

It seems that Wilkins was an urbanely mannered man. Obituaries say that "in society he was cheerful and his conversation displayed a mind stored with various useful information" and mention his "strong and vigorous mind and exceedingly high, correct and polished taste." In contrast to his Neo-Greek contemporary Smirke, who was tiny, "Wilkins' figure was tall and muscular, to appearance strongly framed . . ." He had enough of fantasy in him to have a portrait painted of his family and himself in Caroline dress. In contrast to the cold academic side of his life, he adored the stage and continued to run and to re-build six theatres which he inherited in East Anglia. Soane disliked him, but then Soane disliked most other architects.

In 1826 Wilkins won a limited competition for **University College**, the great secular establishment which was the first constituent part of the University of London, challenging the domination of the Church in higher education. Wilkins's building, built in 1827–29 assisted by J. P. Gandy Deering, faces across a courtyard onto Gower Street to the north of Bloomsbury. The dome and Corinthian portico form a distinguished composition above a

96 *Wilkins. University College, London University, Gower Street, north Bloomsbury (1827–29). The library and the wings around the courtyard were designed later by other architects*

97 *Wilkins. St. George's Hospital, Hyde Park Corner (1827–29)*

fine flight of steps, while the wings are quiet and serious. The internal planning is not so good, reflecting its history; Wilkins thought the selection committee would dislike waste space under the dome, but they took the opposite line, while accepting his plans, and required him to juggle with the arrangement of rooms (these were altered again later). His original design included wing pavilions and a columned screen on Gower Street. These were not built and the later buildings on the other three sides of the courtyard date from 1848 and later to designs by Professor T. L. Donaldson and others. They harmonise well enough with the Wilkins work.

St. George's Hospital, at Hyde Park Corner, was Wilkins's next London work. The fine white building of 1827–29 still survives, with its giant pillared Doric portico between two projecting wings. The severe Greek style, carefully adapted to an early nineteenth-century type of building, is sustained in the few original rooms surviving behind the portico. The Wilkins manner, built in stuccoed brick, was carried on when the building was extended on both sides thirty years later. The future of the building, now that the hospital is moving to new premises, is a matter for much concern.

The governors of St. George's Hospital had simply appointed Wilkins their architect, and it was some years before he won another commission in a competition. It was not for want of trying, for Wilkins had several frustrating experiences of winning competitions for projects never executed or losing narrowly in circumstances which made him cry foul.

In 1832, however, Wilkins won the competition for the **National Gallery**, an institution for which he had been campaigning. The suspicious circumstances here worked out in his favour for once. On the night before entries closed, only Nash and the great C. R. Cockerell had submitted designs. A member of the selection committee that evening urged his friend Wilkins to put in plans. After thinking it over, Wilkins worked all night long and was declared the winner next day.

The National Gallery, as built in 1834–38 with its large rooms for displaying the country's great paintings and its long Neo-Greek range along the top of Trafalgar Square, is Wilkins's most famous building. Unfortunately it is not his best. Using the site of William Kent's demolished Royal Mews, Wilkins was required to use the columns from King George IV's recently destroyed residence, Carlton House. These determined the size of the central portico and partly explain why this, with its four subsidiary porticos, provide such weak and inadequate accents for the length of the range if seen

98 *Wilkins. The National Gallery, Trafalgar Square, Westminster (1832–38). Interiors altered and rear additions done later by other architects. The advance and retreat of forms shown in this photograph belies the blandness of the façade when seen face on*

from a distance. This weakness is emphasised by a flimsy central dome and two smaller cupolas which sit on the roof like pepper-pots.

From close range, however, the succession of porticos forms an impressive enough approach when on foot and the steep staircase up into the central columns heightens the visitor's expectation. Only the rooms along the Trafalgar Square side were in the original building and these were redecorated by E. M. Barry when he added the rear part in 1867–76. Later, the vestibule and central hall were altered again by Sir John Taylor, the government architect, in the late 1880s.

The National Gallery, apart from the now demolished additions of 1828 *etc.* to East India House in the City, completes the short list of Wilkins's London buildings. The last of his four scholarly books on ancient Greek and Roman buildings was published in 1837, and in the same year he succeeded Soane as Professor of Architecture at the Royal Academy Schools. But when the National Gallery opened in the following year Wilkins was acutely distressed by the storm of abuse it provoked from Gothic revivalists such as Pugin. Gout had aged him suddenly and his theatres were now making heavy financial losses. He retired to his house in Cambridge, where he died a year later, and was buried in Corpus Christi College. Elmes called him "a Greek puritan" but, strangely, his Gothic buildings for Corpus Christi are described on Wilkins's tombstone as "the work which found most favour in his own eyes".

Decimus Burton (1800-81)

Decimus Burton, portrait

Putting aside the brilliance of Soane and the high romanticism of Nash, Decimus Burton contributed more gracefully charming buildings to London than any other architect of the Neo-Classical (or Regency) period. Yet his career in public buildings spanned little more than twenty years before he abandoned it for half a life-time of contented semi-retirement on the south coast of England.

Burton's unusual first name was given because he was the tenth son of James Burton (originally known as Haliburton), the favourite building contractor of John Nash. The older Burton was the builder for many of the Regent's Park Terraces, much of Regent Street and the whole of the original Russell Square for various architects. His business acumen was highly valued by Nash in realising his grand schemes and so, after Decimus had trained with his father and in the Royal Academy Schools from 1817, Nash helped him to start as an architect.

In about 1818 Decimus designed the elegant white villa called **The Holme** (now part of Bedford College) on the Inner Circle road of Regent's Park. In 1821–23 his father built Decimus's design for **Cornwall Terrace** on the Outer Circle of the park, and it is likely that **Clarence Terrace**, of the same years, was also designed by him. In 1822 Decimus was the architect of **Grove House** on the north-west side of the park, and in 1823–27 his design for The Colosseum was built on the site of the present Victorian terrace called Cambridge Gate on the Outer Circle. The Colosseum was an enormous amphitheatre for public events under a dome larger than that of St. Paul's Cathedral. It was a huge success and made Decimus Burton's reputation, but it was demolished in 1875.

This success brought him other public commissions quickly. The most lovely and famous of these is the delightful **Ionic Screen** at Hyde Park Corner with its three gateways built beside Apsley House to Burton's designs of 1825. Shortly afterwards he was commissioned to build the series of interesting little **Neo-Classical lodges** around Hyde Park and for St. James's Park in Birdcage Walk. Nash also got him to design the piers and railings around Buckingham Palace in about the same year (they were altered in 1904). Thus by the age of twenty-five, Decimus was described as "in the full tide of professional work".

Many of his buildings have gone, but some of the original buildings Burton did for the Zoological Society Gardens in Regent's Park in 1826–40 survive. Most notably, his fine brick **Camel House** (1830–31) and **Giraffe House** (1836–37) on the Outer Circle of the park are among the visual pleasures of the Zoo. The **Ravens' Aviary** (1827) is

99

also his work.

In 1827–30 Decimus Burton was commissioned to design one of his most celebrated buildings. This was the **Athenaeum Club** in Waterloo Place and Pall Mall, whose membership still includes the cream of influential established professions. The pretty stucco building, with its famous painted frieze and strong Doric portico, is a good example of Burton's simple version of the Greek style (the unfortunate attic storey was added in 1899), and the interiors carry through the manner well. Burton could do such work without the coldness of Wilkins's Neo-Greek designs and with more humanity than Smirke's.

H. M. Colvin describes Burton as having an "amiable and gentlemanly character", and his personal charm probably contributed as much to his success as his charm in building design. He was no scholar, but his use of the Greek Orders was always correct.

In 1828 the King commissioned Burton to build a triumphal arch gateway into the grounds of Buckingham Palace from Hyde Park Corner. Eighteen years after this was built, a huge memorial to the

Duke of Wellington was placed on top of it. This infuriated Burton so much that he added a clause to his will, leaving £2,000 to the government to have the statue removed. In fact, it was removed when the gateway was moved a few yards to its present position facing down Constitution Hill in 1883, but the present angel-driven chariot sculpture was erected on it in 1912 as a memorial to King Edward VII. The gateway is now known as the **Constitution Arch**.

Burton designed several other central London buildings at about this time, of which Nos. 10–14 Spring Gardens (c. 1828) are demolished and **Nos. 3 and 4 Carlton House Terrace** (1828, following Nash's exterior designs) survive. About 1830 he built the present **lodges and gates** at Lord Burlington's old Chiswick House in west London. But his next major commission was the **Charing Cross Hospital** of 1831–34 in Agar Street, with a rounded portico of Corinthian half-columns facing onto the Strand. The site was too cramped and narrow to allow Burton to produce one of his most graceful designs, but the white stuccoed Neo-

100

101

102

99 *Burton. The Athenaeum clubhouse, Waterloo Place, Pall Mall, St. James's (1827–30)*

100 *Burton. Ionic Screen, Hyde Park Corner (1825)*

101 *Burton. Giraffe House, the London Zoo, Outer Circle, Regent's Park (1836–37)*

102 *Burton with the engineer Richard Turner. The Palm House, Royal Botanic Gardens, Kew, south-west London (1844–48)*

Classical building, under threat since the hospital moved out in 1970, would be a sad loss.

After building the hospital, Burton largely withdrew from practising in central London and concentrated on domestic work in the country. Like his father, he built himself a house at St. Leonard's-on-Sea and preferred to stay there. From 1842 onwards he did carry out various alterations to the **United Services Club** in Pall Mall and Waterloo Place, which amount almost to a new design of Nash's building, while in 1840–45 he built a boarding house and the **headmaster's house** at Harrow School.

Burton's last London building of any size is one of his best and most unexpected. This is the **Palm House** which, with other work, he built with Richard Turner the engineer in 1844–48 at the Royal Botanic Gardens, Kew, in west London. It is a giant conservatory, glass-paned on a delicate iron frame which progresses upwards in three stages of seductive yet tautly sprung curves. The interior is seductive too, with the luscious green of the tropical plants filling the warm damp spaces. Burton and Turner's great Palm House was completed three years before the building of Paxton's Crystal Palace for the 1851 Exhibition.

Burton's story, in contrast to some of his eminent contemporaries, ends on a pleasant note. His success achieved and his fortune made, he spent almost the last forty years of his life contentedly by the sea at St. Leonard's, before dying at a great age. He continued to do a little architectural work to keep his mind active, and doubtless the old Neo-Classicist watched with resignation as the Gothic Revival rolled across England.

6

High Victorian Architecture and the Gothic Revival

It is probably still true to say that there are more Victorian public buildings in England than there are of any other period. It was the period of England's fastest growth in its economy and in its population— London, for instance, had a population of a little under a million people in 1800, but four and a half million by 1900.

The Victorian period is particularly associated with the Gothic style, but many of its buildings were generally Classical in manner, and much of its countless acres of new housing development have vaguely Classical detailing. Victorian Classical work varies from the disciplined brilliance of C. R. Cockerell (none of whose London works survives) to the Italianate palace style of Sir Charles Barry and the opulent loose Classicism of his sons, Charles junior (e.g. the Piccadilly range of Burlington House, 1869–73) and Edward (e.g. the Royal Opera House, Covent Garden, 1859). The Royal Exchange, opposite the Bank of England in the centre of the City of London, shows a florid Classicism typical of its 1841–44 date and of its outrageously venial architect Sir William Tite (1798–1873). Other examples of Victorian Classicism in London include what is now The Museum of Mankind (the anthropological section of the British Museum), built in 1866–69 as the first headquarters of the University of London, in Burlington Gardens, Mayfair by Sir James Pennethorne (1801–71). As for Captain Fowke's design for the Royal Albert Hall, Kensington Gore (1867–71), its individualistic manner with Classical details in brick and terracotta is said to be derived from the German Gottfried Semper.

103 *Double plate contrasting what Pugin regarded as the decadence of early nineteenth-century Classicism with the Christian nobility of medieval Gothicism. From Contrasts, Pugin's book of 1836*

Nevertheless, the Gothic style remains the most typical manner of Victorian England. And what Inigo Jones was to Renaissance Classicism in England, what Lord Burlington was to Palladianism, Pugin was to the revival of Gothic architecture which spread through the country between 1840 and 1870. Before Pugin's writings were published at the start of Queen Victoria's reign in 1837, Gothic was a style for cheap churches and schools, or was seen as part of the Picturesque Romantic movement. James Wyatt used the style Byronically, John Nash used it rustically. The entries for the competition of 1835–36 for the new Houses of Parliament were required to be Gothic or Elizabethan largely because of the proximity of Westminster Abbey and Westminster Hall, but Pugin shook his head over Barry's winning design (in whose execution he was later to have such a large part) and called it "Gothic details on a Classic body". Barry himself preferred an Italianate Classicism and used it in almost all his mature buildings except Parliament. It was Pugin's own words, drawings and buildings which convinced most architects and people in a position to commission buildings that Gothic must be scholarly and that it was an approach to building and design, not just another style. And he convinced them that Gothic was the only proper architecture for a Christian country.

The Victorian Gothic revival was a very English phenomenon. Henry-Russell Hitchcock has pointed out that High Gothic was important in America only in the decade 1865–75, and much the same applies to Canada and Australia. Viollet-le-Duc's Gothic work in France gained impetus only after 1850 and the Neo-Gothic churches in the German-speaking countries are almost all of the second half of the century.

In England, a large number of young architects

started their careers during the 1840s under the influence of Pugin's ideas. Of these, Scott, Butterfield and Street are represented in chapters of this book, but there were many others of great distinction. William Burges (1827–81) is perhaps the most eminent of these, but his only remaining building in London is his own Tower House, No. 9 Melbury Road, Holland Park (1875–80).

London has a large number of fine Victorian Gothic churches by architects only slightly less well-known than those already mentioned and some of the best of these must be given here. Pugin's friend Benjamin Ferrey (1810–80) designed St. Stephen, Rochester Row, Vincent Square, Westminster (1845–47), a good earnest design in the Decorated Gothic style. The Roman Catholic Church of the Immaculate Conception, Farm Street, Mayfair is an ambitious and impressive work of 1844–49 by J. J. Scoles (1798–1863) with an altar by Pugin. John Loughborough Pearson (1817–97) and George Frederick Bodley (1827–1907) were among the great masters of Victorian Gothic. Pearson's London churches include St. Peter, Kennington Lane, Lambeth (1863–65) and the glorious St. Augustine, in Kilburn Park Road, Kilburn (1870–80). Bodley built few complete churches in London, but notable early and late designs in his career are St. Michael, Camden Road, Camden Town (1876–81) and Holy Trinity, Prince Consort Road, by the Albert Hall, Kensington (1902–04).

James Brooks (1825–1901) is much better represented in London. All his churches, simplified and powerful designs, are worth visiting although it is often difficult to gain entry. In the East End of London, Brooks built four fine works between 1860 and 1870. These are not all still in use as churches, but they are worth listing; St. Michael, Mark Street, off Paul Street, Shoreditch (1863–65), St. Columba, Kingsland Road, Shoreditch (1867–71), St. Chad, Nichols Square, Shoreditch (1868) and St. Andrew, St. Andrew's Road and Barking Road, Plaistow (1870–71). Later Brooks churches include the Church of the Ascension, Lavender Hill, Battersea (1873–83), St. Andrew, High Road, Willesden Green (1886–87), St. Mary, Church Lane, Hornsey (1888 onwards) and, best of all, All Hallows, Shirlock Street, St. Pancras (1889 onwards).

Other church architects of the mid-Victorian period are too numerous to have their works listed here, but the following are of particular interest; E. B. Lamb (1805–69), S. S. Teulon (1812–73), William White (1825–1900), George Goldie (1828–87), Bassett Keeling (1836–86), George Gilbert Scott junior (1839–97, although almost all his London work has been destroyed) and Basil

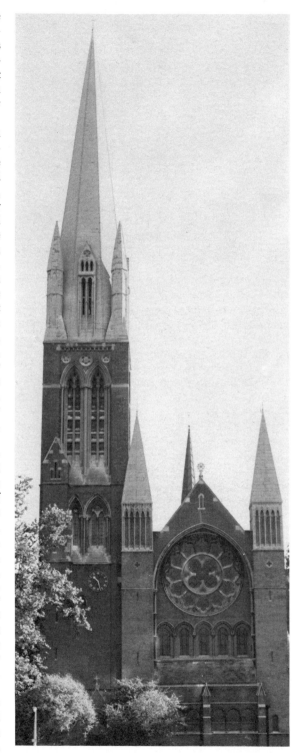

104 *Victorian Gothic. St. Augustine's Church, Kilburn Park Road, Kilburn, north-west London (1870–80) by John Loughborough Pearson. The soaring forms are typical of the best of the serious-minded Victorian Gothic style*

Champneys (1842–1935).

It remains to be noted that the legendarily fat Sir Horace Jones (1819–87) was the City of London official architect in charge of most of the Victorian markets in the City—Smithfield, Billingsgate and Leadenhall—and of the design stage of Tower Bridge, with Sir John Wolfe Barry (built 1886–94). The old Covent Garden market building is older (1828–31) and was designed by Charles Fowler, who was also responsible for the now vanished Hungerford Market of 1834.

The Victorian period saw major advances in the use of iron and steel for structural purposes (see Appendix Three) and of wrought and cast iron for decorative work. The Crystal Palace, built of iron frame and glass around the present site of the Albert Memorial for the Great Exhibition of 1851, was designed by Sir Joseph Paxton. It was later moved to Sydenham in south London and was finally destroyed by fire in 1937. Alexandra Palace by J.

105 *Victorian Classicism. The proscenium arch, interior of the Royal Opera House, Covent Garden, Bow Street (1859) by Edward M. Barry. A good example of the cavalier treatment of Classical forms by many Victorian architects*

Johnson (1872–3 and 1875) still survives in Muswell Hill as north London's equivalent centre for entertainments and culture.

The Crystal Palace was the most famous of London's Victorian buildings of iron, but some of the railway stations were equally notable achievements. The great train shed of St. Pancras, by W. H. Barlow, will be mentioned in the chapter on Gilbert Scott; but those at Paddington (1852–4, by I. K. Brunel with architectural trimmings by Matthew Digby Wyatt), King's Cross (1851–2, by Lewis Cubitt), Victoria (1862, extended 1898 and 1902–08) and Liverpool Street (1875, by the engineer, Edward Wilson, with later additions) are almost as impressive and deserving of mention here.

Sir Charles Barry
(1795-1860)

Sir Charles Barry, portrait

Barry, the chief architect of the Houses of Parliament, is a particularly suitable figure to open the section of this book on the Victorian Gothic Revival. For Barry's buildings range from the timid Gothic of the 1820s to the splendour of his work with Pugin for Parliament. He also initiated an often flamboyant use of Classicism typical of the Victorian age.

Barry's father owned a successful stationery business in London, and the boy was brought up in a fairly prosperous household. When he was fifteen, Charles was articled to a firm of surveyors. His father died, and when Charles inherited his property at the age of twenty-one he decided to study ancient buildings. From 1817 until 1820 he travelled in France, Italy, Greece and the Near East, setting up in practice as an architect in Holborn as soon as he returned to London. This coincided with a series of competitions for the low-cost Commissioners' Churches, following the government decision to provide new churches for many of the spreading suburbs in English cities. Within two years, Barry was designing and supervising a series of these in and around Manchester and Brighton, and in Islington, London.

Barry's churches for the Commissioners are in a simple Gothic manner. They are of brick with stone detailing, competently handled but without the burning conviction of later Gothic revival work by architects inspired by Pugin. The low budgets available for Barry's churches are apparent in these north London buildings. After adding the north aisle of 1824 to **Old St. Mary's Church** in Stoke Newington Church Street, Barry built **St. Paul**, Ball's Pond Road and **St. John the Evangelist**, Holloway Road. Both were built in 1826–28, and both have simple plans with castellated towers topped by four crocketed pinnacles on the street frontage. **Holy Trinity** in Cloudesley Square, Islington, dates from the same years, but here Barry used a more picturesque type of frontage derived from King's College Chapel in Cambridge. There followed St. Peter in Saffron Hill, Finsbury (1830–32) and **St. Peter** in St. Peter's Street, Islington (1834) whose extraordinary spire was added by the eccentric E. B. Lamb nine years later. The interiors of all these churches are decent but austere.

In the meantime, Barry had built some buildings outside London in a style very far from the Gothic. This side of Barry was first seen in London when he won the competition for the **Travellers' Club** in Pall Mall (1829–32), beside Decimus Burton's Athenaeum. The clubhouse is a charming and beautifully detailed adaptation of an Italian Renaissance town palace, its stuccoed façade hand-

106 *Barry. Holy Trinity Church, Cloudesley Square, Islington (1826–28)*

107 *Barry. The Travellers' Club (1829–32) on the left and the Reform Club (1837–41) on the right, Pall Mall, St. James's*

somely proportioned, and the roofline marked by a strong cornice. The interior is fine too, with an internal courtyard and a dignified staircase which runs up to the *pièce de résistance*—the long library which combines grandeur with intimacy in a brilliant way. The club had many wealthy members, and its success brought Barry celebrity and numerous commissions to Italianize large country houses.

In 1834–36 Barry re-built George Dance's **Royal College of Surgeons** in Lincoln's Inn Fields, retaining Dance's Ionic portico but building a good and restrained Classical block around it. The effect has been spoiled by three attic stories added by the surgeons over the years above Barry's cornice.

It was in 1834, too, that Barry saw from a hilltop outside London the smoke and flames of the burning Houses of Parliament. He said later that he immediately thought of the chance which this would offer to some architect. When the competition for the new buildings was announced in 1835, the most important new building opportunity since the Great Fire of 1666, Barry entered it. The style was required to be "Gothic or Elizabethan" so Barry could not use his favourite Italian manner, and he got Augustus Welby Pugin, who had done drawings for him earlier, to help as a draughtsman. In 1836 Barry was declared the winner. The river wall was started in 1837 and in 1840 Barry's wife laid the foundation stone of the building itself.

In the meantime, Barry's fame had increased, and his other commissions with it. He was in that mould of British architect whose whole life seems swallowed by work on their practice. It is hard to get any impression of what he was like as a man beneath the outer manner described by Mark Girouard as "always genial and the best of company". He was devoted to his wife and family, and two of his four sons became architects (one of them, E. M. Barry, later built the present Royal Opera House, Covent Garden). On the other hand, among his countless friendly acquaintances he numbered only one as a close friend. He never seems to have quarrelled with his clients, and perhaps there was little to quarrel about; although he preferred his Italian Renaissance manner, he willingly agreed to fit his designs to his clients' desires. And he produced splendidly rich recipes for any style of architectural cooking.

While the preliminary work for Parliament was under way, Barry was putting up another great Italianate palace for a club in Pall Mall. The **Reform Club**, essentially Whig in its members' politics, was built in 1837–41 right beside his earlier Travellers' Club. The Reform has a Roman splendour about it, both in its noble stone exterior and in the sonorous interiors. After a series of steps rising from the street into the heart of the building, one emerges into an immense central room rising the whole height of the building to a glass roof. With the colonnades around it, this is really a large central courtyard, but roofed over to suit the northern climate. The experience of this breathtaking space continues as one moves up the grand staircase and into the gallery around the central hall which gives access to the long library and other rooms.

Barry's other London works must be described briefly before giving an account of the building of the Parliament buildings. Mount Felix House in Bridge Street, Walton-on-Thames (1837–40) was a typical example of Barry's re-building of older houses in his own early Victorian taste. His Imperial Assurance offices of 1840 in Pall Mall have been demolished, while some of the **gatehouse** of Pentonville Prison in Caledonian Road, Islington is still Barry's work of 1840–42 (the prison itself is by Colonel Joshua Jebb). His lay-out of both **Parliament Square** and **Trafalgar Square** (originally a John Nash idea) have later been altered, although the famous Nelson's Column (1839–42 by William Railton, statue by Baily) and Barry's **terrace** survive of the 1840 work in Trafalgar Square. Barry's Dulwich College of 1841 was entirely re-built by his son Charles. On the other hand, his grand re-building of the **central hall and staircase** (1843) of Benjamin Wyatt's Lancaster House in The Mall remains one of the most impressive spatial experiences in London.

In 1844–45 Barry was working on one of his major Westminster works a few hundred yards from Parliament. This is the new **Treasury** building (now the Privy Council and Cabinet Office) in Whitehall, running north from Downing Street. The commission was to add a storey to Sir John Soane's fine building designed only twenty years earlier, an unenviable task. Barry re-used Soane's columns, raising their bases to the first floor, and re-designed the skyline with the rather spikey urns above the balustrade which became a trade-mark of Barry's later Classical work. Soane's remarkable entrance halls inside the building were left alone by Barry, but the frontage demonstrates the textured surfaces and restlessness of Victorian Classicism in contrast with the exploration of space and solids in Neo-Classical designs of only two decades earlier.

Apart from **alterations to Dudley House** at No. 100 Park Lane, Mayfair, Barry did two more surviving Classical buildings in London. In 1847 he enlarged **St. John's Lodge** on the Inner Circle of Regent's Park, a handsome stuccoed villa. His last major London design was the great mansion **Bridgewater House** of 1847–49 (designs probably 1845),

facing onto Green Park to the north of Stafford House on The Mall. Bridgewater House was built for the Earl of Ellesmere and has fortunately been preserved as a company headquarters. It is not so very far from Barry's earlier Italianate clubhouse *palazzi* in Pall Mall, but the proportions are extraordinarily different. It is their height which gives the Travellers' and Reform Clubs their magnificence. At Bridgewater House the accent is on horizontal expanse with an ornate cornice topped by pillar chimneys and the architect's favourite spiked urns.

While he was working on these Classical London buildings and others elsewhere, Barry's life was dominated for its last twenty-three years by the erection of the great Gothic masterpiece, the **Houses of Parliament**. From the time of the competition designs in 1835, Barry engaged the genius of the Gothic revival, Augustus Welby Pugin, to design the detail inside and outside the building. But the plan of its internal lay-out, the positioning of the towers to form the vertical visual accents, the outline of the building and the long struggle against endless hostile committees to get it built—all these were Barry's greatest triumph. It was the allocation of exactly the right aspects of Barry's and Pugin's talents to the various parts of the work which created this world-famous masterpiece for London.

The fire of 1834 had almost completely destroyed the old accumulation of Parliament buildings except for Yevele's marvellous Westminster Hall of 1395–1402, William Kent's Law Courts of 1758–70 and a few other pieces. Barry pulled down all except Westminster Hall, which is included in the design just inside the public entrance. His plan has a main axis line of public rooms and corridors running from this entrance almost through to the terrace along the Thames river frontage. This axis is crossed by another and they meet in the Central Lobby. Here, coming from the public entrance (St. Stephen's), corridors run to the House of Commons to the left and to the House of Lords to the right. The committee rooms are ranged along the river front on the first floor. Houses for the presiding officers lie at either end of the river front too; the Speaker's beyond the House of Commons, the Lord Chancellor's beyond the House of Lords. Each end has its tower—the Victoria Tower for the House of Lords, the Clock Tower (widely known as Big Ben after its great bell) for the House of Commons.

The interiors will be described in the chapter on Pugin, for they are marked with his Gothic design brilliance, as is the decoration outside. But the buildings as a whole are marked with Barry's genius too. The splendour of his overall plan, the steady

108 *Barry with Pugin. Houses of Parliament, Parliament Square, Westminster (1835–60). The Victoria Tower and the House of Lords are on the left, the high tower in the middle marks the Central Lobby, with the House of Commons and the Clock Tower (Big Ben) on the right*

109 *Barry. Bridgewater House, Cleveland Row, facing onto Green Park, St. James's (1845–49)*

rhythm of his grand frontages punctuated by superb vertical accents, the story of his fortitude in the face of technical difficulties and of successive waves of critical politicians are witness to an extraordinary form of greatness. After the river wall was started in 1837 and the buildings themselves in 1840, the House of Lords was opened in 1847 and the rest of the main buildings in 1852. In that year Barry was knighted and Pugin died. Barry's unfortunate aberrant plan to enclose New Palace Yard with buildings and a spire over a corner gateway was produced in the following year but was not taken up. The inventive Clock Tower was completed in 1858 and the Victoria Tower in 1860, the year in which Barry finally died, worn out by the worry of the work for which he had been ill-paid and inadequately appreciated. The Parliament buildings were not quite finished even then, and his son E. M. Barry supervised the final stages. Apart from his knighthood, the token of burial in Westminster Abbey was the only recognition made by his country for decades of Barry's unsparing and underpaid work to complete the great building.

Augustus Welby Pugin (1812-52)

Augustus Welby Pugin, portrait

Pugin, who designed all the internal and external detail of the Houses of Parliament, was the force behind the idealistic stage of the nineteenth-century Gothic revival. Before his fifteen brilliant and intensive years between 1835 and 1850, the Gothic style was regarded as just one among several available; it was used loosely and often regarded as prettily suitable for the ideas of Picturesque Romanticism. Mention has already been made of Pugin's role in obtaining widespread acceptance for the notion that a correctly used Gothic style was the only fit one for Christians.

Augustus Welby Northmore Pugin was the only child of Augustus Charles Pugin (1762–1832), an aristocratic Frenchman who narrowly escaped from the French Revolution to Wales, where the architect John Nash engaged him as draughtsman in 1793. The older Pugin moved to London with his employer, and his talent soon made him well known. He married Catherine Welby, daughter of a barrister, and prospered. He was a keen student of Gothic work, and his son was brought up with a training which enabled him to design in that style as naturally as if he had been living centuries earlier.

By the time that he was twenty (when his father died) young Pugin was already celebrated for his historical costumes designed for the opera and theatre. In 1833 Charles Barry engaged the young man for the detailed drawings of a Gothic school in Birmingham, and the two men, although not friends, worked together frequently and retained a respect for each other's very different talents. In 1835, Pugin designed the detail and did the drawings for Barry's entry to the Houses of Parliament competition since Barry realised that his own talent for detail design was scanty except in Classical styles. Barry's ground plans and overall visual design were magnificent, and the Barry–Pugin entry gained first prize.

Before describing Pugin's masterly achievement at Parliament, some account of his character and other work should be given. He was a man of extraordinary charm and turbulent energy. Dying at the age of 40, he had had three marriages and built himself two houses. The second wedding, to Louisa Burton in 1833, was followed by a move to Salisbury to a house Pugin designed with an unusual plan that first attracted attention to him as an architect. In 1836, after his impassioned conversion to Roman Catholicism, Pugin published a small book generally known by its short title *Contrasts*. It is an eloquent *paean* to the integrity of Gothic architecture and the goodness of the medieval way of life, illustrated by a

110 *Pugin. St. Thomas of Canterbury Church, Rylston Road, Fulham (1847–49)*

series of Pugin drawings contrasting recent Classical buildings unfavourably with their medieval counterparts shown on the same page.

Contrasts, its revised edition of 1841 and his next book *The True Principles of Pointed Christian Architecture* (also published in 1841) were immensely influential, especially with the recently emancipated Roman Catholics in England. It was these publications which brought Pugin a mass of commissions for churches and cathedrals and started his independent architectural practice. Money for the buildings was not plentiful, for the population was growing and spreading at a faster rate than church-building could be comfortably afforded, and in few of them could he achieve his own ideals of architecture. His best church, St. Giles (1841–46), is far from London at Cheadle in Staffordshire. His first London work, the Convent of Mercy of 1838 at Bermondsey, was destroyed by bombs in 1941. **St. George's Roman Catholic Cathedral** (1840–42) and the **Bishop's Palace** in St. George's Road, Southwark were also bombed and as re-built lack atmosphere—but from the start the cathedral was an austerely low-budget building. **St. Peter's Church** (1843) in Woolwich New Road, Woolwich is again disappointing. The money-saving design is apparent throughout (Pugin put his artistic ideals second to the need to provide places of worship for Catholics) and the chancel was added later by another architect.

The best Pugin church in London is **St. Thomas of Canterbury**, Rylston Road, Fulham. It dates from 1847–49—a late work, for increasing mental illness prevented Pugin from doing much after 1850. The style is of the Decorated period of Gothic with a spired tower at the west front and the entrance from a courtyard at the far end of the church from the street. The interior is good, but still disappointing if compared with Pugin's decorative work on the rare occasions when he had an adequate budget.

For the rest, excepting Parliament, Pugin's surviving work in London consists of stained glass windows, furnishings and, most notably, the **High Altar** and fine standard **candelabra** of *c.* 1848–50 at the **Church of the Immaculate Conception** in Farm Street, Mayfair.

From these works alone one would never guess at the extent of Pugin's influence or at his personal magnetism and romantic nature. The chief record of his personality comes from the *Recollections of A. W. N. Pugin* published by his friend and fellow-architect Benjamin Ferrey in 1861. From this book we know of his wit, the laughter of his friends gathered while Pugin worked at the drawing-board, his outspoken tendency to take offence at careless behaviour by aristocratic clients, his habit of dressing

III

in a seaman's jacket, pilot trousers, long boots and a wideawake hat—and still expecting to be treated as a gentleman. In 1843 he built his own final house at Ramsgate, where he loved to spend days in a boat on the sea. His second wife Louisa died a year after that house was completed, and in 1848 he married Jane Knill who remained devoted during his last four increasingly terrible years.

It is the **interiors** of the **Houses of Parliament** which remain the masterpiece of Pugin in London. The detailing of the exterior panels was apparently to Pugin's designs, executed under the supervision of Barry's master stonemason, John Thomas. From 1844 onwards, however, Pugin's major work commitment was drawing after drawing to bring the great empty spaces provided in Barry's plans to the gorgeous Gothic life which they have today. The overall lay-out has already been described in the chapter on Barry. From the moment one steps inside the St. Stephen's entrance for the public, one is walking through Pugin's rooms and up the steps to his great dim octagonal Central Lobby. Here, his reception rooms along the terrace and committee rooms above lie in front of the visitor. To the left, the

12

111 *Pugin with Barry. External detailing of Houses of Parliament, Parliament Square, Westminster (designed 1835 onwards, the main buildings started 1840 and opened 1852, towers completed 1860)*

112 *Pugin with Barry. Interior, the House of Lords (opened 1847), Houses of Parliament*

Commons interior was spoiled by Parliamentary Committees' own alterations long before it was bombed and re-built differently after the Second World War. But to the right of the Central Lobby lies Pugin's intact masterpiece, the House of Lords.

The House of Lords was opened in 1847. The space is lofty and open, with only shallow galleries to break the vertical rise of the decorated walls. Horizontally, the row of windows high in the walls with large statues of Magna Carta barons between each give a strong rhythm, while the chamber ends in the deep spaces of three lofty arches. Everywhere the texture is rich and warm, the furnishings splendid, and a great climax is provided by Pugin's glorious throne for the Queen. Beyond this end of the chamber there lies a series of other rooms on the grandest scale and with magnificent decoration.

Pugin's last years were tragic. He overworked himself to extremes, and from 1850 onwards periods of madness were frequent, while his kidneys brought him physical illness. By February 1852 he was in constant pain and sometimes violent. For a time his wife Jane committed him to Bethlehem Hospital on the advice of friends. It was in 1852 that the new Houses of Parliament were officially opened by Queen Victoria; in the same year Pugin died. His wife had got him released from Bedlam, but his death followed only three days after his returning home to his house at Ramsgate.

Cardinal Newman said of him, "Mr. Pugin is a man of genius . . . His zeal, his minute diligence, his resources, his invention, his imagination, his sagacity in research, are all of the highest order. . . . But he has the great fault of a man of genius, as well as the merit. He is intolerant and . . . sees nothing good in any school of Christian art except that of which he is himself so great an ornament." Pugin said of himself, "I have lived an hundred years in forty."

Sir Gilbert Scott (1811-78)

Sir Gilbert Scott, portrait

The start of the great years of High Victorian Gothic almost coincided with the death of its prime mover, Pugin, in 1852. From 1850 until 1870 the Gothic style was not only *the* style for churches in England; many Gothic houses and public buildings too were built during this period. The largest architectural practice in England at this time was that of a strong admirer of Pugin and advocate of fourteenth-century Gothic, Sir George Gilbert Scott. Architect of the Albert Memorial, of the front building of St. Pancras Station, of the Foreign Office in Whitehall and of a vast number of churches, Scott was a major contributor to the London scene.

One of thirteen children born to the wife of a poor village clergyman at Gawcott in Buckinghamshire, Scott had little education except drawing lessons from an uncle. At the age of sixteen, he was articled to an obscure London architect called Edmeston, and later worked for a firm of builders. Barely into his twenties, Scott became assistant to Henry Roberts at the time when the latter was designing the resplendent Neo-Classical Fishmongers' Hall (1831–34), for the ancient city guild, which stands beside the northern approach to London Bridge.

Later, he worked for Sampson Kempthorne until, in 1835, Scott's father died and he launched his own practice to try and make more income for the family. These early years of desperate striving for income left Scott with a lifelong anxiety about money which combined oddly with his later taste for a fairly expensive way of life. Scott's partner for the first ten years was W. B. Moffatt (1812–87) and together they built many Gothic churches and about fifty of the workhouses for the poor needed all over the country as a result of recent legislation. It was hard work and poorly paid, but it gave Scott great experience to draw on when he ended the partnership.

Around London, typical examples of Scott and Moffatt's work can be seen in the churches of **St. Peter Norbiton**, London Road, Kingston-upon-Thames (1842), **Christ Church**, Turnham Green, Chiswick (1843), **St. Michael-at-Bowes**, Wood Green (1843), **St. Mary**, Arthur Road, Wimbledon (1843), **St. John**, off the High Road, Wembley (1845–46) and in the **Royal Wanstead School**, Holly Bush Hill, Wanstead (1843). Already, these buildings often show the rather unimaginative design quality difficult to avoid in an architectural practice of so many buildings.

The decision to start practising alone in 1845 was largely the result of Moffatt's worrying extravagance and of Scott's sudden celebrity when he won the commission in 1844 to build the Nicolai-Kirche in Hamburg because of the congregation's distaste for a Neo-Greek design placed first in the competition.

113 Scott. Range of houses on Broad Sanctuary and entrance gateway to Dean's Yard, beside the west end of Westminster Abbey, Westminster (1853)

Scott's career owed much of its success to his captivation with Pugin's books of 1836 and 1841. In 1842 he became an early member of the Ecclesiological Society, an influential High Church of England organisation aiming to reform church practices and architecture along medieval lines.

Apart from the Hamburg commission, 1844 was an important year for Scott. He and his wife moved to a spacious house in St. John's Wood and he travelled abroad for the first time. His early pupils included notable architects such as G. F. Bodley and G. E. Street. In practice by himself, his early London buildings were St. Matthew, City Road (1847, but destroyed in the Second World War), the restoration of St. John the Baptist in East Hillingdon (1847) and St. Peter, Croydon (1849).

In 1849 he was appointed Surveyor of Westminster Abbey, a post he held until his death, and started work on the nearby church of **St. Matthew** in Great Peter Street, Westminster (1849–51). The Kentish ragstone exterior is impressive, but even in this first central London commission of Scott's there was a lack of inspiration in the interior, despite its competence in Gothic design. The chapels added later by other architects gave the church a feeling of organic growth, however. Today one aisle and a chapel on a higher level form the body of the

church, while the nave and the other aisle are a dramatic ruin gutted by fire in 1977.

After building **Emmanuel Church** in Upton Lane, West Ham (1850–52) and **Christ Church** in the Broadway, Ealing (1852), Gilbert Scott started on another work in Westminster. This is the 1853 Gothic range of houses, with the turretted gateway to Dean's Yard, in **Broad Sanctuary** beside the west entrance to Westminster Abbey. It is one of Scott's most remarkable works, with the asymmetrical frontage vertically accented and highly inventive. The **monument** in the centre of Broad Sanctuary is to pupils of Westminster School killed in the Crimea—it is also by Scott and dates from 1859–61.

Scott's **Chapel for Harrow School** (1854–57) in outer north-west London is a fairly convincing Early English Gothic design. In 1856 the competition for the government's new Foreign Office was won by another architect, but a year later Scott's lobbying had gained the commission for himself—more of this story will be told in a moment. His other work of the 1850s included the **chancel** of the Camden Church in Camberwell (1854), **St. John** at Shirley near

114 Scott. *The Albert Memorial, Kensington Gardens, Kensington Gore (1863–72)*

Croydon (1856), **St. Barnabas** at Woolwich (1857), the restoration of Wren's **St. Michael**, Cornhill (1857–60), **St. Matthias** at Richmond (1858), a new church of **St. Mary** in Stoke Newington Church Street (1858) and the **monument** to the engineer Robert Stephenson in Westminster Abbey (1859).

Scott was an earnest and hard-working man, devoted to his wife and family home, enjoying entertaining and pastimes such as the theatre from time to time. On the other hand, he loathed the clerical dinners which his work often involved.

In 1857 Scott had published a book called *Remarks on Secular and Domestic Architecture, present and future* which preached that the Decorated Gothic of the fourteenth century should be applied equally to domestic, public and church architecture, and that modern building techniques could be integrated into the style. In the previous year he had moved for eight years into the Admiral's House, Hampstead and in 1860 he designed the **west gallery** of the nearby church, Christ Church, which he attended. In the early 1860s his many works included in London the **chapel of King's College** in the Strand (1861–62), the **Vaughan Library** at Harrow School (1861–63), **Christ Church** in Wanstead (1861), the **houses at Nos. 1, 3 and 3A Dean's Yard** in Westminster (1862), **Christ Church** in Southgate (1862), **St. Clement** in Islington (1863–65) and **St. Stephen** in Lewisham (1865).

The first of Scott's major public secular buildings is also his most famous, the **Albert Memorial** in Kensington Gardens beside Kensington Gore. The memorial to the Prince Consort was built in 1863–72. Basically it is a realisation on a monumental architectural scale of the type of medieval shrine of metalwork and jewels used to contain the relics of saints. Regarded with derision or affection by later generations of Londoners during the period when Victorian Gothic was unfashionable, the memorial is a concentrated example of the best mid-Victorian craftsmanship. It won a knighthood for Scott when it was completed.

Even more controversial was Scott's largest public work, the **Foreign Office** building of 1868–73 stretching from Whitehall through to St. James's Park. The dubious way in which Scott obtained the commission in 1857 has already been alluded to. Leakage of the fact that Scott was preparing a Gothic design led to a long and bitter dispute in Parliament and elsewhere, known as the Battle of the Styles. Palmerston had been largely responsible for the rejection of the 1856 competition, but went out of office afterwards. Before building could begin, however, Palmerston was back in power, and he

115 *Scott. The Home Office, Whitehall, Westminster (1868–73), which forms one end of a large government building. The other end is the Foreign Office, which faces onto St. James's Park. Scott's use of the Italianate style was dictated by Lord Palmerston*

116 *Scott. St. Pancras Station frontage and hotel, Euston Road, St. Pancras (1868–74). The civil engineer Barlow's great train shed can be seen on the right*

forced Scott to abandon both the Gothic and the freely Byzantine designs which he had prepared. The great politician insisted on a Renaissance design, and so Scott, in his own words, "bought some costly books on Italian architecture and set vigorously to work" before work started in 1868. The final result is Victorian Italianate, presenting a rather ponderous front to Whitehall and a splendidly varied and rich range to the park. From the central courtyard, a great series of Classical halls, corridors and grand staircases leads to the ministerial suite overlooking the park. The building originally housed the Home Office and the India Office as well as the Foreign Office; the India Office courtyard and interiors were designed by Sir Matthew Digby Wyatt, but the rest was one of the designs over which Scott himself took most trouble.

In 1868–74, almost at the same time as the Foreign Office, Scott was at work on one of the great masterpieces of the Victorian Gothic revival in secular architecture. This is the hotel building which provides the frontage of **St. Pancras Station** in the Euston Road, St. Pancras. The approach from the main road and the station entrances are well planned, but it is the brilliant asymmetrical Gothic design and the astonishing romantic skyline which make St. Pancras so breathtaking. Analysis by historians has traced the origin of almost every detail in Italian, French or English Gothic exemplars, but it was Scott's triumph to combine such elements in this particular way. The sumptuous hotel interiors, now used as British Rail offices, are still there and could be reinstated. The train shed of the station itself, for many years the greatest span in the world at 243 feet, was by the engineer W. H. Barlow.

With so much passion and flair shown at St. Pancras, it is surprising to come back to the frequent coldness of Scott's church work. **St. Mary Abbots**, at the corner of Church Street and High Street, Kensington (1869–72) is one of Scott's noblest spired exteriors. The long interior, Early English Gothic in style, is fine too; but there is still that familiar frigidity, as if the architect of so many churches all over Britain and abroad could not devote love to an individual work. With such a huge practice it was perhaps inevitable that much design was done by members of his large staff. Apart from **St. Michael-at-Bowes** in Southgate (1874), this was Scott's last London church.

After 1870 most of Scott's design work in London was concentrated on the **Chancery Lane extensions to Lincoln's Inn** (where he also did the library interior in 1871–73) and on restoration work, particularly at **Westminster Abbey**. Here he re-did the font in the Henry VII Chapel, the Rose Window

117 *Scott. St. Mary Abbots Church, Kensington High Street and Church Street, Kensington (1869–72)*

and the North Transept (up to the level of the porches) on Parliament Square and the Chapter House, among other work. Scott's restorations here and elsewhere were undertaken in a spirit of much devotion. But his hand was heavy and his final year of life was saddened by the sustained condemnation of this work by William Morris, the great designer and reformer, who by then had founded the Society for the Protection of Ancient Buildings (widely known as Anti-Scrape from their campaign to stop Scott and others from "scraping" old monuments and other additions from medieval churches).

Scott's health had been poor since a severe illness in 1871, and he sadly missed the vigour of his wife, who died in 1872. He hated exercise and as a result became stout despite exhausting working hours all his life. On the other hand by the time he died in 1878 he could see his own practice safely in the hands of a son, John Oldrid Scott, while his talented eldest son, George Gilbert Scott the younger, was well set on an architectural career that was too brief but of much distinction. Scott was buried in Westminster Abbey, a worthy tribute to his Victorian virtues.

William Butterfield (1814-1900)

William Butterfield, portrait

Butterfield's polychrome tile and brick buildings, often harsh for all their splendour of form and space, are among the most impressive of all the works of High Victorian Gothic architects. He designed no really large-scale buildings in London, but his churches include two of the most intense architectural experiences to be found in the capital.

One of nine children born in London, Butterfield was the son of a relatively humble chemist, with a shop in the Strand, who prospered during the 1830s. The family's social aspirations rose with prosperity, and so William, who had been apprenticed to a Pimlico builder in 1831, was articled to an architect called E. L. Blackburne from 1833 until 1837. In the following year he became assistant to an architect in Worcester for a year and then in 1840 set up his own London practice in Lincoln's Inn Fields. So Butterfield is unusual in that he started a great practice without having had a connection with any established notable architect. It was the letters about Christian architecture that he wrote to *The Ecclesiologist* magazine (*Instrumenta Ecclesiastica*) in 1842 that started his success. In the same year he moved to an Adam house in the Adelphi, where he practised Gothic architecture all his life surrounded by Georgian furniture and decoration.

Butterfield was a tall thin man, remembered by his contemporaries as always dressed in a frock-coat and bow-tie of black, with a white shirt and grey trousers. Although he and Gilbert Scott were both highly emotional men, Scott's sense of responsibility and occasional sentimentality pale in comparison to Butterfield's suppressed but explosive passions about almost everything.

In 1844 Butterfield became a member of the Cambridge Camden Society and moved into the circles of the Anglican High Church a little later than Gilbert Scott. But it was Butterfield who dominated trends in the architectural part of that reforming movement. Paul Thompson, the biographer of Butterfield, has pointed out that he led the ecclesiologists through a phase when he advocated Pugin's notions of "correct" Gothic, instead of eclectic Gothic, and then after 1849 "to an acceptance of High Victorian originality" within the Gothic style. None of his own significant pre-1849 buildings is in London.

In 1846–49 Butterfield helped the younger Thomas Cundy in his Early English style Anglo-Catholic church of St. Barnabas in Pimlico. Butterfield's own first London church for the movement is also his most ambitious work in the capital. **All Saints' Church**, Margaret Street, Marylebone was built in 1849–59 as an ideal model church for the Cambridge Camden Society.

The church, with its high spire, is tucked into a narrow street north-east of Oxford Circus. It is entered through a courtyard which would be picturesque but for the tall stern brickwork around it, and the visitor's excitement is built up by the time he enters the building. The first view inside is mystifying, for the overall shape cannot be understood from this sideways approach. To the left is the baptistry, with the spaces of four small arches piercing through the solid wall into the nave. The nave itself can be seen ahead and to the right, with a slanting glimpse of the chancel. Moving forward, the high vault of the nave opens above, and the shape clarifies with the sight of the lofty reredos above the altar. The space is small, the scale grand, and everywhere there is a bombardment of colour and decoration and contrasting textures. There is much darkness, while the pervasive smell of incense together with the grilled screens and many small windows contribute to the mysterious quality of the space. This is no "correct" Gothic on any medieval model; it is highly inventive nineteenth-century architecture employing a generally Gothic style.

The Butterfield buildings surrounding the courtyard of All Saints' Church include the **Clergy House** (1849–53) and the **Choir School** (1849–60) while the School (now used for other church purposes) on the opposite side of the street was added by Butterfield in 1870.

In 1849–53 Butterfield built the remarkably forceful church of **St. Matthias** in Matthias Road, Stoke Newington—the church was badly damaged by bombing in the Second World War, but has been refitted—and in 1850 St. Saviour's Hospital in Osnaburgh Street, St. Pancras, now demolished.

St. John's Church, Glenthorne Road, Hammersmith (1857–59), with its parsonage of 1864, shows Butterfield at his most forbidding; it is a great big fierce church with a severe nave and a high polychrome chancel inside (the delightfully decorated organ case is by J. F. Bentley).

Sir Walter St. John's School in the High Street of Battersea (1858) has been much altered, while Butterfield's great **St. Alban's Church** in Brooke Street off Holborn (1859–62) was re-built quite differently within his ruined walls after bombing during the Second World War. His next surviving work in central London is the typically diapered brick old **Vicarage** at No. 14 Burleigh Street, Covent Garden (1859–60, now used as flats). The **Chapel of the Bishop of London's Fulham Palace**, in Fulham Palace Road, Fulham was built in 1864–66 as an independent building whose hard polychrome Gothicism and brick ignore the gentler and older forms of the other palace buildings.

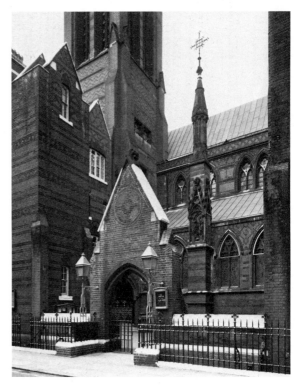

118 *Butterfield. Exterior and courtyard, All Saints' Church, Margaret Street, near Oxford Circus (1849–59)*

119 *Butterfield. Interior, All Saints, Margaret Street (1849–59)*

However, Butterfield's alterations (1867) to Sir James Pennethorne's **Christ Church** of 1838 in Albany Street, Camden Town show the utmost respect to its Classicism. His polychrome **nave of St. Mary Brookfield** in Dartmouth Park Hill of 1869–75 has a chancel added by G. E. Street in 1881.

Butterfield never married. Obituaries describe him as "by nature one of the kindliest and most hospitable of men" with an "old-fashioned courtesy of manner". One of his few close friendships was with Philip Webb, the master of early Arts and Crafts architecture within William Morris's circle, while his family feelings seem to have been poured into the children of his favourite sister Anne Starey. A letter of 1848 survives in which he urges her that they are "no toys to be fondled and caressed. They are intended for God's service . . .". On the other hand he developed a deeply fond relationship with his nephew William Starey as he grew up. In his architectural office he was a recluse, working endless hours alone in his study, calling his assistants in at times and never entering the drawing office next door.

In 1870–77 Butterfield built his other surviving major church near the centre of London. This is **St. Augustine**, Queen's Gate, Kensington. It is an extraordinary work whose multi-coloured splendour is so intense that its interior was thought unsuitable and painted white throughout in the 1920s. Only in 1970 had taste shifted enough for the white to be stripped and the colour restored as far as possible to

its original state. The entrance is almost directly into the end of the nave from the street. It is a great wide nave, blazing with polychrome materials, bounded by two narrow aisles. Reds, yellows and blues mix in the plentiful light. The shallow chancel still retains the amazing Baroque gold reredos (it partly blocks one of Butterfield's huge windows) inserted by Martin Travers when he whitened the church at

120 *Butterfield. Old Vicarage of St. Michael's, No. 14 Burleigh Street, Covent Garden (1859–60)*

121 *Butterfield. St. Augustine's Church, Queen's Gate, Kensington (1865–71)*

the insistence of the vicar in the 1920s, and the fine Stations of the Cross are also by Travers. The coloured tile panels depicting the life of Christ are from Butterfield's original building, dating from 1886 with much of the rest of the decoration. The contrast of the light in this church with the dim mystery of All Saints, Margaret Street is notable. But the religious conviction of both are evident.

Butterfield himself was deeply religious, and orthodoxly religious. He was much shaken by the crisis in the Church of England when many clergy followed Newman into the Roman Catholic Church after 1845, and he was hostile to what he saw as Rome's denigration of worship in church services. Butterfield also believed passionately in the expression of God in his buildings. While St. Augustine, Queen's Gate, was being built, he was also building one of his largest works, Keble College at Oxford University. Of this he wrote in 1873 "we must of course endeavour to stamp upon it what is divine, rather than what is human".

In 1875 Butterfield carried out alterations to Hawksmoor's small masterpiece **St. Mary Woolnoth** at the Bank in the City of London, colouring the walls, removing the galleries and placing their fronts flat against the walls. His **All Hallows**, Tottenham (1876–77) has been largely re-built.

Three more outer London works by Butterfield date from the 1880s. **St. Mary Magdalene**, Windmill Hill, Enfield (1881–83) has a fine polychrome interior with later (1897) chancel decoration by Buckeridge. **Holy Innocents' Church**, Kingsbury Road, Kingsbury (west of Golders Green) was built in 1883–84 in polychrome brick outside with a quirky plaster and tile interior. Finally, **St. Michael** in Borgard Road, Woolwich was built in 1887–90, but it was never completed to the Butterfield designs. Only the nave is his, with its stumpy round piers and a band of coloured tiles above a broad nave—the chancel is earlier, the roof later, neither by Butterfield.

In 1884 Butterfield was at last awarded the RIBA's Royal Gold Medal. This gave him some pleasure but as he grew older his severely orthodox views grew yet harsher. He campaigned against the liberties with the prayer-book taken by many bishops and parsons, and he believed strongly in the existing social structure, both as regards those above and below himself. He mourned deeply the death of his sister Anne in 1891 and retired from most practice the following year. His last architectural work dates from 1895, five years before his own death and six before the death of Queen Victoria. Apart from London, it is in Rugby and Oxford that many of his finest works can be found.

George Edmund Street (1824-1881)

George Edmund Street, portrait

G. E. Street, architect of the marvellous Law Courts in the Strand, was one of the remote idols of the Victorian Gothic revival. Worshipped by countless young architects during the 1870s, his principles remained an ideal to younger men of the Arts and Crafts movement. Yet the lofty splendour of his designs still inspires in many people more admiration than affection—Street's Gothic buildings are peerless in their high quality, but the heights are snow-covered.

Street was born in Woodford, Essex, son of Thomas Street, a London solicitor. Reprimanded for "too much levity" by his teachers, Street left school aged fifteen, wanting to become a clergyman. Thomas Street insisted on his son starting work in his solicitor's office in 1839 but died a year later, after which the young man went to live in Exeter with his mother and sister. There he studied painting and went for a series of long walking tours with his brother, looking at villages and churches. "Tom and I get more fiercely architectural and antiquarian every day," he wrote. In 1841 he was articled to an architect called Owen Carter in Winchester, and in 1844 George Gilbert Scott employed him as an assistant. In Scott's office he became a close friend of G. F. Bodley and William White and in 1849 started his own practice, first of all in Wantage, then in Oxford (where he married Mariquita Proctor) and in 1855 in London. In Oxford he established contact with the Ecclesiological Society and with the Bishop, Samuel Wilberforce, connections which brought him many commissions. In 1854 and 1855 he won much fame by gaining the second prizes in competitions for a cathedral in Lille and a church in Constantinople.

The earliest London building by Street appears to be **St. Paul's Church**, Herne Hill, Camberwell (1858), which gained the praise of the influential art critic, John Ruskin. His next church, **St. James-the-Less**, in Thorndike Street, off Vauxhall Bridge Road, Pimlico (1860–61), is one of the best Victorian Gothic churches in London. Now in the middle of a much-admired housing estate, St. James-the-Less forms a strong composition of church, hall and school built of red brick with black brick decoration. The interior has much mystery and beauty; its wide nave of brick is ornamented by attractive tiles, rather hard carving of foliage and a splendid fresco by G. F. Watts. The style used mixes continental Gothic features with English ones. (See plate 202.)

In 1866 Street entered the competition for the Royal Courts of Justice, the most important public building commission in London since the Houses of Parliament. In July 1867 the assessors announced that no single design was satisfactory: Street and

E. M. Barry were selected to act as joint architects from a field which included Gilbert Scott, Waterhouse, Seddon and Burges (who produced a justly famous but too costly design). Scott protested but got nowhere, for reconsideration by the government led only to Street's appointment as sole architect in June 1868.

Before describing Street's re-designed Law Courts building, built over the next fourteen years, it is worthwhile to look at some of the architect's other London works. One of the finest is **St. Mary Magdalene's Church** (1868–78), occupying an impressively spacious position among recent council housing at the end of Delamere Terrace near Little Venice, Paddington. Built of dark brick banded with stone, the church has a soaring appearance crowned by its slender tower and spire, which have rather a German Gothic character. The interior is unexpected, with rather flat walls of brick and bands of stone, a lofty dim wagon-vault roof and an abruptly raised chancel with more intricate vaulting. The church was built with only one aisle because of the awkward site and it is a curious but dignified space, highly directional towards the altar. The notable crypt beneath is by J. N. Comper.

Street's **St. John the Divine**, Vassall Road, Lambeth (1870–74) has been restored after bombing, but **Holy Trinity, Eltham** (1870) has in effect been destroyed by subsequent alterations. In 1871 Street altered the galleries and stripped the decaying lions and unicorns off the steeple of Hawksmoor's **St. George**, Bloomsbury. **All Saints' Church**, Lower Common, Putney dates from 1874; it is a rather severe low-cost design, but has notable stained-glass windows designed by Edward Burne-Jones. Ironically, in c. 1878 Street designed the **monument** to his old master Sir George Gilbert Scott, for whose work he had little regard, in the nave of Westminster Abbey.

No. 4 Cadogan Square, Chelsea is a rare

122 *Street. Interior of the Great Hall, the Law Courts (1868–82)*

123 *Street. St. Mary Magdalene Church, Delamere Terrace, Little Venice, Paddington (1868–78)*

124 *Street. House for himself, No. 4 Cadogan Square, Chelsea (1879)*

125 *Street. The Law Courts (Royal Courts of Justice), Strand (1868–82). Frontage on the Strand*

123

124

25

example of a town house by Street. It dates from 1879 and is a tall Gothic composition, rather stern, but with an attractive visual play between the three gables at high levels of its corner position. The window detailing and the proportions of each of the five storeys are intriguing.

The list of Street's London works is completed by the **nave of St. James**, Sussex Gardens, the **chancel of St. Mary Brookfield**, Dartmouth Park Hill, and the **chancel of St. Michael**, Highgate, all three dating from 1881, the year of his death.

For Street died just before the Law Courts, his secular masterpiece, were completed. He was an imposingly serious, idealistic and hard-working man, viewed with awe by the many who admired his work. Norman Shaw, who worked in Street's office for some years (as did William Morris and Philip Webb), later wrote, "The rapidity and precision with which he drew were marvellous. . . . He believed in his own work, and in what he was doing at the time, absolutely; and the charm of his work is that when looking at it you may be certain that it is entirely his own, and this applies to the smallest detail as to the general conception. I am certain that during the whole time I was with him I never designed one single moulding."

The Law Courts, as built to Street's designs in 1871–82, run across a large site between the Strand and Lincoln's Inn. Controversial at the time, different individuals still react with strong liking or dislike to the vast building. To the present writer they are one of the great visually romantic places in London. Approached from either direction along the Strand, the row of spired turrets along the stone frontage seem part of some medieval dream. The most massive pair of turrets abutt the layered Gothic arch of the main entrance, with a curious arcaded bridge above, and this doorway opens almost immediately into one of the finest of London's enclosed spaces, the Great Hall. The Hall, with its high stone vaulting, recedes towards the far side of the building. Tall clerestorey windows give enough daylight to show up the details and the series of doorways which lead to stairways that spiral up to the courts themselves. The courts too are impressive rooms and well enough daylighted, although the acoustics are so poor that the barristers and judges seem to be talking in hushed tones. Beyond the Great Hall, a complex of stairways and Gothic vaulted hallways leads to Carey Street and the Judges' entrance. The exterior on this side is of brick with stone bands, distinguished but less over-awing than the Strand frontage.

Accounts survive of Street's constant attendance on site during the eleven year period of building. In the meantime, he designed hundreds of churches and associated buildings elsewhere. He was a strongly religious man and his early successes owed much to that, to two books and to his activities as a member of the Ecclesiological Society. Later, his reputation brought a steady flow of commissions for buildings in many places and he was awarded the Royal Gold Medal in 1874. He died in December 1881, a month after his last visit to the Law Courts and just before the scaffolding was removed from the Great Hall.

7
Late Victorian and
Arts and Crafts Architecture

The three decades of sweeping success for a scholarly and "correct" approach to Gothic design in Victorian architecture ended gradually during the 1870s and 1880s. In London, the office building at No. 19 Lincoln's Inn Fields (1868), by William Morris's friend and collaborator Philip Webb (1831–1915), mixes Gothic with other details in a manner that emerges almost without identifiable style. Waterhouse's approach to style should here be mentioned; his attitude was not too far from Pugin's 1836 statement that "the great test of Architectural beauty is the fitness of the design to the purpose for which it is intended", whatever we may think of the content of beauty in Waterhouse's own taste. Indeed, much of the subsequent development of much Victorian architecture was based on Gothic thought, if not on the Gothic style. The rejection of serene Classical plans in the French *Beaux-Arts* tradition and the preference for shapes and elevations which reflect their interiors, regardless of symmetry, are essentially Gothic in approach.

In 1875 Edward Godwin, architect to the Aesthetic Movement and a former successful Goth, wrote "The day of architectural revivals may be setting—I for one sincerely hope it is." And Godwin's striking artist's house of 1878 at No. 44 Tite Street, Chelsea, expresses this attitude well.

The best known new manner to grow from the Gothic approach combined early eighteenth-century English details with Gothic, Dutch and other features. It was dubbed the Queen Anne style and it first appeared in London in a Bayswater house of 1871 (now destroyed) by J. J. Stevenson, a Scot. It

126 *Early Arts and Crafts architecture. Office building, No. 19 Lincoln's Inn Fields, off Holborn (1868) by Philip Webb. One of the few London buildings by William Morris's partner and co-founder of the Arts and Crafts Movement*

was developed by Stevenson (1831–1908) and by E. R. Robson (1835–1917) in a series of progressive schools for the London School Board all over the city and its outskirts—one good example out of many is Robson's Board School in Anglers' Gardens, St. Pancras (1874). But it was another architect of Scottish origins, R. Norman Shaw, who made the style celebrated and then moved on to develop a number of other styles.

The last third of the nineteenth century in London was dominated by Shaw, and his indirect influence. A group of his former pupils, led by W. R. Lethaby and Edward Prior, played a leading part in putting into practice the Arts and Crafts ideas of William Morris and Philip Webb by founding active guilds and societies during the 1880s. Webb's principles involved starting each architectural design without preconceptions or rules of thumb, relating the building to its site and surroundings, the use of local vernacular building materials and features and the avoidance of scholarly copying of historical styles. During the 1890s these Arts and Crafts principles expanded to include the ideals of an original architecture closely linked to nature and of a unity in buildings of the arts of architecture, sculpture and painting. Mass production was largely rejected by the movement, and its members revived high standards of individual craftsmanship for brick-making, woodwork, metalwork and other decorative arts.

Shaw's Arts and Crafts pupils are not represented well in London buildings, but some other important figures in the Arts and Crafts Movement are. J. D. Sedding (1838–91) and his pupil and successor Henry Wilson (1864–1934) produced a major Arts and Crafts Gothic work in Holy Trinity Church, Sloane Street, Chelsea (1888–c. 1900) while Wilson's Public Library in Ladbroke Grove, North

Kensington (1890–91) and St. Peter's Church, Mount Park Road, at Ealing in west London (1892) are architecturally even more notable. Mary Ward House, Tavistock Place, Bloomsbury (1895–98) by Dunbar Smith and Cecil Brewer was a landmark in Arts and Crafts architecture. Its manner, with the ideas of Philip Webb, was developed by the young architects of the London County Council's Architect's Department in many housing developments such as the Boundary Street Estate, Shoreditch (1895 onwards) and the Millbank Estate behind the Tate Gallery (1899–1902), as well as in public buildings such as the Fire Station on the corner of Euston Road and Eversholt Street, Euston (1901–02). Other notable Arts and Crafts work includes the remaining two houses by C. R. Ashbee (1863–1942) at Nos. 38–39 Cheyne Walk, Chelsea (1899–1901). But the members of the movement who left most mark on London were Harrison Townsend and C. F. A. Voysey, who have individual chapters in the following section.

These buildings are of particular interest but they are far from being typical of late Victorian architec-

127 *Late Victorian eclecticism. Palace Theatre, Cambridge Circus, Soho (1890) by Thomas Collcutt. Built as D'Oyly Carte's opera house (a photograph taken shortly after the opening). A good example of the mixed style typical of late Victorian design*

ture in London. Apart from Shaw and Waterhouse, the most successful architects included Thomas Collcutt (1840–1924), Sir Ernest George (1839–1922) and Sir Aston Webb (whose work will be described in a later chapter). Only the tower remains of Collcutt's huge Imperial Institute (1887–93) off Exhibition Road, Kensington, but his typical banded and mixed-style manner can be seen in the Palace Theatre, Cambridge Circus (1890), the Savoy Hotel, Strand (1889–91), The Wigmore Hall, Wigmore Street (1890) and the office building at Nos. 45–47 Ludgate Hill, City (1890). Sir Ernest George's delightful houses of the 1880s can most easily be seen in Harrington Gardens, Kensington, notably No. 19, of 1882 for W. S. Gilbert. George's later work includes the former Hotel Albemarle (1889) which faces down St. James's Street from the corner of Albemarle Street and Piccadilly. Mention should also be made of the many gorgeous public houses built all over London during the 1890s. Two notably inventive examples are the Old Shades in Whitehall and the Rising Sun in Tottenham Court Road, both of about 1899 and both designed by Treadwell and Martin, who did many other pubs and restaurants.

This was also the period which saw the construction of a number of road bridges across the Thames, several of which still survive. Thomas Page's Westminster Bridge of 1862 and James Cubitt's Blackfriars Bridge of 1869 have both been widened, but the façade designs remain. Further up the river there is a small group of Victorian suspension bridges, some of great charm. The Albert Bridge at Chelsea was built by R. W. Ordish in 1873,

128 *Council Housing. Detail of courtyard frontages of a housing block in the Boundary Street housing estate, Shoreditch (1897–1900), the first of many big estates designed by the London County Council's Architect's Department. The young architects in the Housing Division of the Department were much influenced by Philip Webb and the Arts and Crafts movement*

while Sir Joseph Bazalgette designed both Hammersmith Bridge of 1884 and Battersea Bridge of 1890. The most imposing example of this period, however, is of course Tower Bridge, built in 1886–94 to the designs of J. Wolfe Barry and Sir Horace Jones.

Other architects' secular work of this period will be described in Part Eight of this book, on the Baroque revival and the Grand Manner. As regards church architecture, the Gothic style continued its ascendancy. Most of the High Gothic masters were dead by the end of the century, but there are fine late works by J. L. Pearson at the Catholic Apostolic Church, Maida Avenue, Little Venice (1889–91) and by G. F. Bodley at Holy Trinity Church, Prince Consort Road, Kensington (1902–04). A new generation is represented by Temple Moore (1856–1920) in work such as All Saints, Franciscan Road, Tooting (1905–06) and St. Luke, Westmount Road, Eltham (1906), while Ninian Comper (1864–1960) built St. Cyprian, Clarence Gate, outside Regent's Park in 1901–03. But the great ecclesiastical work of late Victorian London was Westminster Roman Catholic Cathedral, whose Byzantine splendours will be described in the chapter on J. F. Bentley.

R. Norman Shaw (1831-1912)

Norman Shaw, portrait

R. Norman Shaw, who made the Queen Anne style famous and was made famous by it, went on through a number of stylistic phases but remained the most influential figure in English architecture throughout the constant changes of the last third of the century.

Shaw was a Scot through his mother's family and by his birth in Edinburgh, where his father had moved from Dublin and set up as a lace merchant. The father died in 1833 in debt and his mother managed the education of her children with determination despite poverty. In 1846 the family came to London, and Shaw was articled there in about 1849 to William Burn, the successful Scottish architect of many major country houses. In 1851 W. E. Nesfield joined the office and the two young men became firm friends. In 1852 they went to see Pugin's church at Ramsgate and were present by chance at the great architect's funeral. Shaw won the Royal Academy Gold Medal, and the travelling scholarship took him abroad to Belgium, France, Italy and Germany for two years, some of it with Nesfield. After publishing a book of drawings upon his return, Shaw worked for Nesfield's uncle Anthony Salvin and then for four years for G. E. Street. In 1862 he set up his own practice in an unclearly defined partnership with Nesfield, whose wealthy family connections gave both young men a good start.

Shaw's early works are outside London, and his influential New Zealand Chambers (1872–74), a distinguished office building in the City, was bombed in 1941. His earliest important London building to survive is therefore **Lowther Lodge**, now the older part of the Royal Geographical Society, around a courtyard facing across Kensington Gore to Kensington Gardens. It dates from 1872–75 and with its brickwork mixture of tall chimneys, Dutch gable, high windows and some Classical details the house provides one of the major examples of the Queen Anne style in London.

Another Queen Anne style house, No. 196 Queen's Gate (1874–76), has been destroyed, but in the same years Shaw was designing and building for his own use a much more remarkable house. This is **Hampstead Towers**, No. 6 Ellerdale Road, near the top of Fitzjohn's Avenue, Hampstead. Shaw's sheer inventive exuberance as a designer was always extraordinary, but in this house for his own family life he excelled himself with what Andrew Saint, in his notable biography of the architect, describes as a topsy-turvy tease. The staircase divides the plan into two halves of quite different floor heights, and this

129 *Shaw. Swan House, No. 17 Chelsea Embankment, Chelsea (1875–77)*

division is expressed on the street frontage by two long oriel windows topped by gables. One oriel is of the same brickwork as the rest of the house, the other plastered white, giving it a visual impact to balance the greater prominence of the other. The other windows seem randomly placed to suit the needs of the spaces inside, but they are cunningly composed to form a satisfying overall pattern. The highest windows light the most important space in the house, the dining room with its low inglenook fireplace underneath Shaw's *mezzanine* den or small studio where he designed his subsequent buildings—the left-hand porthole in the frontage lights the narrow stairs up from dining room to den. The house transported the Queen Anne style into new realms of free design. It is now a nunnery and difficult to visit.

Shaw was an urbane and charming personality when dealing with the public and was adored in his own office, where he inspired a series of beloved pupils of major talent such as Edward Prior, W. R. Lethaby and Ernest Newton, later to become central figures in Arts and Crafts architecture. He loved his home and family surroundings too and did much of his creative work there. At the start of the 1870s he was respected by a small number of admirers. By the end of the decade his work had made him the most celebrated domestic architect in England, largely due to a series of brilliant London houses.

The most beautiful of these is perhaps **Swan House** at No. 17 Chelsea Embankment (1875–77), with its glorious drawing room and the three-dimensional texture of its elegant and original street frontage. But **No. 8 Melbury Road**, Holland Park (1875–76) is equally striking and **Cheyne House** at No. 18 Chelsea Embankment shows distinguished planning ability. **No. 31 Melbury Road** (1875–77) is less notable and has been altered, as has the fine **No. 61 Fitzjohn's Avenue**, Hampstead (1876–77). Shaw's other embankment works are **Nos. 15 and 9–11 Chelsea Embankment** and the well-known **Clock House** at No. 8 Chelsea Embankment, all of the 1878–80 period.

It was in 1877 that Shaw undertook one of his most famous housing commissions when he succeeded Edward Godwin as estate architect for Jonathan Carr's pioneering garden suburb, Bedford Park at Chiswick in west London. He produced three semi-detached and two detached house designs in 1877–79 which were built many times over—examples are to be seen at **Nos. 19–22 The Avenue, Nos. 3 and 5 Queen Anne's Gardens, Nos. 24–34 Woodstock Road, Nos. 5 and 7 Blenheim Road, No. 6 Bedford Road, No. 3 Newton Grove** and other semi-detached houses in

Woodstock Road. His gabled terrace in **Priory Gardens** dates from *c.* 1881, his **Tabard Inn and shops** in Bath Road from 1879–80. The Tower House of 1879, his most notable house at Bedford Park, was demolished in the 1930s, but his noble church of **St. Michael and All Angels** (1879–87) still provides the central focus of the garden suburb's streets of pretty brick houses.

Another new departure for Shaw was the huge block of flats named **Albert Hall Mansions** (after the neighbouring concert hall) facing Kensington Gardens across Kensington Gore. Built in 1879–86, Shaw had studied French apartment block design before planning the buildings, which by the way overbear his own earlier Lowther Lodge next door. Another block of flats at **Nos. 200–222 Cromwell Road**, Kensington dates from 1882–83. The design of his banking building for Baring Brothers at No. 8 Bishopsgate, in the City, was done in 1879, but this attractive work was destroyed in 1975.

A further group of Shaw houses dates from the end of the 1870s and early 1880s. **Nos. 60A, 62, 68 and 72 Cadogan Square**, Chelsea were all designed and built between 1877 and 1883. No. 6 Fitzjohn's Avenue of 1881 and one of his most original masterpieces, No. 180 Queen's Gate, Kensington (1883–85), have both been wastefully destroyed recently. Among his other buildings, **St. Mark's Church**, Cobourg Road, Camberwell (1877–84), the attractively Flemish-detailed **Alliance Assurance** offices on the south-east corner of St. James's Street (1881–83) and new south rooms and restaurant at the **Royal Academy** (1881–85) still survive.

In the years 1879–81, overwork brought Shaw much illness; his health was always delicate and in future he undertook less work. The middle 1880s produced **Holy Trinity Church** (1885–89) for the Harrow Mission in Latimer Road, Paddington—its glorious tracery window is now divided horizontally inside to provide two levels for the Mission's activities—and two strongly contrasting houses.

130 *Shaw. Lowther Lodge, now part of the Royal Geographical Society, Kensington Gore (1872–75)*

131 *Shaw. Tabard Inn and Shops, Bath Road, Bedford Park, near Chiswick, west London (1879–80). The centre, with the neighbouring church by Shaw, of the pioneering garden suburb*

132 *Shaw. New Scotland Yard, Victoria Embankment, Westminster (1886–90). The companion block shown on the left was added by Shaw in 1897–1907. Interior now converted into offices for Members of Parliament*

Shaw's design for the children's book illustrator Kate Greenaway at **No. 39 Frognal**, Hampstead (1884–85) is a pretty tile-hung house in the Surrey Weald vernacular. Four years later, his design for **No. 170 Queen's Gate**, Kensington (1888–90) shows him striding abruptly into the newly revived Classicism with a manner which mixes Dutch features with the influence of Sir Christopher Wren.

Shaw's transition was not quite so abrupt as that may sound. Swan House had contained hints of East Anglian Classicism, while Baring Brothers' building had a decidedly Baroque doorway. And Shaw's major public building, **New Scotland Yard** (1886–90), the headquarters for the Metropolitan Police on the Victoria Embankment at Westminster, combined Baroque elements with apparently Scottish Baronial turrets and other features of complete originality. The similar south block was added in 1897–1907 and the handsome couple have now had their interiors transformed into office accommodation for Members of Parliament.

The Baroque revival of the 1890s and 1900s was led by architects such as John Belcher, John Brydon and a few others, but Shaw outshone many of them in the panache with which he employed the style. His minor London works of the early 1890s show only restrained Baroque touches—for example, the **Police Stations** in Holmes Road, Kentish Town (1891–96) and Walton Street, Chelsea (1894–95), the **Moreland Hall** in Hollybush Vale, Hampstead (1892, but now altered) and the **Bishop's house** at No. 5 Kennington Park Place, Southwark (1894–96).

With the turn of the century, however, Shaw was involved in several High Baroque designs. By this time he was recognized as the grand old genius of English architecture and, partly retired, he accepted only a few commissions to work on in his den at home in Hampstead. The first of these was for the Gaiety Theatre and restaurant on the west corner of the Aldwych and the Strand (1901–03). Ernest Runtz had designed the building and Shaw was commissioned to provide more distinguished façades. This he did in a full-blooded Baroque manner. The theatre was demolished in 1955, but a remnant of the milder part of Shaw's elevations can be seen, now called **Marconi House**, running through from the Strand to the Aldwych along Montreal Place.

At much the same time, 1901–05, Shaw worked with his former pupil Ernest Newton on new offices for the **Alliance Assurance** at No. 78 St. James's Street, a handsome Baroque design facing along Pall Mall and almost opposite Shaw's earlier building for the same company.

Apart from the small but interesting **Portland House** at No. 8 Lloyd's Avenue in the City (1907–08, with a reinforced concrete structure behind its Portland stone façade), Shaw's final London work was the elevations of the **Piccadilly Hotel** in both Piccadilly and Regent Street (1904–08). Here we see Shaw in old age designing with undiminished power and inventiveness in a freely Baroque style (the interiors were by the architects Woodward and Emden). But the design as built is incomplete. The magnificent colonnade screen of the Piccadilly frontage lacks the second terminating gable which should have matched the existing westerly one—another developer built a quite different building in its place. And the hotel was originally intended to form part of a tremendous Baroque scheme by Shaw, comprising the entire block of the Regent Street Quadrant (replacing Nash's buildings which had long before had their pavement colonnades removed) through to Piccadilly and the north and south side of Piccadilly Circus. Despite long negotiations, nothing came of the rest of Shaw's scheme, and the buildings were finally re-built to the designs done shortly after Shaw's death by Sir Reginald Blomfield; distinguished in themselves, they are the ones we know today.

133 *Shaw. Piccadilly Hotel, Piccadilly and Regent Street, near Piccadilly Circus (1904–08). The interiors were by other architects*

Shaw's last years were saddened by the controversy and frustrations involved with the Piccadilly scheme. Except in his practice, he had no taste for publicity or public life, and he refused a knighthood when it was offered. Life was quiet in the Hampstead house where he produced so many brilliant designs. Neither he nor his wife Agnes had much taste for entertaining or parties. They were devoted to their children and to each other. Andrew Saint quotes a letter from Shaw to his wife which gives something of the flavour of their relationship in old age, ten years before his death. It was written to mark their 1902 wedding anniversary. "My sweet old Mugwump! Do you think it is in the least likely that I should forget it? Only *I* maintain it was the 17th. Dear me, it is a long time ago and many things have happened since. We have been *very* happy, long may it go on!! . . . apart from my tum-tums and fatigue, I don't think I *feel* much older. And you may remember that this time 35 years ago the tum-tum was not much to boast of. Today, *this* day, it is miles better than it was then, with cold veal cutlets in it!"

Alfred Waterhouse
(1830-1905)

Alfred Waterhouse, portrait

The hard terracotta and brick of Alfred Waterhouse's large works, often in a harsh red colour, brought a new Lancashire toughness to London's public buildings between 1880 and 1900. Many of these designs were still generally Victorian Gothic in style, but, to Waterhouse, style was not an expression of an ideal or a principle; he believed that the style should be selected and adapted for its suitability to the planning and structure of that particular building itself. In his own words when presented with the Royal Gold Medal, he wanted "architecture to be considered, on some occasions at any rate, as distinct from style and archaeology." And *architecture*, to this practical Quaker from northern England, was a matter of clear functional planning, the enclosure of spaces, sound structure and suitability of scale.

Waterhouse was born in Liverpool, the eldest of eight children of an eminent Quaker. He wished to become an artist, but the emphasis on worthy practicality of the Society of Friends made his family channel his ambition into architecture—of his brothers, one became a founder of the country's largest firm of chartered accountants, another a distinguished judge. Alfred was articled to a Manchester architect called Richard Lane in 1848–53, travelled in Britain, France, Switzerland, Italy and Turkey, then in 1854 set up his own practice in Manchester. Pugin and Ruskin were both early influences on him, but as a Quaker he was not involved in Church of England or Catholic controversies.

After several small commissions, often for Quaker clients, he gained notability abruptly when he won the competition for the huge Manchester Assize Courts in 1859. The Gothic splendour of this building (now demolished) soon brought him commissions outside Lancashire. In London, his Clydesdale Bank (1864) in Lombard Street and his New University Club (1865) in St. James's Street have been destroyed, leaving the office building at **Nos. 17–18 Lincoln's Inn Fields** (1871–72) as his earliest survivor. The stylistic detailing of the windows is aggressively mixed, and the use of stone rather than brick is unusual for this architect. But the sharp gables and craggy general feeling mark the building immediately as a Waterhouse design.

The Natural History Museum in the Cromwell Road at the southern end of the South Kensington museums site is the first of Waterhouse's public buildings in London. As early as 1866 he had been approached to execute a design for the museum by the architect of the Albert Hall, Captain Fowke. But after Fowke's death Waterhouse put up his own suggestions in consultation with the museum staff.

134

These were accepted in 1872 and the large building was opened in 1881. Fowke had proposed the use of some terracotta, but Waterhouse decided to use this material and no other for the exterior. Within the load-bearing walls, the structure depends on an internal iron frame. The iron can be seen only in the visual *tour de force* of the main entrance hall; otherwise it is covered by terracotta inside the building, but the widespread use of glass daylighting would not have been possible without it. Waterhouse decided on the use of the Romanesque style after Professor Owen, who was in charge of the museum

134 *Waterhouse. Natural History Museum, Cromwell Road, Kensington (1873–81)*

135 *Waterhouse. The King's Weigh House Chapel, Duke Street, off Grosvenor Square, Mayfair (1889–91). Originally Congregational, the church is now used by the American forces*

136 *Waterhouse. University College Hospital, Gower Street, northern Bloomsbury (1897–1906). Like other buildings of this period, the hospital was designed together with the architect's son Paul*

building, had told him of his ambition to harmonise the architectural decoration with the exhibits. Romanesque seemed to Waterhouse the only style suitable to combine with the creation of extensive sculpture depicting the forms of nature—animal, vegetable and mineral.

In 1864 Waterhouse had opened a London office and by the time the museum was being built, he had moved to London and closed his Manchester office. He had married a lady called Elizabeth Hodgkin in 1858 and, a kindly but authoritarian father, sired a dynasty of eminent architects. His nationwide practice grew steadily—he lost the London Law Courts commission to G. E. Street but in 1868 he won the competition for his most famous building, the Manchester Town Hall.

In London, Waterhouse's New Court Buildings of 1875 in Carey Street, Lincoln's Inn, were demolished in 1967. In 1877 he started the earliest part of his Prudential Assurance buildings in Holborn, now replaced by his firm's later work, and in 1878 built **Nos. 11–12 Park Lane**. His building for **Scott's** at No. 1 Old Bond Street, Mayfair (1880), with its chequered terracotta, has no touch of Gothic but is recognisably Waterhouse in manner.

The massive ranges of his St. Paul's School (1881–85) in Hammersmith, with their gables and spires, used to be a landmark on the western road exit from London. It was demolished *c.* 1970 after the school had moved to Barnes. Waterhouse's City and Guilds College in Exhibition Road (1881–84) has also been destroyed, but his excellent brick and

terracotta **Congregational Church** of 1883–84 at the bottom of Lyndhurst Road, Hampstead, survives with its original interior, of the same materials as the outside, painted over in pastel shades.

Terracotta, as used by Waterhouse, is not an endearing material nor one which softens with age. In the **National Liberal Club**, Whitehall Place, on the Embankment facing over the Thames, Waterhouse's 1884 design seems to strive to escape from his usual ruthless rhythms in the façades and the interiors to something more friendly. The effort succeeds to a limited degree and the public rooms are fine spaces, but their hard terracotta is imposing rather than welcoming. His remarkable staircase was re-built in 1950 after war damage.

The street frontage of the **King's Weigh House Chapel** (now an American Forces church) on Duke Street off Grosvenor Square, Mayfair (1889–91) presents an ingeniously broken terracotta composition. As in the Hampstead church, it is hard to attach a style to the building; the rounded windows hint at Romanesque; the spires and gables at Gothic, the sharp angles of the masses at little but Waterhouse's own manner. Behind the street front, the interior of the church itself is a big oval carried on one of the architect's favourite iron frames covered with terracotta. As Stuart Allen Smith has pointed out, Waterhouse rejected the discipline of historical styles—his lifelong attitude is well summed up in a remark of 1859 about an earlier building: "wherever I thought that the particular object in view could not be best obtained by a strict obedience to precedent I

took the liberty of departing from it."

The year 1890 brought British architecture into an age of eclectic Renaissance and Baroque revival (as well as of Arts and Crafts originality), and something of this eclecticism is reflected in Waterhouse's **bank** (now the National Westminster Bank) at Nos. 207–9 Piccadilly (1892–94). His building for the head-quarters of the **Royal Institution of Chartered Surveyors** (1896–98), on the corner of Great George Street and Parliament Square, is more immediately recognisable from its building materials and detail as his work, though untypically formless overall.

University College Hospital, Gower Street, near Euston, dates from 1896–1906. It has an excellently clear and, in its time, functional plan based on an X, built in seven storeys of the architect's usual materials and with his favourite spires and gables to break the sky-line.

The great London splendour of Waterhouse's last years is the blazing red terracotta composition of his re-built and enlarged **Prudential Assurance Buildings** (1899–1906) in Holborn. Here his fa-vourite long ranges, spires and gables are gathered

137 Waterhouse. The Prudential Assurance Buildings, Holborn, near Holborn Circus (1899–1906, designed with his son Paul, replacing Waterhouse's earlier building of 1879 for the firm)

round an internal courtyard and expressed in the overpowering street frontage. Are the details Gothic? Yes, in general they are, but no identifiable Gothic other than Waterhouse's own. And the façade is made up of repeated prefabricated terra-cotta units, another obsession of Waterhouse as he got older.

Waterhouse retired from active practice in 1901. His final London building, Staple Buildings in High Holborn, was designed in that year and has been demolished. He had only four years to enjoy his retirement as a wealthy lord of the manor at Yattendon in Berkshire, though saddened by the fact that public and professional taste had turned against his work, before his death in 1905. His Quaker principles remained staunch to the end, and he refused all honours except those of his fellow professionals, such as the Royal Gold Medal awarded to him in 1878.

John Francis Bentley
(1839-1902)

John Francis Bentley, portrait

Bentley is best known for his Westminster Roman Catholic Cathedral, but that great building's freely adapted Byzantine style is far from typical of its architect's other work. He was in fact one of the most distinguished practitioners of late Victorian Gothic.

The son of a wine-merchant in Doncaster, Bentley went to a private school there and started work in Manchester in a firm of mechanical engineers. He later came to London, where he worked in the yard of a firm of builders called Winsland and Holland. There he became interested in architecture and was articled to Henry Clutton, a Catholic convert, in 1858. Bentley then launched into his own practice in 1862, soon after his own conversion to Roman Catholicism. Before long he was receiving many church commissions.

His earliest London work is already extremely interesting, a brick house at **No. 235 Lancaster Road**, Paddington (1863) whose exterior ignores symmetry, with the windows placed sensitively but according to the needs of the plan within.

Charles Hadfield, a contemporary, described Bentley and his office off the Strand at this time: "He was a fellow of infinite wit, with a . . . personality which surrounded him with friends . . .. There was always, even in his moments of fun, a straying, far-off look . . .. He hated snobbery and shams of all kinds, and denounced them energetically; was a hard hitter in argument, and generally scored. At such times his hair used to bristle up . . .".

A little later, Bentley built a distillery in Bonhill Street, north of Finsbury Square, but these years were typified by many commissions for additions to Roman Catholic churches. These included the presbytery and two altars for **St. Peter and St. Edward** in Palace Street, Westminster (1863–67), the Lady Chapel and Baptistry for **St. Francis of Assisi** in Pottery Lane, Paddington (1863), the lovely Lady Chapel and the aisles of **St. Mary of the Angels** in Moorhouse Road, Paddington (built gradually with other additions in 1869–87, Lady Chapel 1883) and the redecoration of the east end of **Our Lady of the Assumption** in Warwick Street, Pimlico (1874).

Bentley cared nothing for money; for low fees he habitually worked far longer hours than his health, never robust, could stand. His first major London work was the **Convent of the Sacred Heart**, Hammersmith Road, Hammersmith (1868–88). The buildings are of brick with stone dressings, in a dignified but rather fierce Gothic perhaps showing the influence of Butterfield. Bentley's **St. Mary's Church** in Cadogan Street, Chelsea (1877–82) is only adequate, though it has some fine furnishings, while **Our Lady of the Holy Souls** in Bosworth

Road, Paddington (1882) has more distinction. **Corpus Christi** on Brixton Hill (1885–87) is a much more inspiring, lofty design, but work stopped with only the chancel and transepts done, and even those lack the vaulting they need. Nevertheless, the texture of the interior's east end, with deep arcades of Gothic windows penetrating the thick walls, is of great beauty.

Of this period, Bentley's masterpiece is the Church of the Holy Rood at Watford, just outside London, while within the metropolitan boundaries his reputation was sustained largely by minor work such as his complete redecoration (1889) of **St. Botolph**, the eighteenth-century church in Aldgate in the City, the altar for **St. Gabriel** in Warwick Square, Pimlico (1890), his furnishings for the fashionable **St. James**, Spanish Place, Marylebone (1890 onwards) and the north transept of **Our Lady of Victories**, Clapham (1894). Of more substance is his **Redemptorist Monastery** in Clapham of 1891–93, but it is not accessible to the public.

Thus, when Cardinal Vaughan appointed Bentley as architect for the new **Westminster Cathedral** in 1894, he was selecting a man without experience of building large numbers of churches, let alone anything on the scale of the cathedral. Both Vaughan and Bentley were interested in a current revival of the use of early Christian styles and they were inclined to adapt the Byzantine style to modern needs, rather than employing a Gothic or a Classical approach. Bentley, already in ill health, went to Italy to look for inspiration. It was an extraordinarily cold winter and, after visiting and disliking St. Peter's in Rome, he studied Assisi and St. Mark's in Venice at great length. The weather and his health forced him to abandon his plan to visit Greece and Constantinople, but upon his return to London in March 1895, Cardinal Vaughan agreed to the Byzantine style and the design began. Three months later the foundation stone was laid at the site just off Victoria Street, near Victoria Station, Westminster.

The resulting building, as opened in 1903 without internal decoration (which has been added over subsequent years), is one of London's major monuments. The ground plan has great serenity, with four major spaces under broad shallow domes. Breadth of design is the keynote of the exterior, supplying a very necessary contrast, in the wide masses and window spaces, to the busy effect of the banded brick and stone walls and buttresses. This choice of materials, not too dissimilar to that of Norman Shaw's New Scotland Yard, shows clearly how determined Bentley was that this was to be contemporary architecture of the end of the nineteenth century, with the use of the Byzantine style no more than an

138 Bentley. House at No. 235 Lancaster Road, off Tread-gold Street, North Kensington (1863), shamefully neglected

139 Bentley. Our Lady of the Holy Souls Church, Bosworth Road, North Kensington (1882)

acknowledgement of its Christian roots and function.

The soaring campanile of the cathedral is a familiar landmark from many parts of London, while the mounting composition of masses over the main entrance is a breathtaking sight as the building comes into view from Victoria Street. The interior, a huge and calm space, is one of the noblest of English churches—perhaps all the more so for the fact that the intended marbling of the walls has so far reached only balcony level, leaving the heights of the round arches in uncovered brick. Around the cathedral precinct, the **Archbishop's House**, the **Clergy House**, the **Diocesan Hall** and the **Choir School** were all designed by Bentley.

Bentley himself, however, did not live to see his masterpiece finished. A jovial and energetic man, he was overworked and overweight and had suffered from a creeping paralysis since 1889. In 1902, a year before Westminster Cathedral was opened, the paralysis killed him. One obituary ended, "Spectacles and pencil were left upon the unfinished drawing." He left a widow and many children, one of whom became an architect. At the time of his death he was building a Gothic cathedral in Brooklyn, New York, as well as the Byzantine one in Westminster. By a bitter chance, the RIBA met to approve the award of its Royal Gold Medal to Bentley on the day following his death but, after consulting the King, found itself unable to award the medal posthumously.

140 Bentley. Interior, Westminster Roman Catholic Cathedral, Victoria (1895–1903, decoration continued over subsequent years)

141 Bentley. Westminster Roman Catholic Cathedral, Victoria Street frontage, Victoria (1895–1903)

Charles Harrison Townsend (1851-1928)

Charles Harrison Townsend, portrait

For a time the move which started in the late nineteenth century to develop an architecture for Britain which was not just another copy of an historical style resulted in many buildings which were an eclectic mixture of various styles. But some Arts and Crafts architects attempted to develop a really new type of style—one with roots in the British vernacular past but whose expression would be typical only of its own time. Prior, Newton, Lethaby, Voysey and other members of the Art Workers' Guild largely succeeded in this as regards houses. For larger buildings, the architects who found most success with this free style of design were Charles Rennie Mackintosh in Scotland and C. Harrison Townsend in England.

Townsend was born in Birkenhead in Cheshire, son of a poor solicitor and of the daughter of a Polish violinist. He was articled in Liverpool, and then the Townsend family moved to London in about 1880. After working with T. L. Banks for five years, during which he travelled much in Italy, Townsend started his own practice in 1888.

His travels in Italy had produced a passion for the Romanesque and Byzantine work around Venice and for mosaic-work in general. This love is apparent in the new front Townsend designed for **All Saints' Church**, Ennismore Gardens, Knightsbridge in 1892, a free adaptation of the façade of San Zeno Maggiore in Verona. Later he designed a fine, sinuously carved font and other fittings for the church.

Other influences show in Townsend's next London building, particularly his membership of the Art Workers' Guild since 1888 and the influence of the American architect H. H. Richardson. The leading intellectual light of the Guild was William Lethaby, and his 1891 book *Architecture, Mysticism and Myth* apparently had a deep effect on Townsend. The book sought the deep underlying symbols expressed in ancient architecture all over the world and the importance of reference to nature in building.

These ideas and the so-called American Romanesque of H. H. Richardson can be seen in Townsend's **Bishopsgate Institute** in Bishopsgate, City of London (1892–94), intended as a cultural centre for local inhabitants and City workers. The square window in the middle of the highly original street frontage and the carved stone foliage over much of the surface reflect Townsend's interpretation of Lethaby's ideas. The rounded doorway arch and other features show some influence of Richardson. The interiors are functional spaces with little decoration.

In 1894 Townsend wrote "What does much of the work of the present day for which the artist claims

originality show us?... The man of fashion ... calls the result 'the simplicity of originality'. It is not. It is, instead ... a negation that is a poor substitute for invention." His own public buildings exemplify his idea of real architectural invention. He was one of the most active members of the Art Workers' Guild, organising frequent entertainments and expeditions for its members.

Townsend's next commission was for another charitable institution, the **Whitechapel Art Gallery**, in Whitechapel, east London, near the border of the City. His first design of 1895 was an extraordinary composition, with square towers which turned into circles at their tops and much other hidden symbolism in the frontage. The same themes, on a reduced scale, are present in the building as erected in 1899–1901. The Gallery is a remarkable achievement as it stands, though the great mosaic designed by Walter Crane for the high central panel was never executed for lack of funds, and the gap partly spoils the effect of the frontage. Again, the gallery spaces inside are simple, with clever daylighting from above reaching the main lower gallery.

The other major London building by Townsend is the **Horniman Museum** in London Road, Forest Hill in south London (1896–1901). F. J. Horniman M.P. was a wealthy tea merchant who decided to open his anthropological collection to the public. Here Townsend provided an ingenious plan of two long galleries at different levels on the difficult narrow and sloping site. His street frontage combines an extraordinary façade with a big mosaic by Robert Anning Bell and a brilliant tower which blends square and circles in three dimensions. It is one of the most notable London buildings of its period.

Townsend built two typical churches a little way outside London at Blackheath near Guildford and at Great Warley in Essex, and in 1904 he added a third, the **United Free Church** at the end of Links Road, off the High Road in Woodford Green in north London. Its free style has roots in Romanesque and Byzantine. The brick of the exterior is brought inside too, in fine rounded brick arches, although the lack of decoration is austere. In 1910–11 he built the **Library and Lecture Room** to the north of the Horniman Museum, a more rectangular com-

142 *Townsend. The Bishopsgate Institute, Bishopsgate, City (1892–94). The first of the few public buildings by Arts and Crafts architects in London*

143 *Townsend. The Whitechapel Art Gallery, Whitechapel, east of the City (first design 1895, revised design built 1899–1901 without the intended upper mosaic panel)*

position than the museum itself. He built the house at **No. 2 Temple Fortune Lane**, in Hampstead Garden Suburb in about 1912, and probably the houses at **Nos. 135–141 Hampstead Way**. His houses are visually simple, in contrast to the complex free design of his public building frontages. In Townsend's mind the function of these frontages was to demonstrate the nature of the activities within, so there was for him no conflict between their exuberance and the structural simplicity of the interiors.

After the First World War Townsend's practice shrivelled. He never married and aged as a jovial bachelor-uncle figure in his family, spending most of his energy in organising events at his much-loved Art Workers' Guild. The reduction in his practice after the early 1900s is symptomatic of the end of the Free Style. After that time, most of the Arts and Crafts architects (with the major exception of Charles Holden) turned to a freely inventive Neo-Georgian manner, as representing the true vernacular of English towns.

144 *Townsend. The Horniman Museum, London Road, Forest Hill, south London (1896–1901)*

145 *Townsend. United Free Church, off the High Road, Woodford Green, north London (1904). The church shows the usual Arts and Crafts originality of style developed from some historical precedent, in this case Romanesque*

144

145

C.F.A.Voysey
(1857-1941)

C.F.A. Voysey, portrait

Of all the architects who brought about the Arts and Crafts domestic renaissance of the 1890s, Voysey was the only one who built much in London. There are no known buildings by him in the centre, but his influence is seen in almost every London suburb built between 1900 and 1940. Voysey was a leading member of the Arts and Crafts movement, but above all he was an individualistic designer who invented an architectural style of his own.

Charles Francis Annesley Voysey was born at Hessle, near Hull in Yorkshire, of a family claiming descent from the Duke of Wellington. His father was a country parson who was later expelled from the Church of England for denying the existence of Hell. The family moved to Dulwich in 1871, where the sons attended the well-known public school while the father set about establishing his own Theistic Church. Voysey was first articled to J. P. Seddon, then worked for Saxon Snell and for the notable country house architect George Devey in 1880.

In 1882 Voysey set up his own practice. It was to be six years before he got his first architectural commission, and in the meantime he earned his way by designing wallpapers and fabrics at the suggestion of his friend Arthur Mackmurdo, founder of the Century Guild—the first short-lived guild of the Arts and Crafts movement. Voysey married in 1885, living at Bedford Park and later in St. John's Wood.

After an early cottage in Warwickshire, his first work in London is the horizontal **veranda entrance and hall** he added to the front of No. 71 South End Road, Hampstead in 1890. The next year saw two important, though still small, works. The famous three-storey **studio tower** at No. 14 South Parade, Bedford Park (1891) established the simplified manner which was to be his trade-mark— striking forms, white rendered walls, horizontal band windows and hipped slate roof.

Another lifelong characteristic, that of overall horizontal forms, was established in the same year with the charming little studio house which Voysey built at **No. 17 St. Dunstan's Road**, West Kensington. Horizontals again form the dominant feature of his tall houses of 1892 at **Nos. 14 and 16 Hans Road**, beside Harrods Department Store in Knightsbridge.

At this time many Arts and Crafts architects began to experiment with unusual plans for their houses; L-shapes, X-shapes and even Z-shapes, in order to break up the formality of the conventional compact block. Voysey's favourite was the L-plan, and an early use of this can be seen in **Annesley Lodge**, the house he designed for his father on the corner of Platt's Lane and Kidderpore Avenue, Hampstead (1896). The door is in the inner angle of the L, whose

146

147

148

long low arms embrace a pretty front garden. The interiors and furnishings too were designed by Voysey, in accordance with a principle he applied whenever his client would agree.

This was one principle on which Voysey agreed with other Arts and Crafts architects; another was that of seeking to integrate a house with its site. On other matters Voysey disagreed with leading fellow-architects of the movement such as Philip Webb and the group of former Norman Shaw pupils led by W. R. Lethaby and E. S. Prior. They sought to adapt and use the local vernacular, while Voysey developed his own style. They employed local building materials to bring the house close to its surrounding nature, but Voysey almost always used the same white roughcast walls and slate roofs wherever he was building. Voysey felt strongly, and expressed himself strongly, that copies of past styles were wrong and simplicity of design was right. "Begin by casting out all the useless ornaments . . ." he wrote in 1892. "Eschew all imitations. Strive to produce an effect of repose and simplicity."

His next London work was the design of 1897 for

the house called **Dixcote** in North Drive, Tooting Bec Common, Streatham which was built with minor alterations by another architect after Voysey had quarrelled with his client—he had a fiery and rather autocratic temperament which was not always harmonious with those who employed him. The 1898 additions to the front of **No. 16 Chalcot Gardens**, off Englands Lane, Hampstead are typical in detail except that they are of brick and stone to blend with the rest of the house. The house called **Gordon Dene** in Princes Way, Wimbledon (1899) has been partly altered by another architect.

A group of houses followed in Chorley Wood, on the north-west outskirts of London. The most famous is **The Orchard**, built for his own use in Shire Lane (1900–01). Again there are the long white walls, band windows and hipped slate roofs. But the frontage here has a gable at either end with an off-centre front door—the basic form of this elevation has been adapted and copied in countless suburban semi-detached houses all over England and in other countries of the British Commonwealth. In 1903–04 Voysey designed another house, called **Hollybank**,

49

146 *Voysey. Studio house, No. 14 South Parade, Bedford Park, near Chiswick (1891). The early Voysey Arts and Crafts houses set the style for countless estates of suburban houses and country cottages of the early twentieth century*

147 *Voysey. Studio house, No. 17 St. Dunstan's Road, Hammersmith (1891)*

148 *Voysey. Annesley Lodge, on the corner of Platt's Lane and Kidderpore Avenue, Hampstead (1896)*

149 *Voysey. Sanderson Wallpaper Factory, Barley Mow Passage, off Turnham Green, Chiswick (1902–03). A rare example of a factory built by an Arts and Crafts architect*

in Shire Lane, Chorley Wood, and at about the same time made a typical addition to **Hill Cottage** in the same road.

The early 1900s gave Voysey a rare opportunity to show what he could do when designing a larger non-domestic building. In 1902–03 he designed and built a **Wallpaper Factory** for Sanderson's (who had used many of his wallpaper designs) which can still be seen in Barley Mow Passage off Turnham Green,

Chiswick. It is a delightful and elegant building. High piers support the structure and rise the full height to the roof. The windows between these piers are broad, and their horizontals are relieved by lightly arched tops. Most charming of all, the roof at sky level has a wavy outline between the piers. The building has now been well converted into insurance offices and is named Voysey House.

During the 1900s Voysey's practice was reduced. Unlike his slightly younger colleague, M. H. Baillie Scott, he had no stomach for seeking commissions when fashion shifted from his style towards romantic brick and half-timbering, or to the inventive Neo-Georgian of Ernest Newton. Voysey's lovely interiors for the house called Garden Corner at No. 13 Chelsea Embankment (*c.* 1906) have been destroyed except for the staircase. After that, there is only the **War Memorial** (1920) at the corner of Hatfield Road and The Causeway in Potter's Bar to record. Voysey himself had enough private income to live on until 1941 in chambers in Mayfair, doing occasional small architectural jobs. In 1940, a year before he died, he was belatedly awarded the Royal Gold Medal of the Royal Institute of British Architects.

8

Edwardian Baroque and the Grand Manner

From the late 1880s onwards there was a widely voiced demand among architects and their public for a new, specifically English, style for large buildings. Some sought a style with no historical precedents at all, others saw Elizabethan architecture as a suitable basis for modern development. Others again, perhaps thinking of the expression of Britain's importance as the centre of a great Empire, looked for a freely adapted version of the English Baroque architecture of the early 1700s—the age of late Wren, Hawksmoor and Vanbrugh. It had been a style which used Classical forms in a powerful and original Baroque manner typical only of England. It was not subject to the mathematical rules of Classical proportion and planning typical of contemporary Beaux-Arts design, which were the object of xenophobic suspicion in the anti-French political atmosphere of the time. This English Baroque revival, described as late English Renaissance at the time, was to prove far the most successful candidate for a new style and has become known as Edwardian Baroque.

The originator of the idea was probably John M. Brydon (1840–1901), a Scot, who told the Architectural Association in 1889 that the style was "in some respects superior to even the Italian Renaissance . . . a precious heritage to keep and to guard and, above all things, to study and maintain that we . . . may bring forth fruits worthy of the high ideal." Brydon's best works are at Bath, but his older part of the Chelsea Town Hall (1885) and his immense Baroque Government Offices in Parliament Square (1898–1912, though Brydon's design was sadly altered

150 *The Central Criminal Courts, Old Bailey, City (1900–06) by Edward Mountford. High Edwardian Baroque, the style adopted to make London look the great imperial capital it was in the 1900s*

during erection after his death) show his intentions.

The Wren manner was taken up by Norman Shaw before the end of the 1880s and in 1888 the possibilities of Baroque design as a vehicle for Arts and Crafts ideas were demonstrated sensationally by Belcher and Pite's Institute of Chartered Accountants in the City. Belcher's Baroque scheme lost the 1891 competition for the Victoria and Albert Museum to Aston Webb's eclectic design, but by the end of the century the new style had taken most of the major public building works of the time. Baroque town halls and city halls were being built all over Britain, with massive frontages, domes and towers luxuriant with sculpture (often of high quality). In London, apart from Brydon's Government Offices and the work of the architects described in the following chapters, there are some major English Edwardian Baroque buildings, many of them superb. The War Office in Whitehall (1898–1906) was the work of William Young (1843–1900), designer of the earlier Glasgow Municipal Chambers. The Central Criminal Courts building, Old Bailey (1900–06), with its fine interior sculpture, was the design of the prosperous Edward Mountford (1855–1908), who had also done the 1891 Battersea Town Hall on Lavender Hill and many other civic works. Sir A. Brumwell Thomas (1868–1948), architect of Belfast City Hall, designed the Town Hall in Wellington Street, Woolwich (1899–1908). Sir Edwin Cooper (1873–1942) was the architect of the Port of London Authority building on Tower Hill in the City (1912–22) and continued to use the Grand Manner in many later buildings. One firm, Lanchester and Rickards, derived their style more from Austrian and even French Baroque work than from English sources. Their Deptford Town Hall in New Cross Road, Lewisham (1902–04) and Methodist Central Hall, Storey's Gate, Westminster

(1905–11) show off E. A. Rickards' celebrated draughtsmanship and invention well. Norman Shaw's Baroque work must be mentioned here, although it is dealt with in the chapter on the great man. Two of London's main railway stations have Edwardian Baroque frontages, a long way after Belcher. Both are credited officially to otherwise obscure architects: Victoria Station's yard frontage (1906–08) to Alfred W. Bloomfield; Waterloo (1907–22) to J. R. Scott. Their sculpture is splendidly flamboyant, and doubtless the names of their true designers will be revealed in due course. Other large but very varying work of this Grand Manner period includes the Tate Gallery (1897–1900) by S. R. J. Smith and the County Hall of the London County Council (1908–22) by Ralph Knott. The three major theatre architects were Frank Matcham (1854–1920) who designed the Coliseum in St. Martin's Lane (1903) and his pupils W. G. R. Sprague and Bertie Crewe.

About 1906 fashion changed. A campaign for purer Classicism in *The Architectural Review* coincided with the introduction of French ideas and Beaux-Arts designs by Mewès and Davis and by Sir Reginald Blomfield. Mewès and Davis will have a chapter to themselves, while Blomfield's French manner can best be seen in the former United University Club, Pall Mall East (1906–07) and the whole design of the frontages of the north-west, west, and south-west sides of Piccadilly Circus,

151 *Government offices, corner of Parliament Square, Westminster (1897–1912) by John Brydon, the leading campaigner for a new English Baroque style developed from Wren and Hawksmoor*

together with the curving Regent Street quadrant on both sides of Norman Shaw's Piccadilly Hotel. The design was done a year or two after Shaw's death in 1912, and the buildings inside Blomfield's elevations were erected by various architects, reaching completion in 1930. The rest of Regent Street was rebuilt by several designers; Henry Tanner the younger did much of it, notably the Oxford Circus buildings of 1913–28.

The 1914–18 war put an end to most building work for the time being and ended the French architectural fashion too. Both before and after the war, the great Glasgow architect Sir John Burnet (1857–1938) developed a considerable London practice after he had built the King Edward VII Galleries of the British Museum (1904–14) and his post-war work included the impressive large office blocks Vigo House, Regent Street (1920–25) and Adelaide House at the side of London Bridge (1921–25). Sir Edwin Cooper's practice continued to flourish, too, as did that of other Grand Manner practitioners such as J. J. Joass. But the dominant figures in British Classical architecture between the wars were the two designers of New Delhi, Sir Edwin Lutyens and Sir Herbert Baker (1862–1946).

Lutyens will be treated in a chapter to himself. Baker's London work includes the re-building of Sir John Soane's Bank of England in 1921–37, the Grandstand at Lord's Cricket Ground (1926), India House for the Indian High Commission, in the Aldwych (1928–30), Electra House, Victoria Embankment (1931–33), South Africa House for the South African High Commission, in Trafalgar Square (1935–37) and Church House for the Church of England in Dean's Yard, Westminster Abbey (1935–39). Baker was an able and dignified architect, though his work often has an unsympathetic quality and lacks the flair of the great Lutyens at his best.

The other late Classicists who must be mentioned are A. E. (later Sir Albert) Richardson (1880–1964) and E. Vincent Harris (1879–1971). Richardson had a strong liking for French Classicism, but he could strip off most or all of the Classical decoration in buildings such as Moorgate Hall, Nos. 83–93 Moorgate, in the City (1914–16), Nos. 19–23 Wells Street, Marylebone (1931) and Bracken House, Queen Victoria Street, City (1955–58). Harris's works are nearer to Vanbrugh in spirit, though not in detail. They include the vast Government Office Buildings between the Victoria Embankment and Whitehall (1915–61) and the eccentrically charming No. 24 Old Bond Street, Mayfair (1926).

152 *Piccadilly Circus western and northern sides (c. 1913–30) by Sir Reginald Blomfield. Blomfield helped to introduce the more refined forms of French Classicism from 1906 onwards*

153 *South Africa House, Trafalgar Square, Westminster (1935–37) by Sir Herbert Baker. Lutyens, Baker and others designed in a developed Grand Manner right up to the start of the Second World War. The fountains are by Lutyens*

John Belcher
(1841-1913)

John Belcher, portrait

In the early 1900s an advertisement appeared in architectural magazines offering students instruction in the Gothic, Renaissance, Classic and "Belcher" styles—so closely was Belcher's name linked with the freely inventive Baroque which had become fashionable. With his two talented chief assistants, Beresford Pite and John James Joass, he had played a major part in developing what became known as Edwardian Baroque. Belcher and Pite were both involved with the Arts and Crafts architects who founded the Art Workers' Guild, that central organisation of the Arts and Crafts movement whose stated aim was to re-integrate the widely separated arts of architecture, sculpture and painting: but their interpretation of its aims led to a very different style from those of Guild members such as Voysey and Harrison Townsend.

Belcher was born in Southwark, son of an architect of the same name with an established practice in the City of London. The young man studied architecture for a year in Luxembourg and Paris, and then joined his father's firm. He soon took over most of the design work—he was a charming and rather shy man, a fine amateur bass solo singer in oratorios, but restlessly experimental on the drawing board.

The first surviving building by Belcher is the Gothic office building for **Mappin and Webb** (1870–72) on the corner of Poultry and Queen Victoria Street in the City. Belcher admired William Burges at this time and the influence can be discerned. A grimly romantic Gothic church followed, the **Catholic Apostolic Church** (Belcher was a member of the "Irvingite" sect named after the leader of this popular church of the end of the century), Camberwell New Road in south London (1876–77, now used by a Greek Orthodox congregation). A few years later, a tile-hung **Cottage Hospital** in Hermitage Road, Norwood (1881) reflected Belcher's growing admiration for Norman Shaw's manner of that time.

In 1885 Arthur Beresford Pite, then aged only twenty-four, became Belcher's chief assistant, and together they produced the design which won the competition for the **Institute of Chartered Accountants** headquarters in 1888. This building, which was opened in 1893 and stands in the narrow street called Moorgate Place off Moorgate in the City, was a turning point in British architectural history. The Arts and Crafts architects widened their objectives over the years, but Belcher remained

154 *Belcher with Beresford Pite. The Institute of Chartered Accountants, Great Swan Alley, off Moorgate, City (1888–93)*

obsessed by the movement's early aims. The Baroque style seemed to him the ideal medium for their realization—the exterior of the Institute of Chartered Accountants blends rich Baroque architectural detailing with sculpture of high merit by Sir Hamo Thornycroft and Harry Bates, while the interior used sculpture and paintings as ingeniously. The main entrance façade is almost symmetrical, with its massively rusticated central doorway and window surrounds and a notable sculpted frieze behind half-columns at second floor level. The corner is yet more inventive, with a fine oriel sculpted by Thornycroft. The other frontage on Great Swan Alley is highly original too—it was probably Pite who designed the clever break of levels accented by a cupola turret before the other glorious doorway is reached. The interior is as impressive, with a stairway which changes character at each level, a lot of play with scale and a domed main room (originally the Council Chamber) which was carefully converted by William Whitfield when he restored and extended the building in 1969.

Belcher and Pite's building (together with their 1891 competition entry for the Victoria and Albert Museum) started a fashion among progressive architects for a free Baroque style when it was opened in 1893, but rather inexplicably Belcher received no more major London commissions until 1900 (his 1892 house at **No. 2a Melbury Road**, Holland Park for Hamo Thornycroft is charming, however). Pite set up his own independent practice in 1896 or 1897—**No. 82 Mortimer Street**, Marylebone (1896) and **No. 37 Harley Street** (1899) show how he developed the Baroque style at this time—and J. J. Joass, a Highlander trained by Sir John Burnet, became Belcher's assistant in 1898. It was a good time for the firm, for Belcher's success in the 1897 Colchester Town Hall competition and the publication of his big book *Later Renaissance Architecture in England* established that the Baroque of *c.* 1700 was a specifically English style with much appeal to Englishmen of 1900 with Imperial attitudes. New commissions came to Belcher now. These included the dull **Birmingham Post** building at No. 88 Fleet Street (1900–02), the Baroque mass of **Electra House**, No. 84 Moorgate, in the City (1900–03) and the Baroque first section of **Royal London House**, Finsbury Square (1904–05) with its splendid corner tower. Winchester House (1904–05), on the corner of London Wall and Old Broad Street, had notable Baroque sculpture but has been demolished.

In 1904–06 Belcher was President of the Royal Institute of British Architects and presided over the International Congress. He was awarded the

155

Institute's Royal Gold Medal in 1907. During this busy but prestigious period, Joass took over almost all the detailed design work on the commissions attracted by his senior partner's celebrity. Since Belcher's last four years before his death in 1913 were shadowed by illness, this arrangement of the work continued, though Joass later said that they always consulted together about the schemes.

In the years from 1906 onwards the firm produced some very remarkable steel-frame buildings. Following Charles Holden's lead, Joass developed an extraordinary Neo-Mannerism to express the fact that the stone walls of these buildings were really a skin over a steel frame. The first and most remarkable of these designs are the elegant **Mappin House** at Nos. 158–162 Oxford Street (1906–08) and the explosive former **Royal Insurance** building on the western corner of Piccadilly and St. James's Street (1907–08), in which elongated Classical features are used in an extraordinary way to symbolise the fact that they are not load-bearing.

The street frontage of **Mowbray's Bookshop** at No. 28 Margaret Street, Marylebone (1907–08) has the same Neo-Mannerist quality, while in **Whiteley's Department Store** in Queensway,

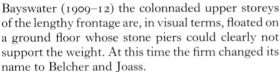

156

157

Bayswater (1909–12) the colonnaded upper storeys of the lengthy frontage are, in visual terms, floated on a ground floor whose stone piers could clearly not support the weight. At this time the firm changed its name to Belcher and Joass.

Holy Trinity Church, Kingsway, Holborn (1910–12) is one of the very few examples of an Edwardian Baroque church. Joass was emotionally involved with this project, which was never completed as money ran out before the brickwork barrel vault of the interior could be stone-clad or the high tower built. He planned to leave money in his will to build the tower, but a later personal financial loss prevented this. In the same years Joass built the office and library building for the **Royal Zoological Society** in the Outer Circle of Regent's Park, and the **Royal Society of Medicine** in Henrietta Place, Marylebone, a handsome building spoiled by the addition of attic storeys. A pretty house at **No. 31 Weymouth Street**, Marylebone dates from 1912, while Joass's last work before the 1914–18 war was the remarkable miniature concrete mountains of the **Mappin Terraces** at the London Zoo in Regent's Park, built in 1913.

Belcher died in that same year. Both he and Joass

155 *Belcher. Royal London House, corner of Finsbury Square and City Road, north of the City (1904–05)*

156 *Belcher with J.J. Joass. Mappin House, Nos. 158–162 Oxford Street, near Oxford Circus (1906–08)*

157 *Belcher with J.J. Joass. Royal Insurance building, western corner of Piccadilly and St. James's Street, St. James's (1907–08)*

were married but remained childless. Joass went on to prosper after the First World War until the start of the Second. He was a dour but humorous man, whose great love was his ocean-racing yacht. Among his large buildings of this period a few must be noted, especially the restaurants and other work at the **Zoo**, the **Lex Garage** in Brewer Street (1927), the astonishing central section of **Royal London House** in Finsbury Square (*c.* 1926–30) with its towering steeple, and **Abbey House**, Baker Street (*c.* 1928–32) with its tower that seems visible wherever you walk in Regent's Park. Finally, **Clarendon House** at No. 17 New Bond Street (1932) shows him coming to terms with the stripped forms of the modern movement.

Sir Aston Webb
(1849-1930)

Sir Aston Webb, portrait

Regardless of the architectural ideals of the time or the distinction of other designers' buildings, the *big* practice at the turn of the century—in terms of the sheer volume of cubic structure or of pounds, shillings and pence—was that of Sir Aston Webb. Nor is he to be derided as a designer. Most of his plans were sound, and in any style—French Renaissance, Gothic, Norman, free Baroque, Byzantine or chaste Neo-Classical—he produced designs of competence and sometimes of real distinction. If some of his contemporaries and some of us today see this multi-faceted quality as showing a lack of integrity, we should perhaps remember that he saw himself as responding to the desires of his clients.

Webb was born in Clapham, in south London, the son of a successful watercolour painter, Edward Webb. He went to school in Brighton, was articled to the London firm Banks and Barry and then travelled on the continent for a year. In 1873 he established his own practice and for most of his career was in partnership with E. Ingress Bell.

In London, his **granary** in Deptford Creek dates from *c.* 1880 and his plain **warehouse** at No. 73 Great Eastern Street, Shoreditch, from 1881. Then, during the 1880s, he was commissioned to put the ruined Norman church of **St. Bartholomew-the-Great**, at Smithfield in the City, into usable order. The long nave was largely destroyed, so Webb closed it off near the crossing, then re-built the transepts and the upper parts and roof of the chancel. He restored one side of the cloister and the Lady Chapel, and added a porch. It was good work and Londoners owe him the salvation of a Norman church and one of the most fascinating places to visit in the city.

A house by Webb at **No. 20 Queen Street**, Mayfair also dates from the 1880s, as does a truly remarkable eclectic composition, with Classical, Romanesque and other details, at **No. 23 Austin Friars** in the City (1888). Almost as original is his office building at Nos. **13–15 Moorgate** (1890–93).

In 1891 Aston Webb and Ingress Bell won the competition for the major building to complete the **Victoria and Albert Museum** on the corner of the Cromwell Road and Exhibition Road, Kensington. It was only in 1899 that the government found funds to start building, and the museum was opened in 1909. It is a curious building outside, in a freely eclectic and rather ponderous manner at the lower levels, but with an exotic array of towers and domes along its skyline. The interior is more distinguished, with a series of lofty and complex spaces providing much pleasure.

Webb's rapidly growing architectural office and his own personality have been evocatively described by a former pupil, H. Bulkeley Creswell. "Webb was

essentially a happy little man; he gloried in his powers and nothing seemed to bother him or to obstruct the fecundity of his ideas. A little man he was, alike in bodily make-up and in his conventional outlook on life. . . . It was beyond thinking that he cared a sniff for the work of Morris, Philip Webb (who was no relation), Nesfield and so forth. His contentment was sumptuous, his demeanour modest to admiration; he was widely esteemed both personally and professionally, and he was truly an artist from his toes to the tips of his fragile lightly boned fingers, characteristically blackened with the soft H.B. lead with which he slapped his designings down on cartridge paper 'because it bites so nicely', hissing through his teeth meanwhile like an ostler curry-combing a horse, in exultation."

Webb once said that his own favourite of his buildings was the terracotta **French Protestant Church** at No. 9 Soho Square (1893). Its **school**, built in 1898, is nearby in Noel Street.

But the French church was Webb's last London

158 *Aston Webb. The Victoria and Albert Museum, Cromwell Road, Kensington (designed 1891, built 1899–1901). The design is in Webb's early eclectic manner, before the Baroque Grand Manner became fashionable*

work in his eclectic terracotta manner, for fashion had changed in favour of a free Classicism. His next building was the **Royal United Services Institute** (1893–95) beside the Inigo Jones Banqueting House in Whitehall. Here Webb used a restrained version of the free Baroque style made fashionable by Belcher and others. In the suburbs Webb and Ingress Bell built the rather original **St. Alban's Church**, Margravine Road, Fulham (1894–96), two houses called **The Gables** and **Pentlands** in Blackheath Park (1895 and 1896) and **Mumford's Flour Mills** in the High Road, Greenwich (1897).

During the following years the number of buildings which Aston Webb had in hand multiplied. Apart from the Victoria and Albert Museum and, outside London, major buildings for the Royal

159

160

161

159 *Aston Webb. The Royal School of Mines, Prince Consort Road, off Exhibition Road, Kensington (1909–13)*

160 *Aston Webb. Admiralty Arch, Trafalgar Square and The Mall, Westminster (1908–09)*

161 *Aston Webb. East Façade, Buckingham Palace, The Mall (1912–13)*

Naval College in Devon and for Birmingham University, his commissions included the huge Classical main building of the **Imperial College of Science and Technology** in Imperial Institute Road off Exhibition Road, Kensington (1900–06), the new lay-out of **The Mall** and the *rond-point* in front of Buckingham Palace (carried out 1901–13) and the **Admiralty Arch** between The Mall and Trafalgar Square (1908–09). Admiralty Arch is an ungainly piece of Classical design, for the Royal Navy insisted on Webb including more offices in the block than it could comfortably contain, but it provides a grand and spatially pleasing screen to terminate the Mall. Webb was knighted in 1904 and was awarded the Royal Gold Medal in the following year.

Webb's favourite eclecticism can be seen at its best again in the dignified **Thames Warehouse** which he built in 1901 in Stamford Street, south of the river near Southwark Bridge, and his eccentric use of Classical detailing is well displayed in the **Canadian National Railways** building of 1907 in Cockspur Street between Pall Mall and Trafalgar Square.

The Royal School of Mines (1909–13) in Prince Consort Road behind the Royal Albert Hall, is the last of Webb's three big buildings on the Kensington Museums site. Its long Classical wings are dull stuff, but the centrepiece is a fine composition of solids and voids.

Webb's pre-war work was completed by a world-famous London building, the main public façade of **Buckingham Palace**. John Nash's fine open-sided courtyard had been closed in with a range by Edward Blore in 1846–47, but Blore's work lacked the distinction which King Edward VII felt desirable for the public aspect of the palace. So Aston Webb was commissioned to design a new frontage. After several attempts, his revised proposal was accepted in 1912 and built rapidly in 1913. It is a noble and chaste Neo-Classical work, its three projecting accents too weak for perfection, but it has become well-loved by the public.

After the 1914–18 war, Webb's practice continued to prosper until his death in 1930. His **War Memorial** of 1920, with sculpture by Alfred Drury, in front of the Royal Exchange in the City is a pretty, minor work. In the 1920s his firm built several commercial blocks in London, such as **Artillery House**, Westminster (*c.* 1925), **24 Bishopsgate**, City (1928) and **36–44 Moorgate**, City (1928). Of this period the **Royal Air Force Club** in Piccadilly (*c.* 1925) is notable. But Webb's period of major public buildings was over and it is probable that his son Maurice Webb, who inherited the practice, did much of this later design work.

Arthur J. Davis of Mewès and Davis (1878-1951)

Arthur J. Davis, portrait

In 1907, four years after King Edward VII's famous visit to Paris and the *Entente Cordiale*, the editor of *The Architectural Review* noted what he called "a recrudescence of the French Renaissance" in London architecture. England had long felt a hostile rivalry with France, and this was reflected in the widespread rejection of current French ideas by English architects. The architects chiefly responsible for altering this trend were Sir Reginald Blomfield, whose United University Club in Pall Mall East (1906–07) and Piccadilly Circus façades (1913 onwards) are in a Classical style of much French influence, and Arthur J. Davis.

Davis was born in London, the son of a successful Jewish businessman, but much of his education was in Brussels and Paris. In 1894 he went to the preparatory *atelier* of Monsieur Godefroy and passed the examination to enter the famous *Ecole des Beaux Arts*. There he was a star pupil of one of the best-known *ateliers*, that of Jean-Louis Pascal, and was invited to help the architect of the Paris Ritz Hotel, Charles Mewès, with some competition designs. Mewès liked his work so much that he asked Davis, aged only 22, to become the London partner in his international firm.

The interiors, now destroyed, which the firm carried out in 1901 for the Carlton Hotel were Mewès designs. The firm's first London masterpiece, the **Ritz Hotel** in Piccadilly (1903–06), was also basically designed by Mewès, but with Davis actively participating. The exterior, with its Mansard roofs, elegant simplified Classical walls and covered pavement arcade, is deeply French in character. The interiors are richly magnificent and planned with truly *Beaux-Arts* clarity. From the Arlington Street entrance a broad and often open-sided corridor runs the length of the building; the sequence of spaces runs from the reception desk with the main staircase curling over it, past the sumptuously decorated "winter garden" saloon and the cocktail bar (now closed) to the climax, the glorious columned restaurant overlooking Green Park.

Davis's personality was admirably adapted to the type of buildings he designed. Darkly good-looking but short in stature, he was a dandy in his dress, a *bon viveur* and loved the company of elegant women. He did not marry until he was forty-five, and then disastrously.

The firm's next London design was arguably the best French-influenced Edwardian building in England, **Inveresk House**, built for the *Morning Post* newspaper in 1906–07. Inveresk House stands on the corner of the Aldwych and the Strand, facing across Waterloo Bridge. Davis solved the problem of the awkward corner angle with sublime ease,

accenting it with a very Parisian dome now un-
believably mauled by the attic additions and a
ludicrous corner aedicule. It is difficult to look only at
Davis's unspoiled work below the high cornice.

In 1908 Davis added a handsome Classical
eastward extension to the **Cavalry Club** at 127
Piccadilly and in 1908–11 he built the **Royal
Automobile Club** in Pall Mall, St. James's. The
R.A.C. was intended to be the apotheosis of the West
End Club. The facilities are varied and lavish, and
the architect was expected to provide a suitably
grandiose setting. Davis certainly did that. The

162 *Mewès and Davis. The Lounge, or Winter Garden, The
Ritz Hotel, Piccadilly*

frontage is still French in character, but the palatial
Parisian of the Louvre rather than the elegant
restraint of the rue de Rivoli. The long frontage, with
screens of giant columns along both wings, has a
good Ionic portico over the entrance as its one accent
(the sculpture includes a cherub on a motor-bike).
Inside there is a dazzling oval entrance vestibule and
then room after room of varied Classical styles.

After the First World War, Mewès and Davis

163

164

165

163 *Mewès and Davis. Exterior, The Ritz Hotel, Piccadilly (1903–06). The French classical manner for grand hotels*

164 *Mewès and Davis. The Royal Automobile club, Pall Mall, St. James's (1908–11)*

165 *Mewès and Davis. National Westminster Bank, Nos. 51–52 Threadneedle Street, City (1922–36). Davis designed many City banks and offices in an Italian palazzo manner after the Great War*

(although Mewès had died in 1914) developed a new type of practice in the City of London. Davis's **Westminster Bank** (now National Westminster) at Nos. 51–52 Threadneedle Street (1922, extended 1936) is a particularly fine work in a manner distantly inspired by Peruzzi's 1535 Palazzo Massimi in Rome. The headquarters of the **Westminster Bank** in Throgmorton Street (1923–29) is the largest of Davis's City works, but not the best. The **Morgan Grenfell** building at No. 23 Great Winchester Street (1925) has a cold character relieved by the three-storey U-shaped recess over the doorway. **No. 52 Bishopsgate** (1928–29), and the courtyard buildings behind, are a distinguished Classical

design done for the Hudson's Bay Company. The **Cunard Building** at No. 88 Leadenhall Street (1930) has a similar cool distinction.

Three other buildings of the 1920s by Arthur Davis should be noted. In 1923, for his marriage, he converted an old pub at **No. 6 Chesterfield Hill**, Mayfair into a charming house. In 1925 he completely remodelled his own favourite restaurant, facing the park in the **Hyde Park Hotel**, Knightsbridge. And in 1928 he did a totally unexpected work, the tiny **St. Sarkis Armenian Church** in Iverna Gardens, Kensington.

During the 1930s Davis's practice was much reduced, although the firm survived and exists today. The last work to be noted here is the reproduction at **No. 21 St. James's Square** of Robert Adam's next-door No. 20 for the Distiller's Company in 1936–38. Davis had suffered a nervous collapse in the army in France in 1915 and he had relapses periodically during the following years. His last years were darkened by such illness. His troubled marriage, by which he had one daughter, ended in 1935 and although he did not die until 1951, Davis was unable to work during the final fifteen years of his life.

Sir Edwin Lutyens

Sir Edwin Lutyens, portrait

Just as Norman Shaw dominated English architecture during the last quarter of the nineteenth century, Sir Edwin Lutyens was the pre-eminent architect of Britain during the first forty years of the twentieth century. And in contrast to the stylistic switches of architects such as Sir Aston Webb, Lutyens' approach to architectural design developed remarkably consistently, once he had made the one major transition of his life in about 1904 from Arts and Crafts vernacular to freely Classical design. That transition was for years regarded by architects as a betrayal of progress—in the light of time it can now be seen as a necessary step in the development of one of the geniuses of British architecture. Lutyens was a flippant man in outward manner, but that should not prevent us from seeing the power and brilliance of the talent beneath.

Edwin Landseer Lutyens was born in London, the eleventh child of a retired army officer and a dominant Irish mother. He was educated privately and then at the Royal College of Art. He joined the staff of Sir Ernest George for under a year in 1887, where he became close friends with Herbert Baker (later Sir Herbert, who re-built Soane's Bank of England in 1921–37 and, among many other London works, built South Africa House in Trafalgar Square in 1935). That was all the formal training that Lutyens had in architecture. Roderick Gradidge has written "Lutyens was almost untrained, perhaps untrainable; as Sir Herbert Baker remembered him 'he seemed to know by intuition'." But he studied the ways of local builders in Surrey where he set up his own practice in 1889, aged twenty. During the 1890s he built up a good practice in middle-sized country houses, chiefly in Surrey, designed in the Arts and Crafts vernacular manner with Elizabethan roots. The best of these houses are among the most beautiful products of the Arts and Crafts movement: Munstead Wood (1896), Fulbrook (1897), Orchards (1899) and Tigbourne Court (1899) are among the best-known, all in the country around Godalming, Surrey. In 1897 he had married Lady Emily Lytton, daughter of a Viceroy of India, and he now began to look for wider horizons.

Lutyens' first London work is the **Country Life** magazine's office building at Nos. 2–10 Tavistock Street, Covent Garden (1904) in an individualistic version of the fashionable Edwardian Baroque style. The same can be said of his **Redland House** at No. 40 Kingsway (1906). Then in 1907 he was appointed architect for the public buildings at the centre of Hampstead Garden Suburb, a model initiated by Canon and Dame Henrietta Barnett near Golders Green. Here in 1909–13 Lutyens built **St. Jude's Church** and the **Free Church**, as well as

166 *Lutyens. Country Life building, Nos. 2–10 Tavistock Street, Covent Garden (1904). The great architect's first London building*

167 *Lutyens. St. Jude's Church, Hampstead Garden Suburb, north of Golders Green (1909–13)*

the two **Parsonages**, part of **The Institute** and some **houses** around the central green of the Garden Suburb. The houses are Neo-Georgian, in the imaginative use of that style developed by Ernest Newton of the Arts and Crafts movement. The churches mix styles freely, or rather blend them into compositions of much originality.

A new development can be seen in three Lutyens buildings of 1911. The age of Edwardian Baroque buildings richly sculpted, in the manner originated by John Belcher and Beresford Pite, was over. It was to be Lutyens and a few others who worked out an imposing style to succeed the Baroque, and the early steps in this process can be seen in the simplified Wren manner ("Wrenaissance", Lutyens called this style) of the original part within the courtyard of the **British Medical Association** in Tavistock Square, Bloomsbury (1911, built originally for the Theosophical Society). And Lutyens took the process further with his Stripped Classical brick buildings at **No. 36 Smith Square**, Westminster and **No. 7 St. James's Square**, both of the same year. In the latter building, only the porch and the high balustrade decorate a plain frontage which depends on the proportions of its windows for its dignity. The imposing pair of houses known as **No. 8 Little College Street and No. 11 Cowley Street**, Westminster, dates from 1912.

In 1912 Lutyens was appointed chief architect for the new Imperial capital of India at New Delhi, and Herbert Baker, who had meanwhile built up a large practice in South Africa, joined him. The two men divided up the major buildings there and developed the grand Stripped Classical style further, integrating some touches of vernacular Indian architecture. After the war had interrupted most building in London, the first fruit of this growth was seen in the famous **Cenotaph** war memorial which Lutyens designed and built in 1919–20 in Whitehall, Westminster. The design, apparently so simple, is in fact an extraordinarily subtle geometrical composition.

In contrast, Lutyens' next London work is positively festive, the joyous little free-standing **Midland Bank** (1922), of brick with playful stone dressings, beside St. James's Church in Piccadilly. His **Mercantile Marine memorial** of much the same time in Trinity Square, Tower Hill, was altered by Sir Edward Maufe in 1952. Lutyens was knighted as early as 1918 and was awarded the Royal Gold Medal for architecture in 1921.

Then in 1924–27, Lutyens built the first of his really large London buildings. **Britannic House** (the name has now been changed since the British Petroleum Company sold the building) occupies a big site running from Finsbury Circus through to

Moorgate. Eight storeys were required, and Classical architecture needs ingenious adaptation to such heights. The curving Finsbury Square frontage is one of Lutyens' most magnificent achievements, rising through two rusticated storeys, and then two plainer ones to a three-storey *piano nobile* with a screen of giant Corinthian columns.

This was followed by what is perhaps Lutyens' masterpiece among his London works: the immense headquarters of the **Midland Bank** running through from Poultry to Princes Street, beside the Bank of England in the City. It was built in 1924–39 and its vast piled-up masses of horizontally rusticated stone, with window arches punched deep into them, are of a power that would have delighted Hawksmoor or Vanbrugh. It was in the vigour of buildings such as this and the Viceroy's residence at New Delhi that Lutyens' talents found full expression.

Lutyens was now famous. he was one of the few British architects (Wren and Nash are the only others that come to mind) whose names were really well-known among ordinary people. His achievements were already great, yet his behaviour remained as irreverent as ever. As Sir Nikolaus Pevsner has written, "He could ask a poor clergyman called Western at a Viceroy's party at Delhi whether he was a relation of the Great Western, but he could also say that the Delhi buildings in their finished form, after all the exasperating quarrels with Baker, were his Bakerloo."

From 1927 Lutyens' practice was so large that, like Norman Shaw in old age, he started to accept commissions to design only the external façades of large commercial buildings. Among the duller of these works are **Terminal House** in Grosvenor Gardens, Victoria (1927) and **Brook House** in Park Lane, Mayfair (1932). His façades for the **C. and A. department store** building, **British Industries House**, at the Marble Arch end of Oxford Street (1927) are more impressive, but only those of **Grosvenor House**, Park Lane (1930), with a series of towers set diagonally to the road achieve high distinction.

168 *Lutyens. The Cenotaph (First World War Memorial), Whitehall, Westminster (1919–20)*

169 *Lutyens. Midland Bank, Piccadilly (1922)*

170 *Lutyens. Midland Bank headquarters, Poultry and Princes Street, beside the Bank of England, City (1924–39)*

171 *Lutyens. Britannic House, Moorgate and Finsbury Circus, City (designed 1920, built 1924–27)*

In 1928–30 Lutyens procured the commission for a large estate of **London County Council flats** at Page Street, Westminster. These are a surprise, given the background of his work, for the external walls are huge chequer-boards of concrete rectangles, brick rectangles and windows. And the courtyards have long horizontal strip balconies of concrete between each level of open connecting passageways.

In the same years Lutyens was building two more **Midland Bank** branches in central London. That at No. 68 Pall Mall (1928) is a strong block with detailing that jokes with traditional Classical features, but it does not quite come off as a composition. The branch in Leadenhall Street (1929) in the City, however, is a highly impressive stone building; a firm overall design with two towers and impressive clean arches at ground level through to the pavement arcade. His **Young Women's Christian Associ-** **ation hostel** in Great Russell Street, Bloomsbury (1930–32) is a chaste return to the rather puritanical brick Stripped Classicism of his earlier No. 7 St. James's Square.

Lutyens was now approaching the end of his career. His last major London building is the headquarters for **Reuter's and the Press Association** (1935), a high Vanbrughesque mass of Portland stone in Fleet Street near Ludgate Circus, topped by a stumpy tower with concave sides. Embedded in its side is a pretty little Lutyens joke, **The Cogers** public house in Salisbury Square. His final work in the West End has been enjoyed by many celebrating Londoners—the spreading pools and **fountains in Trafalgar Square** (1939, Plate 153). Nothing came of the work of his last years designing a National Theatre for a site in the Cromwell Road—that project was realized on a larger site by another architect in a very different style.

9
Modern Design and International Modernism

Simplified modern design in England pre-dated the arrival of the Bauhaus influence by many years. The Arts and Crafts movement in general and W. R. Lethaby in particular had been preaching the need for architectural design based on the new steel and concrete techniques of building structure since before the First World War. Sir John Burnet's Kodak House in Kingsway (1910–11, now owned by Gallaher's) is an early example for England of the expression of structure on the exterior of a building, but it is essentially a Classical design stripped of all decoration. More directly derived from Arts and Crafts ideas, the work of Charles Holden moved towards a powerful manner of its own. Holden's large 1920s buildings express a powerful thrust up from the earth, while his best Underground Railway stations are unmistakably twentieth century in style. Of other buildings of that decade, Easton and Robertson's new Royal Horticultural Hall in Greycoat Street, Westminster (1923–28) has great clarity of structural expression (Robertson later built the Shell Tower of 1960 on the South Bank of the Thames at Waterloo). A little later, mention must be made of the powerful simplified forms of many suburban factories by Wallis, Gilbert and Partners (for example, the Hoover Factory of 1932–35 on Western Avenue) and of cinemas by George Coles, such as the Gaumont State of 1937 in Kilburn High Road. Battersea Power Station (1932–34), beside Chelsea Bridge, was designed by the architect of Liverpool Cathedral, Sir Giles Gilbert Scott (1880–1960), who was also the architect of the lovely Waterloo Bridge (1940–45).

The other Thames Bridges of the twentieth century start with two unexciting examples,

Vauxhall Bridge of 1906 and Southwark Bridge of 1919, for which Sir Ernest George designed the architectural features. Then followed Lambeth Bridge of 1932 by G. Topham Forrest (the LCC architect) and Sir Reginald Blomfield. Chelsea Bridge is a good suspension bridge of 1934 by E. P. Wheeler, also working with the LCC Architects' Department. It was Wheeler again who designed Wandsworth Bridge of 1938. There followed Waterloo Bridge which replaced a famous one by Rennie. The last surviving Thames bridge by Rennie was destroyed when his design of 1823 was replaced by the present London Bridge in the early 1970s.

In a rather different category, Joseph Emberton (1889–1956) was a strong believer in the ideas of Le Corbusier. Without copying the Swiss master's manner, Emberton showed himself of the modern school in his new almost Cubist entrance frontage for Olympia exhibition hall, Hammersmith Road (1930), Simpson's Department Store, Piccadilly (1935) and His Master's Voice building at Nos. 363–367 Oxford Street (1938–39). Sir Owen Williams (b. 1890) was an eminent civil engineer with a considerable talent for simplified architectural design. His work of the 1930s included the black glass block of the Daily Express building in Fleet Street (1931), the Empire Pool and Arena at Wembley (1934) and the Peckham Health Centre in St. Mary's Road, Peckham (1934–36).

During the 1930s, however, the simplified approach to architecture did receive a new impetus with the arrival of a series of distinguished refugees from the pioneering Bauhaus school of design in Germany, following their persecution by the Nazis, and other European architects in search of a new home. Gropius, Mies van der Rohe, Mendelsohn, Chermayeff, Goldfinger, Breuer, Lubetkin and others arrived and left their various marks in

172 Daily Express Building, Fleet Street, City (1931) by Sir Owen Williams, at the time of its completion

74

England. Lubetkin stayed and founded the influential Tecton design group. Goldfinger stayed and built up a successful practice. Gropius formed a brief partnership with the progressive young English architect Maxwell Fry, then went on to America—as did Mies and others.

Fry was one of the first Englishmen to take up the so-called International manner of the Bauhaus and Le Corbusier, but with him must be mentioned the Canadian, Wells Coates (1895–1958), and the partnership of Connell, Ward and Lucas. Coates designed the Isokon communal block of flats in Lawn Road, Hampstead (1933–34) and the flats at No. 10 Palace Gate, Kensington (1938–39). Connell, Ward and Lucas were the architects of the flats called Kent House in Ferdinand Street, off Chalk Farm Road, Camden Town (1936) and the house at No. 66 Frognal, Hampstead (1937–38). Goldfinger's prewar work in London consisted of a number of shop fronts and interiors, and the houses at Nos. 2–6 Willow Road, Hampstead (1937–38). These and a few other buildings mark the extent of the progress made by the international modern movement by the outbreak of war in 1939.

When the war ended in 1945 there was little building for some years. When the great re-building of bombed London did start, however, it was the new architecture and the young architects of the 1930s that found success. One of these young architects, Denys Lasdun, is the subject of an individual chapter. The work of some others will be surveyed briefly in a final summary.

173 *Isokon flats, Lawn Road, Belsize Park, Hampstead (1933–34) by Wells Coates. Coates was one of the small group of young architects who introduced the International Modern style to England from Europe in the early 1930s*

174 *Hoover Factory, Western Avenue (the A40 Oxford Road), Perivale, west London (1932–35) by Wallis Gilbert and Partners, who built many streamlined factories in and around London at this period, reflecting modern developments in the USA and Europe*

Sir John Burnet
(1857-1938)

Sir John Burnet, portrait

The approach to planning and the undecorated detailing typical of modern design did not arrive overnight in Britain; they evolved gradually during the first third of the twentieth century before the arrival of international influences. The development can be seen in the work of John James Burnet, one of the most distinguished of the line of Scottish architects since James Gibbs who have made considerable contributions to London.

Long before his first appearance in London in 1904, Burnet had become the most celebrated Scottish architect of his time. Burnet was the youngest son of the elder John Burnet, who had built up one of the largest Glasgow architectural practices during the long boom growth of that city. The younger Burnet had a good education at the Western Academy and elsewhere, worked in his father's office for two years and then, apparently at the suggestion of R. Phené Spiers, went to study at the *Ecole des Beaux Arts* in Paris from 1874 until 1877. His parents were worried about the effect which Paris, with its alarmingly permissive reputation, might have on their son. But Burnet's character throughout his life was of simple virtue and directness. He was teased for his presbyterian rectitude by his fellow students in the notable *atelier* of Jean-Louis Pascal and his complexion earned the nickname of *"Confiture de Groseilles"*. After distinguishing himself during these years, Burnet returned to his father's firm in Glasgow and soon took over most of the design work. David Walker has pointed out that the disciplined *Beaux Arts* approach to planning and the logical development of designs stayed with him all his life, but the French Classical influence on his detailing was soon dropped in favour of a wide variety of styles which he used with distinction over the years.

By 1900, Burnet had by far the best-known and largest practice in Scotland—baronial houses, Gothic churches, Renaissance flats, Classical institutions and Baroque business premises by him can be seen all over the country and especially in Glasgow and Edinburgh. His office was the goal of most architectural students, for in effect it was as much a teaching centre as a firm. In 1904 the British Museum decided to extend its premises and, after inspecting the work of a dozen architects suggested by the RIBA, they commissioned Burnet.

Burnet's **King Edward VII Galleries** (1904–14) form the northern side of the British Museum in Montague Place, Bloomsbury. The plan is of great simplicity, with a central entrance and staircase. The fine exterior, with its great screen of Ionic columns, is *Néo-Grèc* rather than Neo-Greek; for here the Parisian influence is more apparent than in most of

Burnet's work. The interiors are detailed in a cool *Néo-Grèc* style too, but some of Burnet's best rooms have already been destroyed.

Cool distinction was to be an increasingly important feature in Burnet's work, but his next London building was the end of a series in his previous individualistic Baroque manner. This Baroque design was for **General Buildings**, built for the General Accident assurance company in the Aldwych, Strand in 1909–11. The plan has *Beaux Arts* clarity on a difficult site, but the powerful façade composition, with much sculpture, is in the succession of Burnet's Athenaeum Theatre and major department stores in Glasgow and Edinburgh. On these buildings, the rear elevations often have the simplified detail which was later to appear on his main façades.

In 1905, Burnet had opened a Scottish-staffed office in London in which Thomas Tait (1882–1954) played a growing part and ultimately became a partner. Burnet divided his time between London and Glasgow. His private life was uneven for he, a smallish man, had married a six-feet-tall hypochondriac beauty. They had no children but brought up those of Burnet's dead brother George.

175 *Burnet. The King Edward VII Galleries, British Museum, Montague Place, Bloomsbury (1904–14). Simplified Classicism evolving towards modernism*

Burnet's method of working (in both offices) was to work up the plan of each building himself and then, in many cases, to hand over plan and a sketch design for the exterior to his senior staff to be worked up. In cases such as General Buildings, it is known that he designed the details of exterior and interior himself. In his next London work, the story is more complicated.

The **Kodak Building** in Kingsway (1910–11) is certainly the most startling of the office ranges built after this new street was cut through old slums at the start of the century. It is striking for its simplicity and has been hailed as a precursor of modernism. In fact, it is an Edwardian Neo-Classical design stripped of almost all ornament and has a distinguished *Beaux Arts* axial plan. That is not to deny that it is a pioneering work, but it emphasizes the evolving nature of the growth of British modern design.

The story of the design appears to be that Burnet (after making a study tour in America in preparation for this project) worked out the plans and sketch elevations, which he then gave to Tait for detailing.

176

Tait produced drawings which showed none of the usual decoration and, despite Burnet's doubts about this, the client liked the simplicity. The building still looks modern—the exterior was carefully renovated when it passed into the hands of Messrs Gallaher, its present owners.

Despite his knighthood in 1914 and the commission for the quiet Neo-Georgian **Royal Institute of Chemistry** in Russell Square, Bloomsbury (1914–15), Burnet's practice suffered severely during the building slump caused by the First World War. He had to cut staff and was even forced to sell many of his personal possessions.

After the war, he was appointed one of the architects to the War Graves Commission and was commissioned by Gordon Selfridge to supervise the completion of the massive **Selfridge's Department Store** (1907–28) in Oxford Street. The façades were designed by a young Paris-trained American called Francis Swales, with Daniel Burnham of Chicago and his London representative Albert D. Miller

acting as consultants and designers of the internal steel frame.

Burnet's own design practice gained its first post-war London job with the commission for the large block called **Westmorland House and Vigo House** (1920–25), immediately north of the curving quadrant in Regent Street. It is a design of great strength and distinction, done in a Stripped Neo-Classical manner.

The **Second Church of Christ Scientist**, in Palace Gardens Terrace, Notting Hill, Kensington, dates from 1921. It is a large brick building with an airy space for the interior of the church itself. The style mixes 1920s detailing with references to Byzantine and early Romanesque work.

The last major work in which Burnet's development of simplicity can be seen was the gigantic **Adelaide House** office block at the side of the northern end of London Bridge. Built in 1921–25, numerous favourite themes of Burnet can be seen in modern dress in the building. The most obvious of

these are the increasing shedding of decoration and liking for a strong grid pattern, while the powerful doorways, firm skyline and contrasting vertical corner emphasis are as evident as ever.

From 1920 onwards the firm was called Sir John Burnet and Partners, in recognition of the part taken by Thomas Tait and others. Tait contributed much to the design of the three buildings mentioned above, and after the large Classical **Lloyds Bank** headquarters in Cornhill and Lombard Street, City (1927–30) he took over almost all the firm's design work from Burnet, who was now aged seventy. The final design by Burnet himself was a personal commission for the big **Unilever House** on the embankment of the Thames overlooking Blackfriars Bridge. Carried out in 1930–32 in co-operation with J. Lomax-Simpson, the building is a dramatic Baroque piece of city sculpture on a large scale, but the detail (for which he turned to Tait for some assistance) lacks the punch of his earlier work.

Burnet did not officially retire from practice until 1935, when he moved from his Surrey house to one in Edinburgh. There he and his wife lived for his last three years, contented enough despite the painful skin disease which bothered him and the fact that—as one contemporary put it—in retirement he had "no recreation—nothing of interest for him to turn to, no hobbies of any kind."

77

176 *Burnet with Thomas Tait. Kodak House, Kingsway (1901–11)*

177 *Burnet with Tait. Westmorland House, Regent Street (1920–25)*

178 *Burnet with Tait. Adelaide House, London Bridge, City (1921–25). In the background, Seifert's National Westminster tower, now the tallest in London*

78

Charles Holden (1875-1960)

Charles Holden, portrait

If Lutyens was the late full flower of a development from Edwardian Baroque, Charles Holden was the success story at the end of the efforts in the 1890s and 1900s by Arts and Crafts architects and others to develop a modern Free Style for British public architecture. Heaven knows what Lethaby, Henry Wilson, Harrison Townsend, C. R. Ashbee, Charles Rennie Mackintosh and Voysey thought of Holden's 1920s buildings; but it was his designs, not those of the Bauhaus and Corbusian apostles of the 1930s, which were the outcome of their long struggles.

Holden was born in Bolton, Lancashire, and educated at Manchester Technical School and at Manchester School of Art. He was articled to the Manchester architect E. W. Leeson and later worked for Jonathan Simpson in Bolton. In 1898 he entered the Royal Academy School of Architecture and worked for the great Arts and Crafts designer and architect, C. R. Ashbee, for a year. He then joined the staff of the successful hospital architect, H. Percy Adams, and soon took over most of the design work. He became a partner in 1907, and from 1912 onwards almost all his work was done under the firm's name of Adams, Holden and Pearson.

His first executed design was for the **Belgrave Hospital for Children**, Clapham Road, near Kennington Oval in south London (1900–03). The building, with its austere buttressed masses piling up to high gables and its name cut out in huge stone lettering across the frontage, is still astonishing in its power. At this time, Holden later said, he especially admired Henry Wilson (architect of the public library in Ladbroke Grove of 1891, and of St. Peter's Church, Mount Park Road, Ealing of 1892), and both Wilson's and Ashbee's influence can be seen in his work.

By 1903 many architects of Arts and Crafts principles were concluding that it was not ideologically necessary to exclude all Classical detailing from their buildings since, especially in urban architecture, the nearest thing to a local vernacular style was often a free Classicism. In this respect, Holden's **library block** addition for the Law Society in Chancery Lane, Holborn (1903–04) was a breakthrough—the frontages are elegantly Classical, with touches of Michelangelo's Mannerism, but the power of the piled-up blocks is as impressive as in Holden's earlier hospital. Belcher's partner, J. J. Joass, took up his own version of this theme in a number of buildings.

A similar massive approach to the composition of London buildings, using Classical detailing in a revolutionary way, can be seen in Holden's **Norwich House** at No. 127 High Holborn (1904), in **Rhodesia House** at No. 429 Strand (1907–08) and

179

180

179 *Holden. Belgrave Hospital for Children, Clapham Road, near Kennington Oval, south London (1900–03). An Arts and Crafts design in the tradition of Henry Wilson and C. R. Ashbee*

180 *Holden. Rhodesia House (built for the British Medical Association), Strand and Agar Street, Charing Cross (1907–8)*

in **Evelyn House** at No. 62 Oxford Street (1908–10). Of these, No. 429 Strand is much the most impressive in the mounting forms of its generally Classical elements and much the most important historically. Originally built for the British Medical Association, the eroded remains can still be seen on its walls of the sculpture by Holden's friend Jacob Epstein whose naked realism caused an uproar when the building was opened.

In 1914 Holden built the large **Queen Mary's Hostel** for women students of King's College (University of London) in Duchess of Bedford Walk, Notting Hill. It is a disappointing design, rather dull in its slightly eccentric Neo-Georgian brick elevations. This was Holden's last building

181

before the 1914–18 war. In the previous year he had married Margaret Macdonald, a Quaker widow ten years older than himself. They had no children but seem to have been happy with each other. Holden was an unusual enough man in several ways for a successful London architect, with his small piercing eyes and ginger beard, his Lancashire accent and his height only about five feet four inches. He had strong egalitarian and almost ascetic principles of living; William Gutteridge, later his partner, remembers visiting him at home in a house without a bright colour anywhere and eating puritanically healthy food.

Holden served as a Lieutenant in the Royal Engineers during the war and afterwards was appointed one of the four architects to the Imperial War Graves Commission. In 1923 he started a long collaboration with Frank Pick, later chief executive officer of the London Passenger Transport Board. Together they revolutionized the design style of London Transport, and only a few notable examples of Holden's numerous **stations** will be mentioned here. In 1925 the **Northern Line** of the Underground Railway was being extended to Hendon Central, Burnt Oak, Colindale and Edgware, and Charles Holden designed the new stations. A year later he was at work on a particularly remarkable series for the southward extension of the Northern Line to Clapham, Balham, Tooting, Colliers Wood, South Wimbledon and Morden, whose keynote was a stone frontage with twin Greek Doric columns at the corners of a large three-angled window over the entrance. **Piccadilly Circus**, a large design beneath the ground, dates from 1925–28. Even more extraordinary and advanced are the 1930–34 **Piccadilly Line stations** (designed after a visit to Holland and Hamburg with Frank Pick) on the extensions out to Cockfosters in north-east London and towards Ealing and Osterley in the west. Many of them have brickwork and glass drum or cubical superstruc-

181 *Holden. Broadway House, London Transport headquarters offices, No. 55 Broadway, over St. James's Park underground station, Westminster (1927–29)*

182 *Holden. The Senate House, London University, Malet Street, Bloomsbury (designed 1931, built in stages from 1932 onwards)*

183 *Holden. Arnos Grove underground railway station, Piccadilly Line, north-east London (1930–32). A good example of Holden's many remarkable tube stations*

182

183

tures. Arnos Grove (1930) is a particularly striking example. The later Piccadilly Line extension stations out to Uxbridge, done in 1935–38, are slightly less impressive.

Meanwhile, Holden was responsible for the design of two major buildings in central London, as well as many hospitals and other works elsewhere. The London Transport headquarters building, **Broadway House**, over St. James's Park underground station in Broadway, Westminster, dates from 1927–29. It is the apotheosis on a large scale of Holden's approach to architecture. The block is well broken up to allow optimum daylighting; the style is stripped of all historical references, yet is clearly developed from old traditions. The masses mount in steps and stages towards the high tower, expressing power and strength. The sculpture expresses these qualities, too; again it is by Epstein but here the stone was better adapted to resist erosion than it was in the earlier Rhodesia House. Holden found the site difficult, and in a 1929 lecture to the RIBA he told how the crossing axes of the plan emerged: "I remember the thrill of those crossed lines . . . a plan which could almost be said to design itself externally."

Holden's other major project, the **Senate House** and surrounding buildings of London University in Malet Street, Bloomsbury, was designed in 1931 and built over many years from 1932 onwards. Here the central block is even more huge than in Broadway House, with the same motif of stepped rising masses, with huge buttresses accentuating the upward surge of the big volumes. It has not proved a well-loved building as far as the public are concerned, but it will doubtless come to be well respected, for it is scrupulous in its integrity.

In 1936 Holden received the Royal Gold Medal of the RIBA, but he refused an offered knighthood on the grounds that it would cut him off from ordinary people. Since he lived an insulated and almost obsessively private life, it is hard to see how this could be so, but the reason fits in with his general outlook. In his office, Holden was almost worshipped as the staff's resident genius. And little wonder, as the designs flowed off his drawing board, spreading from buildings to underground trains, London buses and even the standard London telephone booth of his time.

Holden lived on until 1960 and worked until his death. In the post-World War II atmosphere he became something of a symbol of reactionary design to the young modern architects. Certainly his later buildings seem to lack the conviction of his work before 1939, but perhaps that judgement too will change with time.

Tecton and Berthold Lubetkin (born 1901)

Berthold Lubetkin, portrait

During the early 1930s a trickle of talented architects and designers arrived in London, usually as refugees from the spreading blight of Nazism in Hitler's Germany. The refugees included Walter Gropius and Ludwig Mies van der Rohe, both of whom had been in charge of the famous Bauhaus at Weimar and then at Dessau, where the design principles of the International Modern Style of architecture were largely born. Gropius and Mies went on to work in America and to become, with Frank Lloyd Wright and Le Corbusier, the acknowledged masters of the Modern Movement. But other refugees stayed to practise in London. Among these, Erno Goldfinger (later architect of the Department of Health complex at the Elephant and Castle) and Berthold Lubetkin were particularly important. And Lubetkin designed many of the 1930s buildings which brought public attention to the Modern Movement.

Lubetkin was born in the Caucasus in Russia in 1901. He was trained as an architect in Moscow and then there followed some wandering years in which he spent periods in Warsaw and Vienna. He settled for a time in Paris where he studied at the *Ecole des Beaux Arts* and worked for Auguste Perret, a pioneer of modern concrete structure. In his own practice, Lubetkin built an apartment block at No. 25 Avenue de Versailles, Paris in 1927.

A serious and intellectual man of strong left-wing political ideals, he moved to London in 1930 and, following the Bauhaus idea of design groups, founded a team called Tecton. Apart from himself, the Tecton architects included Anthony Chitty, Lindsey Drake, Michael Dugdale, Val Harding and, a little later, Denys Lasdun.

The first major Tecton building in London was the large block of flats called **Highpoint One**, in North Hill, Highgate. The commission was obtained by Lubetkin himself, and it was built in 1933–35. All the trademarks of the International Modern movement are already present. Based on a cross-plan, the building is of eight storeys, the ground floor largely void with round pillars supporting the block above and visually "floating" it. The walls are white-painted concrete, the windows run in horizontal bands with cantilevered balconies. The forms are clean and light, and in accordance with the principles of the new architecture of the time, they largely reflect the structure within. The manner is very similar to that of Le Corbusier's Maison Stein of 1929 and Maison Suisse of 1930.

184 *Lubetkin and Tecton. Highpoint One (1933–35, left) and Highpoint Two (1937–38), North Hill, Highgate*

185 *Lubetkin, and Tecton. Living room in Highpoint One*

84

85

186

187

186 *Lubetkin, Drake and Tecton. The Penguin Pool, London Zoo, Regent's Park, (1935)*

187 *Lubetkin and Tecton. Finsbury Health Centre, Pine Street, off Rosebery Avenue, Finsbury (1938–39)*

In 1934 Tecton was commissioned by Sir Julian Huxley, director of the Royal Zoological Society, to design a new **Gorilla House** for the London Zoo. The small building they produced is between the Outer Circle and the canal, a round drum, half steel caging and half white concrete, with part of the concrete section continued upwards to form a sloping roof and a large clerestorey window to light the indoors part of the house.

Tecton went on to build the **North Entrance** building of the Zoo, with its wavy canopy of light reinforced concrete, and most notably the **Penguin Pool** (1935) on the park side of the gardens. As with the Gorilla House, the Penguins' enclosure is a basically simple geometrical shape treated with elegance and ingenuity. It is formed by a low wall of varying height, oval in plan, most of the wall a comfortable height for leaning and looking. Inside, the penguins have an oval pool with a low surround and two cantilevered interlocking spirals of reinforced concrete curving from higher platforms down into the water. The Penguin Pool remains one of the most popular places in the Zoo today, but its historical importance is that the publicity resulting from its immediate success brought the new style favourably to the attention of the public. Lubetkin and Drake were the Tecton members with particular responsibility for this project and they added a **Studio of Animal Art** in 1938.

The year 1935 saw two other commissions for Tecton members. The terrace of **four houses** at Nos. 85–91 Genesta Road, off Plum Lane, Plumstead (part of Woolwich in south-east London) is a typical Lubetkin design of the time, curvy balconies and all (he collaborated with Pilichowski on this project). The house called **Six Pillars** in Crescent Wood Road, Dulwich is attributed to Val Harding and Tecton and is even more interesting; two storeys of simple form with a high roof terrace above and an eccentric wing at one side.

In 1936 Tecton obtained its first commercial commission, for the original part of the Gestetner duplicator factory in Fawley Road, Tottenham. The factory has now spread immensely along that section of Fawley Road, and the 1936 frontage was finally re-built in 1978.

Another Tecton block of flats, **Highpoint Two**, was built beside Highpoint One in North Hill, Highgate in 1937–38. It shows some marked changes from the earlier block, being simpler in plan and less Corbusian in appearance. The entrance porch has a Lubetkin joke in the form of Caryatids which support the canopy. Both frontages are dominated by large central panels which project slightly. Within these panels, the lay-out of the individual apartments

can be clearly seen on the garden side, with sections of double height alternating horizontally with sections of two single-height floors. One of the members of the team, Denys Lasdun, used a similar approach and expression in a famous block of flats in St. James's designed twenty years later.

Tecton's last London job before the outbreak of the Second World War was one of its largest and most successful. This was the design of the **Finsbury Health Centre** in Pine Street, off Rosebery Avenue in a slum part of Finsbury (1938–39). At that time, health centres were themselves a pioneering concept, and Lubetkin and Tecton produced a shining white symbol which still functions well today. The two-storey building is on an H-plan, its white walls and band windows containing a complex of clinics, offices and lecture rooms. Its whole frontage is angled to lean forward as if to greet the public.

By the time war came in 1939, Tecton—and a few other architects such as Maxwell Fry, Goldfinger, Wells Coates and the partnership of Connell, Ward and Lucas—had built a respectable number of buildings in the new manner. After the war the flood of success came for the International Modern movement everywhere, with the huge re-building of the world's cities in the 1950s and 1960s. But for Lubetkin the new architecture was only a symbol of the new political order that was his justification for his work. Tecton survived for a time, but the participants in the team left and in about 1955 it turned into Skinner, Bailey and Lubetkin. And Lubetkin himself became more and more disenchanted with the events of post-war politics and society in Britain.

The **Priory Green Estate** of Council flats in Collier Street, just off the Pentonville Road near King's Cross was completed in 1951 to designs by Lubetkin and Tecton, then extended in 1958 by Skinner, Bailey and Lubetkin. The **Spa Green Estate** beside Rosebery Avenue, Finsbury dates from 1948–50, and the flats called **Bevin Court** in Holford Place off the Pentonville Road from 1953. In all these, the touch of Lubetkin and the echo of Highpoint Two can be seen. But with the long period of Conservative rule and the evidence that modern design does not produce harmony and progress among its users, Lubetkin lost impetus and finally withdrew from life in London. He now lives quietly in the west of England, doing occasional architectural commissions locally.

E.Maxwell Fry
(born 1899)

Maxwell Fry, portrait

If Lubetkin represents the continental architects who brought the ideas of Le Corbusier and the Bauhaus to England, Maxwell Fry personifies the small group of young English designers who first looked to Europe for a solution to the need for a style which expressed modern building structure and put it into practice in the 1930s. Moreover, for a short period he practised in partnership with one of the fathers of the movement, Walter Gropius, founder of the Bauhaus.

Fry was born in Wallasey, Cheshire. His father was a businessman, his mother a painter. He was educated at the Liverpool Institute in Mount Street and joined the King's Liverpool Regiment in 1917, by which time he was already determined to become an architect. In 1919 he entered the School of Architecture, Liverpool University, against his father's wishes, where C. H. Reilly was Professor of Architecture and Patrick Abercrombie Professor of Civic Design (Town Planning). He received a Classical training. Through Reilly, Fry spent a year in 1922 working for Carrere and Hastings in New York (he had never heard of Frank Lloyd Wright at this time) and through Stanley Adshead—Abercrombie's predecessor—got a job with the town planning firm of Adams and Thompson in London.

Fry tells how he watched C. H. Reilly's designs for Devonshire House in Piccadilly being erected in 1924 and became sure that there must be a more valid exterior to the steel frame than the Neo-Classical stone covering put on that building. He found the Swedish romantic style and Dudok unconvincing, but in 1925 became friends with Wells Coates (later architect of the fine Isokon Flats in Lawn Road, Hampstead of 1933–34, and the flats at No. 10 Palace Gate, Kensington of 1938–39). They became the centre of a group of young designers which also included Jack Pritchard, director of the plywood manufacturers Venesta Ltd., who became a staunch patron. During the 1920s Fry built several simplified Neo-Georgian commissions, the last of them a house called **Ridge End** in Portnall Drive, Wentworth, Virginia Water (1930–31). In 1930 he joined the Design and Industries Association and in 1931 was one of the founders of the MARS (Modern Architectural Research) Group, whose membership included many later notable names, *e.g.* Casson, Gibberd, Gropius, Holford, Lubetkin, Martin, Summerson, Tubbs and Yorke. Both these organizations did much to forward the cause of the new architecture, and Fry's work, enthusiasm and irrepressible good humour contributed a great deal.

In 1932–33 Fry, working with Elizabeth Denby, built his first work in the modern style, the successful block of flats called **Sassoon House** (associated with Sir Owen Williams' neighbouring Pioneer Health Centre), on the corner of Belfort Road and St. Mary's Road in Peckham, south London.

Three houses followed in 1935; **No. 21 Queensmere Road** in Wimbledon, **Miramonte** in Warren Rise, Kingston, and one of Fry's best-known works, **Sun House** in Frognal Way, off Frognal in Hampstead. Sun House stands on a slope, slender pilotis supporting the front of its upper two storeys, whose horizontal band windows have now been slightly altered. Both ends of this simple quadrangular block are given interest by projecting cantilevered balconies and canopies.

A more ambitious work was built in 1936. This is **Kensal House**, a curving H-plan estate of flats consisting of three blocks of different heights with a nursery school and other amenities on the site. The

188 *Fry. Sassoon House flats, corner of Belfort Road and St. Mary's Road, Peckham, south London (1932–33)*

189 *Fry. Sun House, Frognal Way, off Frognal, Hampstead (1935)*

190 *Fry with Elizabeth Denby, Grey Wornum, C. H. James and Robert Atkinson. Kensal House estate, Ladbroke Grove North Kensington (1936–38)*

buildings stand beside the railway towards the north end of Ladbroke Grove, North Kensington and, despite some years of dilapidation, they still look remarkable after recent repainting. The blocks of flats are of reinforced concrete, the low nursery school behind has a steel frame structure. Fry worked here with a design team consisting of himself, Elizabeth Denby, Grey Wornum (architect of the RIBA building in Portland Place), C. H. James and Robert Atkinson—a remarkable mixture of young and old.

In 1935 Walter Gropius left Nazi Germany and came to live in one of Wells Coates' Hampstead co-operative flats. Fry and Gropius entered a partnership together which produced two major works, a well-known school at Impington outside Cambridge and a house for the farce playwright Benn Levy, at **No. 66 Old Church Street**, Chelsea (1936).

Gropius moved on to America in 1938 and Fry continued work by himself. **The Cecil Residential Club** at No. 95 Gower Street, Euston (1937) is a crisp compact block. Fry's block of flats at **No. 65 Ladbroke Grove**, North Kensington (1938) has been less noticed than it deserves, for the use of brick

as the basic material in this well articulated design makes it less visually striking than the earlier white buildings. But this was the start of Fry's lasting preference for the texture and fittingness of brick in the London climate.

After the outbreak of war, Fry joined the Royal Engineers as a Major. In 1941 his unsuccessful marriage of eleven years was dissolved and in the following year he married Jane Drew, a young architect who later became his partner. He was posted to West Africa as a town planning adviser in 1943, and went into practice there with Jane Drew and later Denys Lasdun and Lindsey Drake. In 1951 he and Jane Drew invited Le Corbusier to join them in designing buildings for the new Punjab capital, Chandigarh, where they worked for several years.

Since then Fry, Drew and Partners have designed buildings in many countries. Their post-war London work includes the **Passfields Estate**, Danewood Avenue, Catford in south London (1950), the **entrance gates** of the Festival of Britain exhibition in 1951, the **Wates building firm's headquarters** in London Road, Thornton Heath, north of Croydon (1960), the flats called **Chelwood House** in Gloucester Square, Bayswater (1968), and the **Woodsford Square** houses and flats, Addison Road, Holland Park (1968–70). Fry was awarded the Royal Gold medal of the RIBA in 1964.

Sir Denys Lasdun (born 1914)

Sir Denys Lasdun, portrait

The International Modern style of architecture has had many variations and sub-movements since it was introduced to England in the 1930s: Festival of Britain frivolity, concrete Brutalism, the brick impact architecture of James Stirling and James Gowan, the plastic fantasies of the 1960s. But the direct legacy of Le Corbusier *via* Lubetkin in England has been transformed by a series of buildings adapting it to British ways by a few men. The most eminent of these is Denys Lasdun.

Lasdun was born and brought up in London. He was educated at Rugby School and at the Architectural Association. While Lasdun acknowledges his debt to the technological innovations of the pioneers of the Modern Movement, he has always rejected their Utopian visions of the city, disliking their lack of continuity with historical surroundings. His often-stated concern for context and detail in buildings has led him to a technique of design which makes extensive use of models rather than drawings.

After leaving the Architectural Association, Lasdun worked with Wells Coates in 1935–37 and joined the Tecton team, led by Lubetkin in 1937. Together with Le Corbusier and Frank Lloyd Wright they provided a formative influence on his early career.

The house at **32 Newton Road**, Paddington (1937–38) is his earliest individual work. Built for a painter, it is a clean rectangular block. The ground floor is recessed a little, the two storeys above have horizontal band windows and the uppermost level of the block is pierced by a large recessed balcony. The concrete is faced in dark brown tiles. The influence of the tradition of Le Corbusier's "five points in architecture" can be traced in the design.

Lasdun's character is outwardly of kindness and quiet charm, but beneath this lie obsessive qualities, passion and concentrated energy. A Canadian architect who worked for Maxwell Fry recalls a short period when Fry was in Chandigarh and Lasdun looked after the Fry Drew office—the Canadian watched him at work with awe, for he says that he never knew anyone give such unremitting intensity to design work from beginning to end of the day.

After the war Lasdun rejoined Tecton and remained there until the firm's dissolution in 1948. During that time the immense **Hallfield Housing Estate**, Bishop's Bridge Road, Paddington (1951–59) was initiated. It was subsequently developed and executed in partnership with Lindsey Drake. This project, of fifteen large blocks and some smaller ones on a flat but well-treed site, is still recognisably in the Tecton manner with echoes of High Point Two and details such as curved concrete balconies. The blocks are varied in design and one can see in it an attempt to realise Le Corbusier's city in a park. But the sheer size of the complex is somewhat overbearing.

Behind the estate in Porchester Terrace, however, is a gem—the **Hallfield Primary School** (1951–54). Here can be seen Lasdun's growing interest in a more organic architecture, all detailed on the right scale for small children, the low arms of the building curving out into gardens. The work started the growth of Lasdun's reputation and marks the beginning of a departure from the influence of his predecessors.

In independent practice he designed two more housing projects which caused something of a sensation. The first was the housing **Cluster Block** in Usk Street off Roman Road, at Bethnal Green in the East End of London (1952–55). Eight storeys high, the design provides four towers of maisonettes set at different angles to each other, each maisonette connected by a bridge to a central tower of lifts and staircase. Not far away, Lasdun built a second Cluster Block of fifteen storeys (1955–58). This block is called **Keeling House**, in Claredale Street off Cambridge Heath Road, Bethnal Green. Part of Lasdun's idea was to provide independent houses in the sky, each with its own front door and each with a kitchen balcony at the rear from which people could see and talk to their neighbours. These remarkable buildings certainly provide a visual contrast with the miles and miles of rather characterless housing development in the East End. Both blocks have much quieter low horizontal blocks of brick and

191 *Lasdun. Keeling House cluster block housing, Claredale Street, off Cambridge Heath Road, Bethnal Green, east London (1955–58)*

192 *Lasdun with Drake. Hallfield Junior and Infants School, Porchester Terrace, Paddington (1951–54). The school was built at the same time as the large neighbouring Hallfield Estate of flats (1951–59, by Lasdun and Drake with Tecton)*

193 *Lasdun. Royal College of Physicians, Outer Circle, Regent's Park (1960–64)*

concrete by Lasdun near them.

In 1958 Lasdun designed two very different buildings in central London. The **Peter Robinson department store** at 65 Strand (now offices of the Government of New South Wales), near Charing Cross Station, is a distinguished piece of street architecture with a long horizontal window at ground level, a band of stone with clerestorey lighting and then three bands of bronze-framed office windows above. His famous block of flats overlooking Green Park, at **26 St. James's Place** (1958–60) expresses the idea of split-level apartments—used earlier in Tecton's pre-war Highpoint Two and by Wells Coates on his Palace Gate flats (on which Lasdun had worked as a young assistant)—in a finely articulated building which still remains respectful to its neighbouring Classical mansion. (See plate 47.)

In 1960 the firm of Denys Lasdun and Partners was founded with Alexander Redhouse and Peter Softley. One of Lasdun's most successful and elegant designs dates from this time. This is the **Royal College of Physicians** in St. Andrew's Place on the outer circle of Regent's Park (1960–64). The plan is a T with some projections from it. The rear part is offices, the downstroke of the T coming forward towards Regent's Park and containing members' functional and ceremonial parts and the library. The low lecture room projects to one side—it is of a subtle curving design in dark brick, unlike the light concrete and mosaic finishes of the rest of the long building. (The brick parts have a special significance for Lasdun who said in a 1965 RIBA lecture that they "can be altered, adapted, extended, through a century of occupation.") The main mosaic-covered concrete levels, with slit windows, project over each other with three slender piers supporting the overhang above the main entrance. The library is in the upper part of this end. Beyond it, the interior of the building opens up into the complexities of the big staircase hall, one of the finest modern interiors in Britain and presaging the form and atmosphere of the National Theatre foyers. Above the building rise the twin service towers of concrete and, beyond the lecture hall, another projection at ground level contains the seventeenth-century panelling of the Censor's Room from the College's previous premises.

Lasdun's major projects include buildings elsewhere in Britain, notably the new University of East Anglia in Norwich. Due for completion in 1980 is the new Luxembourg headquarters building for the EEC's European Investment Bank.

In London, his **Wartski shopfront** in Regent Street dates from 1962, as does his exciting but unbuilt design for the Royal Institution of Chartered Surveyors in Parliament Square. In 1965 he was

194

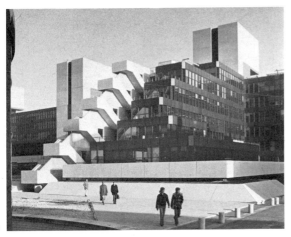

194 *Lasdun. The National Theatre, South Bank, beside Waterloo Bridge (designed 1967, built 1969–76)*

195 *Lasdun. Interior of the foyer, the National Theatre (1969–76)*

196 *Lasdun. Institute of Education and Law building, London University, Russell Square and Bedford Way, Bloomsbury (designed 1965, built 1973–78 but still incomplete)*

given the commission of the decade in London: the new **National Theatre** and Opera House on the South Bank of the Thames. The site was to be south of the Royal Festival Hall, and Lasdun produced an imaginative design with tiers of long terraces rising to the two flytowers. In 1967 the idea of the Opera House was abandoned and the site changed to the one alongside Waterloo Bridge. Lasdun had to start again.

The National Theatre, as designed in 1967 and built in 1969–76, is a happy addition to the cultural life of London and a highly distinguished building well blended with its riverside site. The form is a varied series of long horizontal terraces mounting like a hillside on the river frontage to the two high flytowers above, though the rear elevation presents a rather harsh face. The terraces penetrate to the interior too, where rich spaces for people to wander during the intervals flow around the auditoria of three theatres of different types and sizes. The architecture rejects vertical façades and uses levels of building like geological strata connected in such a way that they flow into the surrounding riverscape and city. The building is thus intended as an extension of the spaces of the theatre into the everyday world. After its completion Lasdun was knighted and was awarded the 1977 RIBA Royal Gold Medal for Architecture.

1965 was also the year of design of a large redevelopment project for London University on the site of Woburn Square, Bloomsbury. Of this project, the new building for the **School of Oriental and African Studies** (1972–74) and the highly imaginative **Institutes of Education and of Law**, backing onto Bedford Way (1973–76), have been completed. The latter building is designed to have five cascading terraced arms extending towards the eight-storey block of the SOAS building and is soon to be joined by a new building for the **Courtauld Institute** which will complete at least part of the conception of a precinct. To date only one of the arms has been built. Under the open space beside it lies a large auditorium of unusual structural design. The completion of the whole development lies far into the future. But then Lasdun projects have a way of taking many years to reach completion. Indeed, at the time of writing, Lasdun's ideas of architecture as urban landscape, embodied in the National Theatre and Opera House scheme, has again been presented with a challenge, this time of placing a new headquarters building on the river front adjacent to the National Theatre. These two buildings taken together will be on the scale of Somerset House opposite, providing an intriguing comparison between public buildings of the 1770s and of the 1970s.

Some London Architects and Buildings since 1945

So great has been the number of new buildings in London since the end of the Second World War that it is only possible to mention a few especially notable buildings and their architects. Lasdun has been given an individual chapter for the number of his major buildings in central London as much as for their high qualities. One other architect's firm, Richard Seifert's, has contributed even more large buildings to London's appearance today and he will end this chapter. Meanwhile there are some other designers, among many, who must be mentioned.

After the war Sir Robert Matthew (1906–75) was appointed Architect to the London County Council, a post in which he was assisted and later succeeded by Sir Leslie Martin (b. 1908). Under them the Department's architects produced acre upon acre of new housing to replace bombed areas and slums. The Lansbury Neighbourhood, off Commercial Road, Poplar of 1950 onwards, is a fair example. Another housing estate, Alton East and Alton West, Bessborough Road, Roehampton (1954–61) was acclaimed as a realization of Le Corbusier's dream of a town of high blocks among open parkland. The Festival of Britain in 1951 celebrated the emergence of the country from the war and the centenary of the Prince Consort's Great Exhibition. Among the numerous temporary but spectacular buildings by leading architects erected for the Festival on the South Bank of the Thames, the Royal Festival Hall was intended to remain. Built in 1948–51, the design of the concert hall was done under the supervision of Matthew and Martin, assisted by Peter Moro, Edwin Williams and others. The river frontage was extended by other L.C.C. architects in 1964.

Both Matthew and Martin went on into successful private practice, and Robert Matthew, Johnson-Marshall and Partners designed New Zealand House, Haymarket and Pall Mall (1960–63) and the Commonwealth Institute, Holland Park (1960–62), as well as the Hillingdon Civic Centre (1973–78). Of the same generation, Sir Frederick Gibberd (b. 1908) was the architect of the London Airport buildings at Heathrow (1950 onwards) and of the new Mosque in Regent's Park (1973–77). Sir Basil Spence (1907–76) spread his big practice to central London comparatively late—his works include the Public Library and Swimming Pools at Swiss Cottage, Hampstead (1963–64), the thuggish Knightsbridge Barracks, Hyde Park, Kensington (1967–69) and the new Kensington and Chelsea Town Hall, Hornton Street, off Kensington High Street (planned 1967, built 1970–77). Ernö Goldfinger (b. 1902) has built much in London in his very individualistic manner, including the Department of Health and Social Services headquarters, the Alex-

197 *Interior, Royal Festival Hall, South Bank, Waterloo (1948–51) by the London County Council Architect's Department under Sir Robert Matthew, Sir Leslie Martin, Peter Moro, Edwin Williams and others. Extended by other architects in the department in 1964*

ander Fleming House complex at the Elephant and Castle, Southwark (1960–67), as well as the large tower block flats at Rowlett Street, Poplar (1965–67) and Trellick Tower, Edenham Street, Paddington (1968–73). H. T. Cadbury-Brown (*b.* 1913) designed the Royal College of Art in Kensington Gore (1961–65, with interiors by Sir Hugh Casson, former architectural director of the Festival of Britain and designer of the Zoo's notable Elephant House). David Aberdeen (*b.* 1913) built Congress House (T.U.C.) at Nos. 23–28 Great Russell Street, Bloomsbury (1948–57) and the Swiss Centre building in Leicester Square (1964–68). Sir Eric Lyons (*b.* 1912) designed many pleasing housing estates in Blackheath, Twickenham and other suburbs before the immense World's End Estate of tower blocks and low-rise flats on the King's Road, Chelsea (designed *c.* 1962, built 1970–77). Robert Maguire built a number of notable churches such as St. Paul's, Burdett Road, Stepney (1958–60).

Of the next generation of architects, Powell and Moya (Philip Powell *b.* 1921 and John Hidalgo Moya *b.* 1920) won a much publicized competition in 1946 with the notable design for the Churchill Gardens housing estate in Grosvenor Road and Lupus Street, Pimlico (built 1950–62). Their later

London work includes the London Museum, on the corner of the London Wall Extension and Aldersgate, City (designed 1966–68, built 1973–76). No British architects have had more ideological influence on post-war architecture than Peter and Alison Smithson (*b.* 1923 and 1928). Their few buildings include the Economist Building group of three blocks in St. James's Street (1960–64) and the Robin Hood Gardens ranges of flats, East India Dock Road, Poplar in the East End (1967–72). Another major post-war influence on British architecture, but by example rather than words, is James Stirling (*b.* 1926)—his major works are in other parts of Britain but comparatively quiet works in London include the Langham Close flats in Ham Street, south Richmond (1958), the Children's Home at Nos. 11–12 Frogmore, off Putney Bridge Road, Wandsworth (1963) and the flats at No. 37 Gloucester Avenue, Chalk Farm (1967).

Some other notable major schemes and their

99

architects must be mentioned. Chamberlin, Powell and Bon designed the Bousfield Primary School, The Boltons, Kensington (1955), the Golden Lane housing estate off Old Street, Finsbury (1955–63) and the immense Barbican area scheme, north of the London Wall extension, City of London (1957–79) with housing for 6,000 people, a school and an arts centre around an old church and other fragmentary survivors of the Second World War bombing. Gollins, Melvin, Ward and Partners built the first International Modern style London office tower, Castrol House in Marylebone Road (1960), the Commercial Union and P. and O. Line blocks in Leadenhall Street, City (1966–69) and the new Covent Garden Market at Nine Elms, Vauxhall (1970–75). Ronald Ward and Partners were the architects of the Vickers building, the Millbank Tower, beside the Tate Gallery on Millbank (1960–63).

More recently, younger architects have introduced their own manners. Darbourne and Darke (b. 1935 and 1929 respectively) have built the famous Lillington Gardens housing estate, around the Victorian church of St. James by G. E. Street, beside the Vauxhall Bridge Road, Victoria (1961–72) and other work including the Marquess Road Housing in Canonbury, Islington (1974–76). Norman Foster has introduced his own use of sheer glass walls which

200

198 *The Economist Building, St. James's Street, St. James's (1960–64) by Peter and Alison Smithson*

199 *The Barbican Area, housing and other buildings north of the London Wall extension, City (1957–79) by Chamberlin, Powell and Bon*

200 *Trellick Tower, Edenham Street, North Kensington (1968–73) by Ernö Goldfinger*

201

202

act as mirrors of their surroundings—in London, his Fred Olsen Centre in Millbank Dock in the East End (1967–69) is an example of such work.

Three famous projects remain to be mentioned. Thamesmead is a complete modern suburb built on wasteland near the river in Woolwich, south-east London; designed by the Greater London Council Architect's department and others, the first part was opened in 1972 and it is expected to be half completed by 1985.

The Post Office Tower, near Fitzroy Square, off Tottenham Court Road, has already become an optional international visual symbol for London— built in 1960–64, it was designed by Sir Eric Bedford, Chief Architect of the Ministry of Public Building and Works, and his staff.

Last of all there is Centre Point and the myriad other works of Richard Seifert (b. 1910). Trained at the Bartlett School of University College, London University, Seifert started his own practice in 1934 and then served in the Royal Engineers and the Indian Army during the Second World War. Returning to private work in 1948, he built up the largest practice of his time by combining large-scale design ability with good contacts and a mastery of the complex planning regulations as they changed during the phenomenal building boom of the 1960s.

His Tolworth Tower at Surbiton on the Kingston By-pass road, the elegant National Westminster Bank headquarters tower at Drapers Gardens in the City, and the Royal Garden Hotel overlooking Kensington Palace all date from 1962–68. But his fame among the public came through the strange story of Centre Point, the thirty-four storey office tower of 1961–68 above Tottenham Court Road underground station. Its extraordinarily slender shape when viewed from the north or south, and its individualistic surface texture of glass within a frame of pre-cast concrete sections, have made it a popular

201 *Thamesmead, a new suburb built on waste land near the Thames in Woolwich, south-east London (first part 1969–72, the rest still growing) by the Greater London Council Architect's Department*

202 *Lillington Street housing estate, Vauxhall Bridge Road, Victoria (1961–72) by Darbourne & Darke. The photograph shows how the estate incorporates G.E. Street's church St. James the Less. The low-rise but high-density housing, around attractive courtyards, expresses a reaction against the fashionable tower-blocks of the time*

203 *Post Office Tower, near Fitzroy Square, off Tottenham Court Road (1960–64) by a group led by Sir Eric Bedford, Chief Architect of the Ministry of Public Building and Works*

landmark for Londoners and tourists. Through a series of misfortunes with tenants Centre Point stood empty for many years and was invaded and besieged in a famous protest by the homeless in 1975.

Seifert's other huge buildings are too numerous to name here, but now in 1979 the highest of all his works is being completed. The sixty-storey tower for the National Westminster Bank between Old Broad Street and Bishopsgate, in the City, was designed in 1971 and replaces the Post Office Tower as the tallest building in the capital. It dominates distant views of the City as St. Paul's used to do (see Plate 178). With this and his other buildings, it can truly be said that Seifert has changed London more than any other architect since Sir Christopher Wren.

In the late 1970s, some writers are saying that we are moving into an age of Post-Modern architecture. Certainly the age of the tower blocks seems to be ending. High-density low-rise housing and the rehabilitation of existing buildings are the fashion of the present. What will Post-Modern design consist of? Perhaps a revival of a historical style again— perhaps something quite unforeseeable: new materials and building techniques are still being developed. Moreover, it is extraordinary that only three women architects have been mentioned even briefly in this book—the potential of the female contribution to large-scale architecture is still unknown.

204 *Centre Point, office block, Tottenham Court Road (1962–66) by R. Seifert*

APPENDIX ONE
Sir Christopher Wren

CHRONOLOGICAL LIST OF LONDON WORKS

Re-built Gothic **St. Sepulchre-without-Newgate**, Holborn (*c.* 1668–80)

The Custom House, Lower Thames Street (1669–74) burned 1718

St. Lawrence Jewry, Gresham Street (1670–77) bombed 1941, restored

St. Mary-at-Hill, Love Lane, off Eastcheap (1670–76)

St. Mary-le-Bow, Cheapside (1670–73, steeple 1680) bombed 1941, restored

St. Bride, off Fleet Street (1670–78, steeple 1701–03) bombed 1941, restored

Deanery (house), Dean's Court, opposite St. Paul's Cathedral (*c.* 1670) (attributed to Wren)

St. Benet Fink, Threadneedle Street (1670–73) demolished 1842

St. Christopher le Stocks, Threadneedle Street (1670–71) demolished 1781

St. Dionis Backchurch, Fenchurch Street (1670–74, steeple 1684) demolished 1878

St. Dunstan-in-the-East, off Lower Thames Street (1670–71), **tower** (1699) only survives 1941 bombs

St. Edmund King and Martyr, Lombard Street (1670–79, steeple *c.* 1707)

St. Mary Aldermanbury (1670–76) gutted by bombs 1941 and now re-erected at Westminster College, Fulton, Missouri as Churchill memorial

Repaired St. Mary Woolnoth (1670–77), re-built by Hawksmoor 1716

St. Michael, Cornhill (1670–72, tower by Hawksmoor 1718) much altered 1857

St. Michael, Wood Street (1670–75) demolished 1894

St. Mildred, Poultry (1670–76, steeple after 1711) demolished 1872

St. Olave, Old Jewry, Poultry (1670–76) demolished 1888, **tower** remains

St. Vedast, Foster Lane (1670–73, steeple 1709–12) bombed 1941, restored

St. Magnus the Martyr, Lower Thames Street (1671–76, steeple 1705)

The Monument, by London Bridge (1671–76) (attributed to Wren and to Hooke)

St. George, Botolph Lane (1671–74) demolished 1903

St. Nicholas Cole Abbey, Queen Victoria Street (1671–77) bombed 1941, restored

Temple Bar (gateway to the City in Fleet Street, 1672) now gateway of Theobald's Park, North of Enfield, Hertfordshire (moved 1878). May be put up beside St. Paul's Cathedral

St. Stephen Walbrook, by Mansion House (1672–79, steeple 1717)

Drury Lane Theatre, Drury Lane (1672–74) altered 1775, re-built 1791

Cupola, St. Martins-in-the-Fields (*c.* 1672) demolished 1722

The Navy Office, Seething Lane (1674–73) demolished (attributed to Wren and to Hooke and to both jointly)

St. Bartholomew-by-Exchange (1674–79) demolished 1840.

St. Stephen, Coleman Street (1674–76) bombed 1941 and demolished

Royal Observatory, end of Blackheath Avenue, Greenwich Park (1675–76)

St. Paul's Cathedral (1675–1711) west front and towers designed *c.* 1703

Pedestal for Charles I statue, Charing Cross (1675) (attributed to Wren)

St. James Garlickhythe, Garlick Hill (*c.* 1676–83, steeple 1713–17)

St. Anne and St. Agnes, Gresham Street (1676–80, steeple *c.* 1714) now Lutheran

St. Michael, Bassishaw (1676–79) demolished 1899

St. Michael, Queenhythe (1676–87) demolished 1876

St. Peter upon Cornhill, Cornhill (1677–81)

St. Martin, Ludgate Hill (1677–84)

All Hallows the Great, Upper Thames Street (1677–83) demolished 1893, **tower** remains

All Hallows, Watling Street (1677–84, steeple 1697) demolished 1876

St. Benet, Paul's Wharf, Queen Victoria Street (1677–83) now Welsh Church

Christ Church, Newgate Street (1677–87, steeple 1704) bombed 1941, only **tower** remains

St. Swithin London Stone, Cannon Street (1677–85) gutted 1941, demolished *c.* 1960

St. Antholin, Watling Street (1678–82, tower 1688) demolished 1875

King's Bench Walk Houses, Temple (No. 1 re-built, No. 2 1678, Nos. 3–6 *c.* 1678, No. 7 *c.* 1685, Nos. 8–12 18th/19th centuries) Nos. 2–7 have been attributed to Wren

St. Clement Danes, Strand (1680–82, steeple by Gibbs 1719)

Cloisters, Pump Court, Middle Temple (1680–81) bombed 1941, restored

St. Anne, Soho (c. 1680–86, steeple by S. P. Cockerell 1802) bombed 1941, tower only remains

St. Augustine, Watling Street (1680–83, steeple 1695) bombed 1941, tower only remains

Reconstructed Gothic St. Mary Aldermary, Queen Victoria Street (1681–82, tower 1702–04)

St. Mary Abchurch, Abchurch Lane, off Cannon Street (1681–86)

St. Mildred, Bread Street (1681–87) destroyed by bombs 1941

St. Benet, Gracechurch Street (1681–86) demolished 1867

St. Matthew, Friday Street (1681–85) demolished 1881

Chelsea Royal Hospital, Royal Hospital Road, Chelsea (1681–86), Wren added some of the flanking outbuildings in 1691, while Soane added others in 1809–17

St. James, Piccadilly (1682–84) bombed 1941, restored

Gallery for St. Margaret, Westminster (1682) removed 1877

Refitted the Temple Church, Temple (1682–83) removed 1840

St. Alban, Wood Street (1682–85, steeple 1698) bombed 1941, tower remains

St. Clement, Eastcheap (1683–87)

St. Mary Magdalen, Old Fish Street (1683–85) burned 1886 and demolished

St. Andrew, Holborn (1684–90, steeple 1703)

St. Margaret Pattens, Eastcheap (1684–87, steeple 1698)

St. Michael, Crooked Lane (1684–88, tower 1698) demolished 1831

Chapel, Privy Gallery and other additions, Whitehall Palace (1685–87) burned 1698

The Great Armoury, Tower of London (1685–92) burned 1841

St. Andrew by the Wardrobe, Queen Victoria Street (1685–95) bombed 1941, restored

St. Margaret, Lothbury (1686–90)

All Hallows, Lombard Street (1686–94) demolished 1939

Enlarged the French Protestant Church, The Savoy (1686) demolished

St. Mary Somerset, Upper Thames Street (1686–95) demolished 1871, tower remains

St. Michael Paternoster Royal, College Hill (1686–94, steeple 1713) bombed 1944, restored

Houses in Bridgewater Square, Barbican (1688 on, speculation) all demolished

East and South Wings, Hampton Court Palace (1689–94)

Kensington Palace, Kensington Gardens (1689–95 and 1702)

Queen's Apartments, Whitehall Palace, including terrace and river steps (1691–93) burned 1698

Sir John Moore's Writing School, Christ's Hospital (1693–95) demolished 1902 (probably by Hawksmoor under Wren)

Morden College, off The Paragon, Blackheath (1695–1700) (attributed to Wren)

Royal Naval Hospital for Seamen, Greenwich, lay-out and design of King William and Queen Mary Buildings (1696–1702)

Repairs at Westminster Abbey (1698–1713)

State apartments, St. James's Palace (1703) (attributed to Wren)

Enlargement of House of Commons for 45 Scottish Members (1706) altered 1800, burned 1834

Marlborough House, Pall Mall, St. James's (1709–11) upper storeys and entrance added later by others

Chapter House, St. Paul's Cathedral churchyard (1712–14) (attributed to Wren)

The Royal Society's Repository, Fleet Street (1711–12) demolished

APPENDIX TWO
Architects' Appointments to the Royal Office of Works and other major London Surveyorships etc.

The eminent historian of the Royal Office of Works is Howard Colvin, who has traced the holders and functions of the main appointments in detail. A summary of these will be useful to readers.

The Royal Office of Works developed from the medieval office of the King's Mason, held by such dimly recorded individuals as Henry of Reyns in 1243–53, John of Gloucester in 1254–60 and Robert of Beverley in 1261–84. In 1360 Henry Yevele was appointed Disposer of the King's Works for Westminster and the Tower of London and was in charge of most of the royal works until 1400. The size and activity of the office of works varied with individual kings and queens during the following centuries until in 1615 Inigo Jones was appointed King's Surveyor and transformed the post's largely administrative duties into the direction of a considerable royal building programme for James I and Charles I.

In 1663 King Charles II issued royal orders setting out a new organisation for the Office of Works. These orders established the post of Surveyor-General and below it those of Comptroller, Paymaster, Purveyor and Chief Clerk (or Engrosser) of the King's Works. The level below these officials consisted of Patent Artisans to the Office—Master Mason, Master Carpenter, Master Bricklayer, Master Plasterer, etc.

The work of the Office of Works was to maintain or build the royal palaces and subsidiary royal buildings. From 1716 onwards all this work was controlled from the main Office in Scotland Yard, near the north end of Whitehall. The Surveyor-General's post became a politician's appointment in 1718, likely to change with the fall of a government, and the Deputy-Surveyor was in charge of the architectural work from then until 1761, when two Architects of the Works were appointed.

In 1782, with the reform of the Civil Service, the Office of Works was greatly reduced and its posts altered. The appointment of Comptroller was joined with that of the Surveyor-General, and an architect was given the combined post.

A further reorganization followed in 1813–14. The post of Surveyor-General was abolished, and three Attached Architects of the Office of Works were instead appointed to carry out its architectural work; at the same time the Office's responsibilities were extended to include state buildings other than the royal works.

From 1832 the Office of Works was combined with the Office of Woods, Forests and Land Revenues, until 1852. Thereafter it became independent again, first as the Office of Works and then as the twentieth-century Ministry of Works, until it was merged into the Department of the Environment in the 1960s.

Well-known architects who held royal offices include the following: Sir Christopher Wren was Surveyor-General in 1669–1718, after which the post was held by politicians until the appointment as Surveyor-General and Comptroller of Sir William Chambers in 1782–96 and James Wyatt in 1796–1813. The post was then abolished.

Deputy Surveyors included John Webb in 1664–69, Colen Campbell in 1718–19, William Kent in 1735–48, Henry Flitcroft in 1748–58, Stephen Wright in 1758–80 and Sir Robert Taylor in 1780–82.

Architects of the Works were appointed two at any time. They were Sir William Chambers with Robert Adam in 1761–69, then Sir Robert Taylor in 1769–77 with James Adam in 1769–82, then Thomas Sandby in 1777–80 and James Paine in 1780–82.

Comptrollers included Hugh May in 1668–84, William Talman in 1689–1702, Sir John Vanbrugh in 1702–25, Thomas Ripley in 1726–58, Henry Flitcroft in 1758–69 and Sir William Chambers from 1769 until the post was merged in 1782. Chambers retained the joint title until 1796.

Chief Clerks of the King's Works had the job of examining the accounts for building materials and works done by the individual Clerks of Works at each royal palace. Holders of the post included the elder William Dickinson in 1660–1702, Wren's son the younger Christopher in 1702–17 and Colen Campbell in 1718–19.

The Secretary to the Board of Works was responsible for the Minutes of the Board's meetings and for other secretariat duties. Nicholas Hawksmoor held the post in 1715–18 during Wren's last years as Surveyor-General. Then Hawksmoor was reappointed in 1726 until his death in 1736. His successors were Isaac Ware in 1736–66, William Robinson in 1766–75 and Kenton Couse in 1775–82.

Westminster Abbey

The Abbey was built largely at royal expense under the supervision of the King's Mason in medieval times and was maintained by an official called the College Surveyor. In 1698 Parliament started to make an annual grant for the upkeep of the Abbey and a post called Surveyor to the Fabric was created. Those holding this appointment have included Sir Christopher Wren in 1698–1722, Nicholas Hawksmoor in 1723–36, John James in 1736–46, James Wyatt in 1776–1813, Benjamin Dean Wyatt in 1813–27, Edward Blore in 1827–49, Sir George Gilbert Scott in 1849–78 and William Lethaby in 1906–28.

St. Paul's Cathedral

The Surveyor to St. Paul's Cathedral (as against the Surveyor to the Dean and Chapter) was appointed by the Lord Mayor and the Bishop of London and the Archbishop of Canterbury. Surveyors have included Sir Christopher Wren in 1675–1723, John

James in 1724–46, Henry Flitcroft in 1746–56, Robert Mylne in 1766–1811, S. P. Cockerell in 1811–19 and C. R. Cockerell in 1819–52.

The Bank of England
The post of Architect to the Bank of England was created in 1732. Those appointed include George Sampson in 1732–65, Sir Robert Taylor in 1765–88, Sir John Soane in 1788–1833 and C. R. Cockerell in 1833–63.

Other Appointments
Other major appointments relevant to London public buildings included the Clerk of Works to the Chelsea Royal Hospital, the two Commissioners for Building Fifty New Churches between 1711 and 1733, the Architect to the Commissioners for Building New Churches between 1821 and 1857, the Surveyor and Clerk of the Works to Greenwich Royal Hospital, and the Clerk of the Works to the City of London.

APPENDIX THREE
London Building Materials

Brick
Brick is the most widely used material for London buildings erected after 1650, with the exception of public buildings which could afford stone, for there are hardly any building stone quarries in south-eastern England. Bricks were manufactured in England under the Roman Empire, but the industry ended after Roman withdrawal until after A.D. 1200. At that time, the manufacture of large bricks ($10 \times 5 \times 1\frac{3}{4}$ inches or more) started in East Anglia (which remains a major centre of brick manufacture today). Before 1300 many Flemish bricks, as small as $8 \times 3\frac{3}{4} \times 1\frac{3}{4}$ inches, were imported into London, and this became the approximate size of the English "statute" brick. From 1550 onwards, brick gradually started to replace timber for ordinary London houses, and it became the usual material after the great fire of 1666. Despite the competition of cheaper stone from Bath after 1770, the popularity of brick continued in London houses, often with stone or terracotta trimming. The introduction of the Hoffman kiln in 1858 made possible the large-scale manufacture of the identical and cheaper mechanically moulded and fired bricks typical of Victorian buildings. The Arts and Crafts Movement encouraged a return to hand-moulded bricks in the 1890s but with limited success as their cost was three times that of the mechanical products. Brick sizes have altered many times over the centuries, depending on brick taxes and on firing techniques, and only in the twentieth century reached the standard size of $8\frac{3}{4} \times 4\frac{3}{16} \times 2\frac{5}{8}$ or $2\frac{7}{8}$ inches.

Brick colour depends on the clay used and on the temperature at which the bricks are fired. Most clays produce red bricks if they are fired in an oxidising atmosphere at 900° to 1,000° centigrade. Firing at a slightly higher temperature produces darker reds or purples, while bricks fired at 1,200° centigrade are often brown, yellow-brown or grey. The well-known London Stock brick, so widely used in the eighteenth and nineteenth centuries and later, is typically yellow-brown in colour. The Staffordshire Blue brick, popular from the late nineteenth century onwards, is fired at about 1,200° centigrade with a restricted draught in the kiln reducing the supply of oxygen to obtain the colour.

Coade Stone—*see* Terracotta

Concrete
Writing in 1906 in *Modern Buildings*, H. Y. Margary commented, "It is only in quite recent years that the custom of ancient Rome and Byzantium, of casting edifices in concrete, has come into use to any extent in England. Engineers have for a long time realized the great constructive value of this material, but architects have considered it to be a material unworthy of their notice. . . ."

The Romans used various types of concrete made from cement, sand and pebbles or some other bulk materials, initially for fillings or for facing walls, and later for rounded vaults or domes. After the Roman Empire, concrete was hardly used in England until the discovery of Portland Cement in 1824 led to its use in civil engineering works. Reinforced concrete, using steel bars to overcome concrete's lack of tensile strength especially in horizontal spans, was developed in the latter half of the nineteenth century and introduced in English buildings at the end of the century. Arts and Crafts architects such as William Lethaby, Edward Prior and Edgar Wood developed the use of concrete gradually in English buildings outside London shortly after 1900. An English architectural magazine held a competition for an office block with a reinforced concrete structure in 1909, and the Liver Building of 1908–11 in Liverpool is an early example of a reinforced concrete frame building. But in London steel frame buildings preceded concrete frame buildings by several years. Only in about 1930, with the introduction of new German and French architectural ideas, did the series of London buildings start which explored the plastic and structural possibilities of concrete and led up to such recent buildings as the Royal Festival Hall, the National Theatre and countless tower blocks of flats and offices.

Faience—*see* Terracotta

Glass

The use of glass in windows goes back to Roman times but because of its high cost it was rarely used in England before the sixteenth century except in churches and the houses of the wealthy.

Stained coloured glass in churches was used as early as A.D. 532–37 in Constantinople, and its use spread into western Europe. After A.D. 1000 strongly coloured windows with human figures became increasingly popular, followed by the *grisaille* period in the thirteenth century with greyish glass and more restrained colouring. The broader areas of church window with less stone tracery built during the 1400–1550 period (late Perpendicular) were accompanied by a return to richer colouring in large windows such as those in King Henry VII's Chapel at Westminster Abbey. Little stained glass was made during the seventeenth and eighteenth centuries, and the Classical churches built at that time are better suited to clear glass windows. During the nineteenth century, Victorians such as A. W. N. Pugin revived stained glass making for the Gothic churches they were building. The art was brought to a new high point by William Morris, Edward Burne-Jones and others in the late nineteenth century. After 1945, some stained glass artists started to produce abstract designs for windows.

Domestic window glazing became usual in large London houses by 1600. By 1700, after the great fire in London, glass windows were commonly used in all but the poorest houses built. Early window glass was blown in discs and then cut into rectangular pieces. This limited the size of the individual pieces and necessitated the division of windows by many glazing bars of metal, stone or wood. Good cheap glass in large sheets became increasingly available after 1840, and bars were no longer necessary.

Slate Tiles

Slate is a hard stone which can easily be divided along the strata into large pieces of exceptional thinness and durable flat surface. The colour is usually grey, but a variety of blues, greens, reds and purples are found in combination with the grey. Slates from Devon and Cornwall have been widely used as roofing material in southern England since A.D. 1200 and even earlier. During the nineteenth century slate from Wales dominated the London market, since it was cheaply quarried and has a wide range of colours.

Steel

During the nineteenth century, and especially after the building of the Crystal Palace for the Great Exhibition of 1851, the use of iron frames for buildings such as warehouses was steadily developed in Britain. Wrought iron, iron columns with stanchions and rolled iron joists were increasingly used as frames for commercial buildings with walls of brick. After 1890, with the building of the Forth Bridge, mild steel gradually replaced iron in use for engineering and warehouse frame structures (following the American example), since its strength was greater. An emporium of 1896 in West Hartlepool is possibly the earliest steel frame building in Britain for general public use, and the Ritz Hotel of 1903–06 is usually quoted as the first large London building to use the new type of frame. The thin walls needed with steel frame buildings allowed the client the use of significant areas previously occupied by load-bearing masonry, and the method of construction gained popularity quickly. At the same time, the slender structure led London architects to new sorts of expression in their fashionable Classical frontages of stone. This produced many strikingly original Classical elevations using stone and glass skins on steel frames and then simpler façades which reflected the grid frame within especially after the Second World War of 1939–45.

Stone

The builders of the Roman Empire quarried building stone only from workings close to the surface. Saxon builders cannibalized old Roman buildings for their comparatively rare stone edifices or carried out primitive quarrying of local rough stone. After the Norman conquest, good limestone from Caen in Normandy was imported to build the prestigious strongholds such as the White Tower of London and the great keep at Rochester. During the fourteenth century the demand for better squared and smoother faced building stone increased, and limestone quarrying was developed in Oxfordshire, Dorset and elsewhere.

Stone is of three main types. *Igneous rock* has been

produced from the molten material inside the planet. *Sedimentary rock* combines the eroded remains of igneous rock with the remnants of ancient organic growth and creatures. *Metamorphic rock* can be igneous or sedimentary stone or both which has undergone a physical alteration through great pressure and great heat. Limestone and sandstone are both sedimentary rock, the former containing a high proportion of formerly organic material fossilized. Limestone is especially prized as a building material for it has an optimum combination of ease for quarrying and carving with durability when exposed to the weather. A great band of limestones, of varying characteristics, lies diagonally across England from the Humber and the Wash in the north-east to Somerset and Dorset in the south-west.

Sir Christopher Wren claimed in 1713 that the Gothic Westminster Abbey of 1243–c. 1400 was built of Reigate stone (with Purbeck marble inside) because the Norman Caen stone was by then too expensive. Whatever the reason, English quarrying increased during the following centuries and the Lord Protector's original Somerset House (started in 1547) and Sir Richard Gresham's Royal Exchange (1566–71) were extravagant examples of stone-faced London buildings.

After that, quarrying dwindled until Inigo Jones renewed the demand for stone in the 1620s and a royal decree revived the ailing quarries on the peninsular of Portland in Dorset. Portland stone was from that time onwards to become the prestige building material of London. For more than a century, including the great re-building of London and St. Paul's Cathedral following the fire in 1666, the Portland quarries had the great advantage of a nearby pier to load stone into sea transport—the only economical method of carrying such weights from the building stone areas of England to the capital. Portland is an excellent limestone, basically pale honey-coloured, but with a variety of shades and fossil content at different levels and in different areas of the peninsular.

Other quarries were soon supplying stone to London on a smaller scale—Taynton from the upper Thames valley, Reigate from Surrey, Purbeck marble from Dorset, Clipsham from Rutland and Kentish Rag, a hard limestone from the Medway valley. But Portland's great rival, Bath stone, is hardly mentioned before the 1720s in London. It only gained a large share of the market when its fine buildings and the fashion for Bath as a spa made the name familiar. Then in 1810 the Kennet and Avon Canal opened waterborne transport from Somerset to London (overtaken by the Great Western Railway in 1841) and the low cost of Bath stone, combined

with qualities nearly as good as Portland, brought it the mass market which its quarrymasters wanted.

Despite the rivalry of Portland, Clipsham and the cheap but excellent Kentish ragstone, Bath production boomed. Seven Bath firms combined to form Bath Stone Firms Ltd. in 1887; the company quarried one and a half million cubic feet of stone in its first year and three million cubic feet a year by 1900. In 1899 the Bath and Portland firms combined and the company name became Bath and Portland Stone Firms Ltd. Portland was fully stretched in supplying public and large prestige buildings such as the Law Courts and the War Office, leaving the domestic market for Bath.

Early in the twentieth century the role of stone became largely that of a skin for the steel or concrete frames which replaced load-bearing masonry in large buildings. But Portland stone in particular has retained its reputation to the present day, often cut into panels $2\frac{1}{2}$ inches thick to clad structures whose finishes would otherwise have a less warm and traditional London appearance.

Stucco

Stucco is an adhesive material applied to external or internal walls to prevent the weathering of the basic building material or to give a smooth finish. The word is used to describe a variety of renderings or coatings or plasters of many different thicknesses, made from cement or lime and gypsum mixtures with other additives, applied wet to the wall and allowed to dry. Most stuccoes can be sculpted or moulded easily or painted for decoration. Most types, if used on the exterior of buildings, need to be painted to weather well.

Like other building materials still in use, stucco was used during the Roman Empire. It was brought to England again by Italian stucco craftsmen in the late 1500s. English plasterers soon acquired some of the range of techniques—early English mixtures combined lime with organic substances such as vegetable juices or blood to make it adhere.

In Italy, the architect Palladio used stucco with much effect during the sixteenth century, and his English admirer Inigo Jones used it in several London buildings of the early 1600s. In the eighteenth century, stucco of lime and sand became fashionable as "Roman cement". In 1708 Sir Christopher Wren wrote, "The vaulting of St. Paul's is a rendering as hard as stone; it is composed of cockleshell lime well beaten with sand: the more labour in the beating, the better and stronger the mortar. . . . Chalk-lime is the common practice . . ." By the 1770s, oil mastic stuccoes were in use in London. The Adam brothers bought the first patents and publicized their "Adams cement" as obligatory for use over brickwork if a mean look was to be avoided. Other new stuccoes were introduced in 1815, using linseed oil and porcelain clay or a mixture of limestone with brick dust, sand, litharge and linseed oil. These mixtures were much used in the major white stuccoed London buildings designed by John Nash, by Decimus Burton and others.

The Victorians to some extent reversed accepted opinion about stucco, since their hard machine-made bricks weathered formidably and needed no covering. But at the end of the nineteenth century Voysey and his followers rendered the brickwork of their houses with textured mixtures called roughcast and later with the even coarser pebbledash.

Terracotta

Terracotta means baked earth. It has been used in many different ways as a building material, and the term is sometimes loosely applied to tiles or pottery in general. The normally accepted definition, to differentiate it from other clay materials, is that terracotta is clay mixed with sand or a proportion of already fired clay to reduce shrinkage during firing. After mixing with this "grog", the material is kneaded, left to stand, pressed into moulds of plaster of Paris, dried and then fired. If the terracotta is to be glazed, it is fired twice. "Faience" is twice-fired terracotta, firstly at a high temperature for the clay, then at a low temperature for the glaze and the clay together.

Reaching London from Europe shortly after 1500, terracotta was fairly widely used until about 1550. After that the material was hardly used at all until the Holt and Ripley factory opened in Lambeth and flourished from 1722 until 1750. After a gap, the works were revived in Lambeth by George and Eleanor Coade, whose "Coade Stone" was extremely popular in London from 1767 until closure in 1835.

In 1850 the Doulton factory started to manufacture terracotta again in Lambeth, chiefly as decorative panels for the Victorian Gothic architects, and this use was continued by the late Victorian architects of the "Queen Anne" style with their well-known sunflower panels. At the end of the century, Arts and Crafts promotion of individual, rather than manufactured, sculpture ended the great period of terracotta's popularity for domestic work. But Alfred Waterhouse and some other architects continued to use the material for large buildings.

Tiles of clay

Baked flat clay tiles were in increasingly frequent use as roofing materials from shortly after A.D. 1200,

when they were introduced from the Netherlands, until they were largely outpriced by cheaper Welsh slate in the nineteenth century. In 1212 the City of London enforced the building of new roofs in clay tiles, rather than wooden tiles, to reduce fire risks. Curved pantiles first appeared in eastern England about 1600, imported from the Netherlands, and were manufactured in East Anglia from the eighteenth century onwards.

Tiles of slate—see Slate

Timber

Early London houses were mostly of timber construction of various types. The most common in medieval times was a timber frame wall (usually oak or elm) with infilling of wattle and daub. Thin staves were fitted vertically into holes bored in the horizontal timbers, then flat and flexible wooden withies were woven horizontally between the staves to form the wattle. This was made solid by a daub of mixed clay, horsehair and organic material such as dung. These panels were then sealed by a layer of plaster if the customer could afford it. Preconstructed frame panels were developed from 1400 onwards, at first with narrow gaps between the timbers, but by 1600 with wider gaps in which the plaster was often decorated. Infills of brick and other materials were occasionally used, while weatherboard or tile coverings of timber frames were sometimes used after 1700.

Timber frames are still commonly used as the supporting structure for roofs and as the general structure for domestic outbuildings.

References

Brunskill, Ronald. *Vernacular Architecture* (London, 1971)

Brunskill, Ronald and Clifton-Taylor, Alec. *English Brickwork* (London, 1977)

Davey, Norman. *A History of Building Materials* (London, 1961)

Davey, Norman. *Building Stones of England and Wales* (National Council of Social Service, London, 1976)

Hudson, Kenneth. *The Fashionable Stone* (Bath, 1971)

Middleton, G. A. T. (ed.). *Modern Buildings : their Planning, Construction and Equipment* (London, 1906)

Information was also given privately by Vanessa Debenham.

Short Glossary of Architectural Terms

AEDICULE Two columns surmounted by a pediment, usually framing a door or window

AMBULATORY The curved aisle around an apse

APSE Semi-circular area, backed by a wall or arcade with a curved vault, often forming the east end of the chancel in a church

ARCADE A row of columns or pillars supporting arches

ARCH A rounded or pointed solid form, spanning the space between two vertical solids in a building, and usually supporting the structure above

ARCHITRAVE See *Entablature*

ARTS AND CRAFTS A revival of British traditional crafts and original design started by William Morris about 1860 and widespread by the 1890s

ASHLAR Stone structure of large blocks, flat-faced and flat-edged

ATLANTES Male sculptured figures used as columns in Classical architecture. See also *Caryatid, Herm*

ATTIC Top storey of a building, above the main floors

BALDACCHINO Architectural canopy, usually supported by four columns, often above an altar or throne

BALUSTER A small column or pillar

BALUSTRADE A row of balusters topped by a rail or a coping, often used along the side of stairways or along the top edge of buildings

BAPTISTRY The part of a church, with a font, where baptism takes place

BAROQUE A style developed from Classical architecture with powerful forms but not following Classical rules of proportion and detail. First developed in Rome in the 1630s

BARREL or TUNNEL VAULT A roof formed by a long rounded arch, without diagonal ribs

BASILICA An early church plan with a nave rising to a clerestorey (*q.v.*) and lower aisles

BATTER The slope of an inclined wall face

BATTLEMENT A parapet with frequent lowered edges, giving a toothed effect

BAUHAUS A German design school which, under the direction of the architect Walter Gropius, became internationally influential in modern design in the 1920s and later

BAY The area or space between one vertical division of a building and the next vertical division, whether inside or on the external frontage

BAY WINDOW A window which projects beyond the general wall of a building. If the window curves, it is sometimes called a bow window. If the projection is not supported by the ground, it is usually called an oriel window

BEAM A large horizontal timber supporting a ceiling or roof

BEAUX ARTS The *Ecole des Beaux Arts* in Paris was the most influential force in stimulating the spread of Neo-Classicism in the nineteenth century in many countries throughout Europe, and its educational system was widely copied

BELFRY Turret with open sides, for a bell or bells

BELL STAGE The storey of a tower with openings in the walls to let out the sound of bells suspended within

BLIND ARCH or ARCADE An arch or row of arches against a plain wall

BOARD OF WORKS The department in charge of royal buildings. See Appendix Two

BOND The way in which rows of bricks are laid on each other, *e.g.* English bond is composed of alternate rows of headers (*q.v.*) and stretchers (*q.v.*), while in Flemish bond each row is composed of alternate headers and stretchers

BOSS A projecting feature where the ribs of a vault meet

BOW WINDOW See *Bay Window*

BOX PEW A church pew with high wooden sides enclosing it

BRACKET A projecting feature of stone or wood to support a beam or other projecting structure

BRICK Building material of baked clay (see Appendix Three). See also *Bond, Header* and *Stretcher*

BROACH A truncated pyramid to effect a transition from a square plan to an octagonal superstructure *e.g.* in broach spire

BROKEN PEDIMENT See *Pediment*

BUTTRESS A supporting structure against a wall, often sloping inwards towards the top

BYZANTINE The forms of architecture derived from Constantinople and the Byzantine Empire of early Christian times

CAMPANILE A free-standing bell tower

CANTILEVER A projecting structure supported by weight or ties only at one end

CAPITAL Top part of a column, which is usually decorated. See *Doric, Ionic, Corinthian, Tuscan* and *Composite*

CARTOUCHE A plaque, often inscribed with writing or a shield, with an ornamented surround

CARYATID Female sculptured figure used as columns in Classical architecture. See also *Atlantes*, *Herm*

CASTELLATED Battlemented (see *Battlement*)

CEILING Material suspended beneath roof or floor beams to cover them and to insulate the room below

CHANCEL The part of a church where the altar is usually placed, normally at the east end. Parts of the chancel may be described as the choir, the presbytery, the sanctuary, *etc.* (*q.v.*)

CHOIR Part of the church, usually between the main part of the chancel and the nave, where the service is sung (choir stalls or seats are usually provided for a trained choir of singers)

CLASSIC An exemplary work in a particular style or manner

CLASSICAL The forms of architecture derived from ancient Greece and Rome

CLERESTOREY or CLERESTORY Upper part of a church nave or chancel which rises above the rest (*e.g.* the aisles) and has windows in its walls

CLERK OF WORKS The supervisor of the erection of a building, not necessarily its designer

COADE STONE Artificial stone of baked clay formerly made in a London factory (see Appendix Three)

COFFERING A ceiling composed of sunken decorative squares, quadrangles or polygons

COLONNADE A row of columns

COLUMN A cylindrical free-standing vertical support conforming to one of the five orders (*q.v.*) of Classical architecture. See also *Pillar*

COMPOSITE A mixture of Classical (*q.v.*), Ionic and Corinthian orders (*q.v.*), developed in the late Roman Empire

COMPTROLLER An official post often held by architects (see Appendix Two)

COPING The stone or other covering on top of a wall

CORBEL Stone feature protruding from a wall to support a vault or other projecting feature above it

CORINTHIAN A Classical (*q.v.*) order (*q.v.*) with a capital (*q.v.*) composed of sculpted acanthus leaves

CORNICE The top part of the entablature (*q.v.*), often used by itself as a horizontal decorated projection at the top of or high up on a wall

COVE or COVING Decorated concave moulding at the top of a wall where coving makes the transition to the ceiling

CRENELLATION Battlement (*q.v.*) often on a projecting parapet (see *Machicolation*)

CROCKET Decorated feature in Gothic architecture protruding on the slope of a roof, particularly on spires or pinnacles

CROSSING Area at the intersection of nave with chancel and transepts

CRYPT Underground room or rooms beneath a church

CUPOLA A domed turret

CUSP Projecting point in Gothic decoration

DADO Decorated lower area of a wall

DECORATED Gothic architecture of the sort typical of English work of the late thirteenth and first half of the fourteenth century, after the Early English and before the Perpendicular periods (*q.v.*). The spaces are wider and the decoration and structure more complex than those in Early English work

DIAPER Patterns, usually in brick or tile work, formed by geometrical designs in different colours or shades

DORIC The simplest of the Classical (*q.v.*) orders (*q.v.*). The Greek Doric has no base or plinth, and a simply moulded capital. Roman Doric columns have bases and plinths, with more complex mouldings but no volutes (*q.v.*) or acanthus leaf decoration in the capitals. See also *Tuscan* for comparison

DORMER Window projecting from a sloping roof

DRESSED In masonry, a stone chiselled to a flat surface

DRESSING Stone door or window surrounds or quoins (*q.v.*), often found in brick buildings

DRUM Vertically-walled cylindrical section beneath the curve of a dome

DUTCH GABLE A gable tall in proportion to its width, often with a shape more complex and decorated than a simple gable

EARLY ENGLISH Gothic architecture of the sort built in England in the thirteenth century, the earliest Gothic phase after the Norman, typified by strong solid forms and lancet windows with comparatively little elaboration

EAVE Edge of a roof overhanging the wall

ELEVATION In architecture, the design of a building (or object) as if seen horizontally, looking at a wall

ENGAGED Architectural features joined together and one sunk into the other

ENTABLATURE The horizontal features placed above a column in Classical architecture. From top to bottom, these are cornice, frieze, and architrave

ENTASIS Slight curve introduced to a generally straight line (*e.g.* in columns) to achieve a desirable visual effect

FAN VAULT Late Gothic vault whose many ribs spread widely and are of equal lengths, thus forming an uninterrupted fan curve around their ends

FESTOON A sculpted bunch of flowers and fruit curving down as if suspended from both ends

FINIAL Decorative feature at the tip of a spire or pinnacle

FLÈCHE A slender spire on a roof

FLUTING Decorative vertical lines carved into a column

FLYING BUTTRESS Free-standing buttress (q.v.) whose top joins and supports the side of a roof or wall

FOIL A lobe between the cusps (q.v.) in Gothic decoration. Cusps and foils form leaf shapes. Thus, trefoil is a decorative form divided into three leaf shapes, quatrefoil into four, etc.

FOLIATED Leaf-like forms in decoration

FREE STYLE Some British architecture of around 1900, which sought a new modern style, free of revived historical styles

FRIEZE Middle part of an entablature (q.v.), often painted or sculpted

GABLE The inverted V formed by a wall rising to support the edges of sloping roofs. The basic triangular shape is sometimes decoratively varied, as in Dutch gables

GALLERY Upper part of a building, especially of a nave of church, with arches opening into spaces behind. Also used to describe balconies of seating above the church floor level, and suspended upper levels of seating in a theatre

GIBBS SURROUND Blocks of masonry, alternating large and small, used as decoration around a Classical doorway or window. An English term used to describe a Classical form of decoration favoured by the architect James Gibbs

GOTHIC The architectural style of c. 1200 until c. 1530 (with later revivals) in England, following the Norman (q.v.) Romanesque. It is typified by pointed arches, shafted piers, rib vaulted roofs and flying buttresses

GREEK The Classical architecture of ancient Greece, before the introduction of arches and other features in ancient Rome. Greek Cross—one with all four arms of even length

GROIN The line where two vaults meet to form an edge

HALF-COLUMN As a pilaster (q.v.) but round in section

HALF-TIMBERED A timber-framed construction with the outer timbers left uncovered on the external walls and the gaps in the frame infilled with plaster, brickwork or other materials

HAMMER BEAM A horizontal beam cantilevered from a wall and supporting a vertical beam which in turn supports a roof, thus avoiding the need for beams at low level across a wide space

HEADER A brick laid so that its smallest surface appears on the face of a wall

HERM or TERM A column, pillar or pilaster whose upper part is sculpted as the upper part of a human or mythical figure, or of a creature.

HIPPED ROOF A sloping roof whose ends also slope to the top of the walls, rather than ending vertically in a gable

INTERNATIONAL MODERN The style or styles of architecture (based on the relatively new building materials of steel, reinforced concrete and plate glass) developed by the Bauhaus in Germany and by Le Corbusier in France and elsewhere in the 1920s, and spread across the world by its disciples in the mid-twentieth century. It aimed to express its own building materials on visible surfaces, rather than following traditional appearances

IONIC A Classical (q.v.) order (q.v.), with a capital (q.v.) composed chiefly of four volutes (or scrolls)—two showing on the outer face of the building, and two on the inner side

JAMB The vertical side of an archway or other opening in a wall

KEYSTONE The central stone at the highest point of an arch

LANCET A tall and narrow window topped by a pointed arch

LANTERN A term used in architecture for a turret or cupola with windows in its sides which bring daylight to the internal space below it

LINTEL A horizontal stone or beam across the top of a door or window, usually supporting the structure above the opening

LOGGIA A colonnaded balcony recessed (q.v.) into the side of a building

LUNETTE An arched semi-circular window or opening. Sometimes used to mean a semi-circular surface. See also *Tympanum*

MACHICOLATION A parapet, usually battlemented (q.v.) projecting from a fortress wall, with openings in its floor so that boiling oil and other things can be dropped onto any attackers beneath it

MANNERIST In architecture, a style in which Classical features are employed in a way which makes it obvious that they are not fulfilling their ancient functions (e.g. columns which support little or nothing), especially associated with Michelangelo's designs. Occasionally the term is used to denote a rigid Classical manner which followed the Renaissance and Baroque periods in Italy. See also *Neo-Mannerism*

MANSARD A roof whose lower slope is steeper than its upper slope, forming an angle where the two slopes meet. The name is derived from the seventeenth century architect François Mansart, who established it as a favourite feature in French Classical architecture

METOPE The area between the triglyphs (*q.v.*) in a classical frieze (*q.v.*)

MEZZANINE A storey of low height between storeys of greater height

MOSAIC See *Tesselation*

MULLION A fixed vertical stone or timber, dividing up the glazed area of a window. See also *Transom*

NEO-CLASSICAL In architecture, a revival of Classical architecture following its rules of proportion and of the use of its traditional features in ancient Greece and Rome (as against Renaissance, Baroque or Mannerist *etc.* Classicism, *q.v.*)

NEO-GEORGIAN A revival after *c.* 1900 of the English vernacular forms of domestic Classical architecture common in the 1720–1830 period

NÉO-GRÈC The specifically French forms of Neo-Classical architecture deriving from ancient Greece

NEO-MANNERISM A revival of Mannerist (*q.v.*) design in the 1900s to express the fact that the Classical detailing of stone walls was not load-bearing in the steel-frame buildings of the time

NICHE A platform recessed into the mass of a wall

NORMAN The round-arched and massive walled Romanesque (*q.v.*) style typical of English buildings from 1066 until about 1200

OBELISK A pillar which tapers towards its top and is capped by a pyramid shape, supporting nothing

OGEE A pointed arch whose concave curves dip into convex curves before reaching the topmost point

ORDER In Classical (*q.v.*) architecture, an order is any one of the five widely accepted combinations of the column with its substructure and superstructure, each according to set rules of proportion, decoration and permissible features. See *Doric, Ionic, Corinthian, Tuscan* and *Composite*

ORIEL A bay window (*q.v.*) projecting from an upper storey, the projection being supported by a bracket or other support

PALLADIAN In British architecture, the type of Classical design practised by Andrea Palladio (1508–80) in Vicenza and Venice and by other Italian Renaissance architects, much copied by Lord Burlington and his disciples in England from 1720 until about 1780

PANTILE A roofing tile, S-shaped when viewed from its top or bottom end

PARAPET A low wall on the edge of any sudden drop of level, as on the edge of a flat roof or the sides of a bridge

PEDESTAL The base of a column or pillar in Classical architecture. Also used as a term to describe the structure underneath a statue. See *Plinth*

PEDIMENT In Classical architecture, a triangular or round-topped feature, basically a low-pitched gable, above a portico (*q.v.*) or an aedicule (*q.v.*), also used by itself above doors or windows. A Broken Pediment has a gap in the lower line or lower and upper lines. An Open Pediment has a gap in the lines forming the upper part of its shape

PENDANT In architecture, a boss (*q.v.*) extended downwards so that it hangs from the joint of the vaulting ribs well down into the space beneath

PERPENDICULAR Gothic architecture of the sort typical of English work after the Decorated period. Perpendicular Gothic dominated the buildings done in Britain from the middle of the fourteenth century until about 1530

PIANO NOBILE In Classical Italian Renaissance architecture, and its English equivalent, the grandest storey of a house containing the main reception rooms, often above a ground-floor level containing functional or less formal rooms

PIAZZA In Italian, an open space, usually in a town and often square in shape, surrounded by buildings

PIER A massive vertical support, usually of stone. Used to describe a variety of architectural features for this purpose, all clearly thicker in proportion than a column or a pillar (*q.v.*)

PILASTER A pillar, of one of the five orders (*q.v.*) of Classical architecture, square in section, apparently protruding slightly from a wall. If round in section, see *Half-Column*

PILLAR A free-standing vertical support, usually of stone, which does not necessarily conform with one of the five orders (*q.v.*) of Classical architecture—as does a column (*q.v.*)—and may be square or round in section. In Classical architecture, a pillar is usually square in section and conforms with one of the five orders. See also *Pilaster* and *Pier*

PILOTI Pillars or piers used in twentieth century International Modern (*q.v.*) architecture to raise the bulk of a building from the earth, leaving the ground floor open

PINNACLE A steep pyramid or cone of stone, usually decorated with crockets (*q.v.*), crowning a roof or spire, *etc.* Most frequently found in Gothic architecture

PITCHED Sloping

PLAN In architecture, the design of each storey of a building, as if uncovered and seen from directly above it

PLINTH The protruding base of the pedestal (*q.v.*) of a column or of a wall in Classical architecture

PORCH A projecting roofed entrance to a building

PORTICO A projecting part of a building in Classical architecture, usually with a row of columns surmounted by a pediment (*q.v.*) and often containing the main entrance

PRESBYTERY The area of a church chancel where the high altar is placed, east of the choir

PUTTI Sculpted cherub boys

QUATREFOIL A four-leaved Gothic decorated feature. See *Foil*

QUOIN Vertical rows of dressed or rusticated stone blocks at the corners of a building

RECESSED A portico or other feature built within the wall of a building, rather than protruding from it

REEDING Decoration by a continuous series of thin straight convex mouldings, as if a row of stalks side by side

REFECTORY Dining hall, as in a monastery

RENAISSANCE In architecture, the style of Classical design developed in Italy from 1400 onwards, based on ancient Roman remains, and spread through Europe in various forms from the sixteenth century onwards

REREDOS A sculpted screen rising behind an altar

REVEAL The part of a jamb (*q.v.*) between any door or glass in an archway or other opening and the outer surface of the wall which the opening pierces

ROCOCO A late development of continental Baroque architecture (*q.v.*) typified by lightness and complexity of form and by *rocaille* decoration (curling shapes like corals, rocks and shells)

ROMAN Architecture derived from the Classicism (*q.v.*) of ancient Rome. Roman Cross—a cross with one of the four arms longer than the others

ROMAN CEMENT See *Stucco* and Appendix Three. An oil-based cement often applied to the exterior of the late Georgian buildings

ROMANESQUE The strong-walled and round-arched style of architecture widespread in Europe from the end of the dark ages before A.D. 1000. In England it is often called Saxon, and then Norman (*q.v.*) from 1066 onwards, and was in use until Early English (*q.v.*). Gothic replaced it gradually after 1200

ROOD SCREEN A screen of wood or stone, often open-work, between the nave and the chancel of a church, beneath a Rood (a large crucifix with accompanying figures, in a high position normally under the chancel arch)

ROOF The upper covering of a building, flat or sloping. See *Eave, Gable, Hammer-beam, Hipped, Mansard, Pitch, Slate, Tile*, and Appendix Three

ROSE or WHEEL WINDOW A circular window, with stone tracery (*q.v.*) within it in Gothic architecture

ROTUNDA A building of circular plan, often domed, in Classical architecture

RUSTICATION Blocks of masonry in Classical architecture cut so that the face of each block bulges forward, rather than aligning smoothly with its neighbouring blocks (as in Ashlar, *q.v.*). The bulging face is usually textured, rather than smooth. See also *Vermiculation*

SANCTUARY The area around the altar in a church, often within the area called a presbytery (*q.v.*)

SECTION In architectural drawing, the design of a building or object as if it were cut away along any particular line and the resulting interior or shape were seen

SCREEN A wall or row of columns or pillars *etc.* dividing one area from another, but, if inside a building, often not rising to the roof of the space

SEGMENT(AL) Part of the perimeter of a circle, less than a semi-circle. A segmental arch thus forms a shallower curve than a full round arch

SILL The fixed horizontal at the bottom of a window

SLATE A roof tile of the naturally stratified flat thin stone, slate. See Appendix Three

SOUNDING BOARD or TESTER A wooden board or other device constructed above a pulpit or the proscenium arch of a theatre to project sound outward

SPANDREL The triangular solid area between two arches in an arcade. More precisely, half of this area divided by a vertical line down to the top of the column

SPIRE An elongated cone or pyramid often built on top of a tower or above a crossing in Gothic architecture

SPRING In architecture, the point at which an arch rises in a curve from its support

SQUINCH An arch built across the angle between two walls to support a superstructure or to effect a transition *e.g.* from a quadrilateral below to an octagon above

STALL A carved ritual seat of wood or stone, or in the plural a row of carved seats, *e.g.* for a choir in a church

STRAPWORK A type of decoration imported from Flanders and common in the eclectic English Renaissance style of the 1500s. The stone is carved in flat bands of low-relief, detailed as if they were leather straps of decorated form

STRETCHER A brick laid so that its longest side appears on the face of a wall

STUCCO An oil-based cement widely used for rendering the surface of brick buildings in the late eighteenth or early nineteenth centuries. See Appendix Three

SURVEYOR A professional qualification in construction work and calculation of measurements and quantities. The supreme post in the Royal Office of Works in Stuart and Georgian times was the Surveyor-General, often an architect (see Appendix Two)

SWAG A decorative feature in Classical architecture,

carved to represent a cloth curving down from two points

TERMINI or TERMS See *Herm*

TERRACOTTA Building material of baked but unglazed clay, often in decorated moulded blocks. See Appendix Three

TESSELATION A pavement or wall of tesserae (small pieces of coloured glass or stone, embedded in cement and arranged to form a picture or pattern) as in mosaic

TESTER See *Sounding Board*

TILE A flat unit of roofing material, usually of baked and glazed clay. See also *Pantile, Slate* and Appendix Three

TILE-HANGING Tiles suspended on a vertical wall, rather than on a sloping roof

TOMB-CHEST A large box of stone, usually decorated with sculpture, used as the monument and coffin of a person of importance in medieval times

TRACERY Decorated ribs of stone, intersecting with each other in various patterns, within the upper part of the glazed area of Gothic windows and in arches and vaults

TRANSEPT The side arms of a church of cross-shaped plan. Transepts meet the nave and the chancel at the crossing (*q.v.*)

TRANSOM A fixed horizontal stone or timber, dividing up the glazed area of a window. If vertical, see *Mullion*

TRIFORIUM In Gothic architecture, a passage in the wall above the side arches of a nave, with small arches between the passage and the space of the nave, below the level of the clerestorey (*q.v.*)

TRIGLYPH Stone blocks, with vertical grooves, in a Classical frieze (*q.v.*)

TROPHY In Classical architecture, a sculpted decorative composition of weapons, sometimes with a coat of arms and other objects included

TUNNEL VAULT See *Barrel*

TURRET A small tower

TUSCAN A Classical (*q.v.*) order (*q.v.*), said to have been derived from Etruscan temples, and widely used by the Romans and later for simple or rustic buildings. The order is similar to Roman Doric, but the columns have no fluting (*q.v.*) and have broader proportions

VAULT Arched roof of a church or other internal space, built of stone or brick or, recently, concrete. See *Barrel, Fan, Groin, Rib, Tunnel* and *Waggon*

VERNACULAR In architecture, the traditional building manner and materials of the neighbourhood, as against fashionable styles common to larger areas or whole countries

VENETIAN WINDOW An English term for the Serlian window of Renaissance (*q.v.*) architecture consisting of a central window topped by an arch, with a narrower flat-topped window on either side of it

VERMICULATION Decoration like wriggling worm tracks in the blocks of stone on the exterior of buildings

VESTIBULE A room of secondary importance, opening into a principal room

VILLA A house in the country

VOLUTE A decorative feature of Classical architecture, consisting of a spiralling scroll carved in stone. Widely used in decorative buttresses or brackets (*q.v.*) and in the capitals of Ionic columns (*q.v.*)

WAGGON ROOF or VAULT Another term for a barrel vault (*q.v.*)

References and Select Bibliography

Publication was in London unless stated otherwise

General

A Biographical Dictionary of English Architects 1660–1840. H. M. Colvin (1954)

A Biographical Dictionary of British Architects 1600–1840. Howard Colvin (1978)

The Buildings of England—London, Volumes 1 and 2. Sir Nikolaus Pevsner (1957 and subsequent revisions, and 1952)

London the Unique City. Steen Eiler Rasmussen (1934)

Handbook to the Environs of London. James Thorne (1876)

London Past and Present. H. B. Wheatley (1891)

The Survey of London. Detailed volumes, each on the buildings *etc.* of a small area or parish of London by various authors. Published by the London County Council, or later the Greater London Council, and the London Survey Committee (in progress since 1896)

Lost London. Hermione Hobhouse (1971)

The History of the Squares of London. E. Beresford Chancellor (1907)

Architecture in Britain, 1530 to 1830. Sir John Summerson (1953)

The Growth of Stuart London. N. G. Brett James (1935)

English Baroque Architecture. Kerry Downes (1966)

Georgian London. Sir John Summerson (1945 and subsequent revisions)

The Greek Revival : neo-classical attitudes in British Architecture 1760–1870. J. Mordaunt Crook (1972)

English Architecture since the Regency. H. S. Goodhart-Rendel (1953)

Early Victorian Architecture. Henry-Russell Hitchcock (1957)

Victorian Architecture. Edited by Peter Ferriday (1963)

Victorian Architecture. R. Furneaux Jordan (1966)

Victorian Architecture. Roger Dixon and Stefan Muthesius (1978)

Architecture : Nineteenth and Twentieth Centuries. Henry-Russell Hitchcock (1958)

Style and Society, 1835–1914. Robert Macleod (1971)

Seven Victorian Architects. Edited by Jane Fawcett (1976)

Victorian and Edwardian Theatres. Victor Glasstone (1975)

Edwardian Architecture and its Origins. Edited by Alastair Service (1975)

Edwardian Architecture. Alastair Service (1977)

Representative British Architects of the Present Day. Sir Charles H. Reilly (1931)

A Visual History of Twentieth Century Architecture. Dennis Sharp (1972)

The Politics of Architecture. Anthony Jackson (1970)

New Architecture of London. Sam Lambert (1963)

Modern Buildings in London. Ian Nairn (1964)

Architecture in Britain Today. Michael Webb (1969)

Guide to Modern Buildings in London 1965–75. Edited by Charles McKean and Tom Jestico (1976)

New British Architecture. Robert Maxwell (1972)

Henry Yevele

Henry Yevele. John Harvey (1944)

Henry Yevele Reconsidered. John Harvey (1952)

The Renaissance and Inigo Jones

The Growth of Stuart London. N. G. Brett James (1935)

Architecture in Britain, 1530 to 1830. Sir John Summerson (1953)

Inigo Jones

The Life of Inigo Jones. P. Cunningham (1844)

Inigo Jones. J. A. Gotch (1928)

The Age of Inigo Jones. James Lees-Milne (1953)

Inigo Jones. Sir John Summerson (1966)

Wren and the English Baroque

English Baroque Architecture. Kerry Downes (1966)

Architecture in Britain, 1530 to 1830. Sir John Summerson (1953)

Sir Christopher Wren

(a small selection of numerous books)

Parentalia, Christopher Wren the younger. Volumes I–XX (written *c.* 1750, published by the Wren Society in the twentieth century)

Memoirs of Sir Christopher Wren. Harvey Elmes (1823)

Wren the Incomparable. M. S. Briggs (1953)

Sir Christopher Wren. Sir John Summerson (1953)
Wren and his Place in European Architecture. E. Sekler (1956)

Nicholas Hawksmoor
Nicholas Hawksmoor. H. Goodhart-Rendel (1924)
Hawksmoor. Kerry Downes (1959)
Hawksmoor. Kerry Downes (1969)

Sir John Vanbrugh
Sir John Vanbrugh. A. E. Street (1891)
Sir John Vanbrugh. C. Barman (1924)
Sir John Vanbrugh. Laurence Whistler (1938)
Vanbrugh. Kerry Downes (1978)

Thomas Archer
Thomas Archer. Marcus Whiffen (1950)
Baroque Inspiration. H. B. Leather (RIBA Manuscripts)
St. Philip, Birmingham and its Architect (RIBA Library, leaflet)

James Gibbs
Manuscript Memoir in Sir John Soane's Museum
Manuscript thesis. H. B. S. Gibbs (*c.* 1912, in RIBA Manuscripts)
The Life and Work of James Gibbs. B. Little (1955)

Georgian Palladianism
Architecture in Britain, 1530 to 1830. Sir John Summerson (1953)
Georgian London. Sir John Summerson (1945)
Palladio and English Palladianism. Rudolph Wittkower (1974)
The Palladian Style in England, Ireland and America. D. Guinness and J. T. Sadler (1976)

Lord Burlington
Earls of Creation. James Lees-Milne (1962)
"Young Lord Burlington". *Country Life,* 30 June 1960
"Burlington and Kent". *Archaeological Journal,* February 1947
"Hogarth against Burlington". *The Architectural Review,* August 1964

William Kent
William Kent—a chronology (RIBA Manuscripts)
The Work of William Kent. M. Jourdain (1948)
Earls of Creation. James Lees-Milne (1962)
"Houses of Parliament Designs". *RIBA Journal,* 1932 p. 733 and p. 800

Sir Robert Taylor
"Villas". Marcus Binney. *Country Life,* 6 July 1967

"Work at the Bank of England". Marcus Binney. *Country Life,* 13 and 20 November 1969
Biography by Marcus Binney forthcoming

Sir William Chambers
"Chambers as a Professional Man". *The Architectural Review,* April 1964
"Chambers at Kew". *Apollo,* August 1963
Sir William Chambers. A. T. Edwards (1924)
Sir William Chambers. John Harris (1970)

Adam, Neo-Classicism and the Regency
The Greek Revival: neo-classical attitudes in British architecture 1760–1870. J. Mordaunt Crook (1972)
Architecture in Britain, 1530 to 1830. Sir John Summerson (1953)

Robert Adam
"Adam and Piranesi". D. Stillman in *Essays presented to R. Wittkower* (1967)
The Age of Adam. James Lees-Milne (1947)
Robert Adam and his Circle. J. Fleming (1962)
Robert Adam and his Brothers. J. Swarbrick (1915)
Robert Adam. Doreen Yarwood (1970)

George Dance the Younger
"George Dance". *Official Architect,* August 1949
"Dance, Town Planner". *Journal of the Society of Architectural Historians,* December 1955
George Dance, Architect. Dorothy Stroud (1971)

Sir John Soane
The Life and Works of Sir John Soane. T. Donaldson (1837, RIBA Manuscripts)
The Portrait of Sir John Soane. A. T. Bolton (1927)
Sir John Soane. Sir John Summerson (1952)
The Architecture of Sir John Soane. Dorothy Stroud (1961)

John Nash
John Nash—architect to King George IV. Sir John Summerson (1935)
The Architecture of John Nash. T. Davis (1960)
John Nash, the Prince Regent's Architect. T. Davis (1966)

Sir Robert Smirke
"Architect of the Rectangular: Sir Robert Smirke". J. Mordaunt Crook: *Country Life,* 1967, Volume 141 p. 846
"Sir Robert Smirke: a Centenary Florilegium". J. Mordaunt Crook: *The Architectural Review,* 1967, Volume 142 p. 208
Letters (RIBA Manuscripts)

Benjamin Dean Wyatt
"James Wyatt and his Sons". *Architect and Building*

News, 26 March 1948
James Wyatt, Architect. A. Dale (1936)

William Wilkins
"William Wilkins". *RIBA Journal*, 24 December 1932
Manuscript by G. Walkley (1946, RIBA Manuscripts)
"Haileybury and the Greek Revival". J. Mordaunt Crook: *The Haileyburian and ISC Chronicle 1964*

Decimus Burton
"The Life and Works of Decimus Burton". R. F. Jones: *The Architectural Review*, 1905
Decimus Burton. C. H. Strange (RIBA Manuscripts)
Decimus Burton. P. A. Clarke (RIBA Manuscripts)

Victorian Architecture and the Gothic Revival
Style and Society—Architectural Ideology in Britain 1835–1914. Robert Macleod (1971)
Victorian Architecture. Edited by Peter Ferriday (1963)
First and Last Loves. John Betjeman (1952)
Seven Victorian Architects. Edited by Jane Fawcett (1976)
Victorian Architecture. Robert Furneaux Jordan (1966)
The High Victorian Movement in Architecture 1850–1870. Stefan Muthesius (1972)
Victorian Architecture. Roger Dixon and Stefan Muthesius (1978)

Sir Charles Barry
The Architectural Career of Sir Charles Barry. Digby Wyatt (1859)
The Life and Works of Sir Charles Barry. Rev. Alfred Barry (1867)
"Sir Charles Barry". Peter Fleetwood-Hesketh, in *Victorian Architecture* edited P. Ferriday (1963)

Augustus Welby Pugin
Recollections of A. W. N. Pugin. Benjamin Ferrey (1861)
Pugin, a Medieval Victorian. M. Trappes-Lomax (1932)
Lord Shrewsbury, Pugin and the Roman Catholic Revival. D. Gwynn (1946)
Pugin. Phoebe Stanton (1971)
"A. W. N. Pugin". Alexandra Gordon Clark, in *Victorian Architecture* edited P. Ferriday (1963)

Sir George Gilbert Scott
"Sir Gilbert Scott". David Cole, in *Victorian Architecture* edited P. Ferriday (1963)
Recollections, annotated by G. E. Street (RIBA Manuscripts)
Tributes. Transactions of the RIBA, 1878–79 p. 3

William Butterfield
William Butterfield. Paul Thompson (1971)
"William Butterfield". Paul Thompson, in *Victorian Architecture* edited P. Ferriday (1963)
List of works. *Transactions of the Ancient Monuments Society* 1963

G. E. Street
Memoir of G. E. Street. A. E. Street (1888)
"G. E. Street, the Law Courts and the Seventies". Joseph Kinnard, in *Victorian Architecture* edited P. Ferriday (1963)
Manuscript notes etc. (1916, RIBA Manuscripts)

Late Victorian and Arts and Crafts Architecture
Victorian Architecture. Edited P. Ferriday (1963)
Edwardian Architecture and its Origins. Edited A. Service (1975)
Style and Society—Architectural Ideology in Britain 1835–1914. Robert Macleod (1971)

Norman Shaw
Richard Norman Shaw. Andrew Saint (Yale 1976)
R. Norman Shaw—A Study. Sir Reginald Blomfield (1940)
"Richard Norman Shaw". Nikolaus Pevsner, in *Victorian Architecture* edited P. Ferriday (1963)

Alfred Waterhouse
"Alfred Waterhouse". Stuart Allen Smith, in *Seven Victorian Architects* edited J. Fawcett (1976)
Typescript Chronology 1950, revised 1954 (RIBA Manuscripts)
Letters to T. L. Donaldson (RIBA Manuscripts)

John Francis Bentley
J. F. Bentley. W. Scott-Moncrieff (1924)
"John Francis Bentley". Halsey Ricardo, in *Victorian Architecture* edited P. Ferriday (1963)
Westminster Cathedral and Bentley, 1902 (RIBA Manuscripts)
"John Francis Bentley: a memoir". T. J. Willson, in *RIBA Journal* 1902, p. 437

C. Harrison Townsend
C. H. Townsend. Thesis by Richard Woollard, 1971–72 (School of Architecture, Cambridge)
"Charles Harrison Townsend". A. Service, in *Edwardian Architecture and its Origins* (1975)

C. F. A. Voysey
C. F. A. Voysey—A Memoir. John Brandon-Jones (undated reprint of special 1957 issue of *Architectural Association Quarterly*
"C. F. A. Voysey". John Brandon-Jones, in *Victorian Architecture* edited P. Ferriday (1963)

Edwardian Baroque and the Grand Manner
Edwardian Architecture. Alastair Service (1977)
Edwardian Architecture and its Origins. Edited A. Service (1975)
The Turn of the Century. Sir John Summerson (Glasgow 1975)

John Belcher
"Belcher and Joass". A. Service, in *Edwardian Architecture and its Origins* (1975)

Sir Aston Webb
"Sir Aston Webb and his Office". H. Bulkeley Creswell, in *Edwardian Architecture and its Origins* (1975)
Articles, obituaries *etc.* in *RIBA Journal* 1916–17, p. 91; 1930, p. 710; *Builder* 1930(2), pp. 329 and 1034; *Building* 1930, p. 100

Mewès and Davis
Chapter on Davis in *Representative British Architects of the Present Day.* Sir C. H. Reilly (1931)
"Arthur Davis of Mewès and Davis". A. Service in *Edwardian Architecture and its Origins* (1975)

Sir Edwin Lutyens
Life of Sir Edwin Lutyens. Christopher Hussey (1950)
The Architecture of Sir Edwin Lutyens. A. S. G. Butler *et al* (1950)
A Blessed Girl—Emily Lutyens' letters (1953)
Sir Edwin Lutyens. Robert Lutyens (1942)
Chapter on Lutyens in *Representative British Architects of the Present Day.* Sir. C. H. Reilly (1931)
"Sir Edwin Lutyens". Roderick Gradidge, in *Seven Victorian Architects* (1976)

Free Design and International Modern Architecture
English Architecture since the Regency. H. S. Goodhart-Rendel (1953)
The Politics of Architecture. Anthony Jackson (1970)

A Visual History of Twentieth Century Architecture. Dennis Sharp (1972)
Architecture in Britain Today. Michael Webb (1969)

Sir John Burnet
"Sir John James Burnet". David Walker in *Edwardian Architecture and its Origins* (1975)

Charles Holden
"Charles Holden's Early Works." Sir Nikolaus Pevsner in *Edwardian Architecture and its Origins* (1975)
"Charles Holden". Sir C. H. Reilly, in *Building* 1931
"Charles Holden and his London Underground Stations". Grahame Middleton in *Architectural Association Quarterly* 1976 Vol. 8 No. 2
Further information given personally by Mr. W. A. Guttridge, Holden's partner and successor

Tecton and Berthold Lubetkin
Article in *The Architectural Review*, July 1955
The Politics of Architecture. Anthony Jackson (1970)
Further information given by John Allan

E. Maxwell Fry
The Politics of Architecture. Anthony Jackson (1970)
Maxwell Fry : autobiographical sketches (1975)
Leaflet by Sir Nikolaus Pevsner (RIBA Library)
Further information given personally by Mr. Fry

Sir Denys Lasdun
A Language and a Theme—the Architecture of Denys Lasdun and Partners. William Curtis and others (1976)
"My Four Gurus". Helen Dawson in *The Observer Supplement*, 16 September 1973
"Denys Lasdun, his Approach to Architecture". RIBA lecture on 9 February 1965, in *Architectural Design*, June 1965.
Information on dates given by Sir Denys Lasdun

Some London Architects and Buildings since 1945
New British Architecture. Robert Maxwell (1972)
Modern Buildings in London. Ian Nairn (1964)
New Architecture of London. Sam Lambert (1963)
Guide to Modern Buildings in London 1965–75. Edited by Charles McKean and Tom Jestico (1976)

Index

224